Kitchen Planning and Management

Kitchen Planning and Management

John Fuller and David Kirk

Butterworth-Heinemann Ltd
Halley Court, Jordan Hill, Oxford OX2 8EJ

 PART OF REED INTERNATIONAL BOOKS

OXFORD   LONDON   GUILDFORD   BOSTON
MUNICH   NEW DELHI   SINGAPORE   SYDNEY
TOKYO   TORONTO   WELLINGTON

First published 1991

© John Fuller and David Kirk 1991

British Library Cataloguing in Publication Data
Fuller John. *1916–*
    Kitchen planning and management.
    1. Catering establishments. Kitchens. Management
    I. Title   II. Kirk, David. *1945–*
    647.95

ISBN 0 7506 0011 X

Typeset by MS Filmsetting Ltd, Frome, Somerset
Printed and bound in Great Britain by
Thomson Litho Ltd, East Kilbride, Scotland

Contents

Preface

The catering kitchen has undergone many changes over the last twenty years. The increased diversity of meals in restaurants, diners, bars, at work, in hospitals and schools has been accompanied by equally significant changes 'behind the scenes'. In some cases these changes have resulted in the kitchen becoming a much more complex and technological place. In other situations, the kitchen and its processes have been greatly simplified, through the use of prepared foods, a wide range of which is now available to the caterer.

In the kitchen, we see a blend of art, science and business, with the three working together to produce foods which are both satisfying to the customer and profitable to the caterer. Without the art, we are in danger of losing our customers through boredom or positive dislike of the meal on offer. Without the science, we are likely to give the customer food poisoning and poor nutritional value, to misuse equipment and to waste energy. Without the business we will not be able to produce an experience which the customer wants, at a price he or she is prepared to pay.

Food is an emotive issue, about which most of us hold strong views concerning the types of raw material used, the method of preparation and the method of service. This 'mix', which goes to make up the catering experience, will continue to evolve as:

- Customers' needs and wants change.
- The availability of food materials develops.
- Catering technology and information technology progresses.

Kitchen Planning and Management provides a basis for analysing and evaluating the value, applicability and significance of current and future changes in these elements of catering.

It is aimed primarily at students of hotel and catering at all levels, including:

City and Guilds 706/1, 706/2 and 706/3.
BTEC and SCOTVEC first certificate and diploma; national certificate and diploma; and higher national certificate and diploma.
HCIMA certificate and diploma.
Degree courses in hotel and catering management.

The approach has been to provide a systematic framework, which integrates scientific and technical principles with the catering application. This is in line with the approach adopted by many courses. In order to cover the broad spread and level of educational readers, full reading lists are provided to allow more advanced students to take the subject matter further. This also aids the student centred approach adopted by many courses.

The book should also be of interest to people in the hotel and catering industry: those involved with the management and supervision of kitchens; those involved in the catering equipment supply industry; and those involved with kitchen planning.

This new book reflects much of the content of *Professional Kitchen Management*, written by John Fuller and published by Batsford and, indeed, started life as a revision of that book. Changes in content have been necessary in the light of some of the changes within the professional kitchen which are outlined above. The structure of the book has been changed to introduce the subject of catering systems at an early stage, so that this can form a framework to the development of the rest of the technical material in the book.

The book opens with a brief history of the development of the catering kitchen, together with some background statistics on the structure and size of the catering industry.

This is followed by an introduction to systems concepts and the use of systems as a means of analysing what takes place in the kitchen. Examples are developed to illustrate the variety of catering systems which are in use.

Chapter 3, which is on the menu, emphasizes the importance of the menu as a blueprint for the catering operation. The various types of menu together with the impact of the computer on menu planning are described.

Next comes a chapter on production planning and control. The production, or operational plan, develops from catering policy via the menu. The success of the plan is monitored, controlled and corrected as an integral part of the planning cycle.

Chapter 5 covers the topic of food hygiene, an area of increasing concern to the Government and the consumer. The catering industry has come in for much criticism in this area. For this reason, bacteriological food poisoning is covered in some depth, together with systems for maintaining control over hygiene using the hazard analysis and critical control point approach.

Chapter 6 is concerned with accidents in the kitchen and with the specific responsibilities of the caterer under the Health and Safety at Work Act and the Fire Precautions Act.

Catering equipment is covered in Chapters 7 and 8, with the first of these chapters providing the basic principles of equipment and equipment selection. This is followed by a description of the most important types of small and large equipment available in the kitchen. It is important that all students of catering are aware of recent developments in equipment and are aware of their uses and suitability.

Chapter 9 covers the topic of kitchen planning. As with production planning, the starting point of kitchen planning is an analysis of catering policy and the menu. Because of the increasing diversity of catering operations, there are few hard and fast rules about kitchen planning. A thorough analysis of each situation is required, if costly mistakes are to be avoided.

The book concludes with a chapter on maintenance and energy management. Maintenance has often been a neglected area within catering, with preventative maintenance forming the exception rather that the rule. As the catering industry develops, companies are now giving much more thought to the true cost of equipment and are including maintenance in their planning and budgeting. The same points can be made about energy management. Many companies now have energy management policies and are making a significant investment in energy conservation.

John Fuller and David Kirk

Acknowledgements

Thanks are due to: staff in the School of Leisure and Food Management at Sheffield City Polytechnic for help and advice; to John Kay and colleagues at that Polytechnic involved with CATERCAD for the origination of catering equipment diagrams; to Mike Olsen and staff in the department of Hotel, Restaurant and Institutional Management at Virginia Polytechnic and State University during David Kirk's sabbatical at that institution which afforded both stimulus and a unique opportunity to complete this book. Particularly acknowledged is help by Mike Evans during team teaching sessions on a Facilities Planning course when many ideas in this book were debated, developed and honed.

The publishers are thanked for art material used from R. E. Maitland's and D. A. Welsby's *Basic Cookery* (Heinemann, 1981) and for diagrams from Anthony Milson's and David Kirk's *Design and Operation Catering Equipment* (Ellis Horwood, 1981).

As this book started as a revision of John Fuller's *Professional Kitchen Management* (Batsford, 1962, final revision edition, 1981) the aid in that former book is acknowledged of colleagues from Strathclyde and Surrey Universities.

Finally, thanks to our wives, Pamela Honor Fuller and Helen Kathleen Kirk, for their patience and support.

1
The development of the professional kitchen

This book is concerned with the planning and management of production and service systems for the catering or food service industry. The catering industry is now a very large and important industry. It is usually defined as those activities concerned with the provision of food and drink away from home and, as such, it covers both food consumed on the premises of the caterer and also food bought and consumed off the premises.

It is impossible to produce a precise definition of the catering industry since many activities overlap with other industries, such as food retailing. For example, many shops and supermarkets sell hot and cold snack foods, sandwiches, etc. for consumption off the premises. On the other hand, many restaurants now sell 'take-away' foods which are consumed away from the premises of the caterer, and often in the home. Another example of a hard-to-categorize activity is the home delivery of fast-food products such as pizzas. These are normally considered to form a part of the catering industry, even though the product is consumed at home.

Catering is concerned not only with a product but also with a service. When people go to a restaurant to eat, they have expectations about the total experience – the ambience and décor, the style of service and other customers, as well as the food itself. Although the emphasis of this book is on the production aspects of catering, it is important not to forget the customer and the service aspect since this forms a major component of what the customer wants.

Factors affecting the development of the professional kitchen

Catering as an industry has seen rapid development this century. The professional catering kitchen as it exists today has developed because of the combined effects of a number of changes, as shown in Figure 1.1.

Early development of catering

The present methods of preparing foods in catering can be traced back for thousands of years. Cooking, which forms the basis of most types of cuisine and most forms of catering, predates history. It is difficult to know when man started cooking food. Evidence shows that fire was first used 500,000 years BC and that Neanderthal man cooked his food. All three of the basic methods of heat transfer used in cooking – conduction,

- The development of culinary methods and practices through the development of the vocation of the chef and of professional cookery.

- Changes in the organization of staff within the kitchen and with the methods used to supervise them.

- The development of agricultural/food supplies, food distribution and processing techniques.

- Changes in the demands for eating out – marketing/consumer sociological trends.

- Changes in the types of food available, its quality, shelf life etc.

- Technological changes in fuel supplies and catering equipment.

- An understanding of the scientific basis to nutrition and food hygiene.

Figure 1.1 *Factors influencing catering*

convection and radiation (see Chapter 7) – have their roots in prehistory.

However, early forms of cooking would have been primitive. Initially, the roasting of meat would have been carried out by placing it in the embers of a dying fire. Later, metal spits were used to suspend roasting meats over the fire. The earliest baking would have been done on a flat stone next to the fire. Pit ovens were developed, using holes in the ground lined with hot embers. The earliest known method of heating liquids was by dropping hot stones from the fire into containers of water. By 7000 BC there is evidence of the use of stone cooking pots, which could be heated directly by the fire. Later, fired pottery and bronze and iron cooking vessels were suspended over the fire.

Babylonian tablets from around 2500 BC contain the first written reference to food and cooking. By the time of the Egyptians, baking technology had developed into the use of clay-lined ovens which were preheated internally with burning charcoal. Once the charcoal had finished burning, the ashes had to be scraped out before the cooking could commence. This internal method of oven heating survived in Europe through until the eighteenth and nineteenth centuries. The

Egyptians also learned how to make leavened bread.

The development of catering, in the sense of the provision of food for the traveller and for banquets and celebrations, is lost in prehistory. However, it is certain that the professional cook was known in the time of the Greeks who developed culinary skills. The provision of food for large banquets was also recorded by this period.

The development of catering equipment has been a slow process. Indeed, the Romans had many cooking implements that would be recognized in the kitchens of today – tripods and grid irons used over open fires, crescent-shaped blades with wooden handles for chopping, strainers, colanders. There is also evidence of the existence of restaurants and inns in Rome and this practice spread throughout the Roman Empire.

Medieval and pre-Industrial Europe

These inns survived throughout Europe after the decline of the Roman Empire. In addition to the inns, which provided accommodation, there were also ale and wine houses, and monasteries, which provided food for the traveller. The professional kitchen would also have been found in such places as castles, fortified manor houses and châteaux of medieval Europe.

At this time, cooking techniques had not advanced very far and cooking was mainly confined to two methods: either by cooking in an iron cauldron and or by spit roasting. Nevertheless, these methods did see some developments. For example, techniques were devised for raising and lowering the cauldron and for the mechanical rotation of the spit. Baking was also very important, since bread formed an important part of the diet. However, ovens were still internally heated with wood. During the eleventh to nineteenth centuries the influence of French cooking methods and terminology had a profound effect on European cookery. By 1652, the first coffee houses were established in London (Hackwood, 1987).

The Industrial Revolution

The Industrial Revolution at the end of the eighteenth century saw major changes to the structure of society and these changes had significant effects on the diet of the British

for the next fifty years (see Figure 1.2). This period also saw the start of the catering industry as we know it today.

During the Industrial Revolution, and for some time afterwards, there was considerable poverty and hunger among agricultural and industrial workers. Therefore, these groups of workers rarely ate away from home in either the traditional inns or the new chop houses which were being opened in towns and cities. Some enlightened employers provided meals for their employees, but this practice did not become widespread until the twentieth century.

However, for the more affluent members of society, the choice of foods, the way in which they were prepared and cooked, the order of their service and time of dining all became matters of social significance. At this time the formal dinner party became an important part of both the social and business scene. In towns and cities, business and professional men started to frequent clubs and chop houses for luncheon.

French dishes began to become popular at the table of the rich as an alternative to the simpler traditional methods of preparing foods by roasting, boiling and baking. French service also became fashionable. Instead of all the dishes being placed on the table at the

---

- Rapid increase in population.

- A concentration of this population in towns and cities.

- Farms supplying local markets could no longer cope with the demands of large urban populations.

- The need for transport of food by road and rail.

- Decline in domestic skills such as home baking and brewing.

- Changing food habits, i.e., an increase in the demand for tea rather than ale and white refined bread rather than brown bread.

- The replacement of wood by coal as the source of heat for cooking.

Figure 1.2 *Influences of the Industrial Revolution on food and diet*

same time, this type of service comprised three or four courses, each course being made up of several different dishes. With French service, waiters assisted in the service but diners served themselves from the dishes. When looking at menus of this time, it must be remembered that diners did not normally eat all of the separate dishes before them, but would select from those available.

In contrast to the high standards of catering in these locations, the inns, taverns, eating houses and hotels had a poor reputation for their catering. Food in the inns and taverns of Britain would have been a very humble affair, consisting in the main of plain roast and boiled meats with vegetables and bread.

The French influence on British catering was marked throughout the nineteenth century, encouraged by the employment of chefs of considerable stature and influence to the clubs and palaces of Britain. For example, Antonin Carême accepted an invitation to act as maître chef to the Prince Regent at his London residence and at Brighton. During the middle of the nineteenth century the use of the term 'hotel' began to take over from 'inn' and the first restaurants were opened with à la carte menus.

At about this point in time, we see a divergence between domestic cooking and professional catering. Professional chefs started to produce books on the subject. For example, Carême, through his written work, influenced the development of cookery and pastry. Although he is often remembered for the introduction of an architectural aspect to his work, he also developed dishes on a smaller and simpler scale.

Alphonse Gouffé, who was chef to Queen Victoria for over a quarter of a century, translated the work of his brother, Jules Gouffé, a student of Carême, into English.

The development of cookery took place not just in the palaces and great houses but also through the development of gentlemen's clubs. Here, too, the influence of

French chefs was considerable. For example, Louis Eustace Ude was responsible for catering at Crockford's Club and St James's Club. He did much to encourage the development of culinary methods in Britain, particularly through his book, *The French Cook*. He also developed the idea of using technical terminology as a shortened explanation and directed particular attention to sauces which he described as 'the soul of cookery'.

These French influences continued into the second half of the nineteenth century. One of the greatest influences, Alexis Soyer, was head chef at the Reform Club during this period. However, his concern was not only with that of feeding the wealthy in their London clubs. He was also involved in military catering during the Crimean War and developed soup kitchens and low-cost cookery books for the poorer members of society.

Charles Elmé Francatelli, who was a contemporary of Soyer, became chief cook to Queen Victoria after holding positions at Crockford's Club and the Reform Club. He led a number of important trends in catering practice, such as a simplification of dishes and menus and a reduction in the number of courses at dinner. He, like Soyer, had an influence on young chefs through his book, *The Modern Cook*.

By the end of the nineteenth century the range of food items available in Britain had considerably expanded through the import of fruits, cereals, meat and fish. The work of Pasteur in the mid-eighteenth century led to a better understanding of heat preservation. The mechanical refrigeration cycle was invented about this time. Through scientific knowledge such processes as canning and refrigeration, although invented earlier in the century, started to take on commercial significance. The availability of canned, chilled and frozen foods revolutionized the food distribution system.

The use of coal as a source of fuel required a change in the design of the open fire since a much greater draught was required. This required the fire bed to be raised off the ground and for a flue to be provided to draw off the products of combustion. It then became possible to box in the fire and divert the flue gases around an oven, leading to the development of the closed range. By the end of the nineteenth century the closed range had superseded the open fire as a method of cooking, allowing a greater variety of cooking methods.

The closed range, with its solid top and oven to one side, was much more controllable and helped the development of the culinary arts. It also meant that the kitchen environment could be made more comfortable for the kitchen staff.

Although gas had been used as a source of fuel for cooking as early as 1841 in the kitchens of the Reform Club, it was much later in the century before it completely replaced coal. The end of the nineteenth century saw the development of specialized catering equipment, different in nature from its domestic counterparts. These new items of equipment saw a move away from the range to the use of deep fat fryers, steamers and grills. Electrical appliances such as mixers, slicers and refrigerators were also introduced. Electricity, as an energy source in the professional kitchen, was first available at the end of the nineteenth century but, particularly in the UK, gas has remained the favourite fuel among chefs.

Dining out was still unusual in working class communities, but the provision of pie-shops, chop houses and public houses selling food at modest prices was on the increase. By the 1890s the family café was beginning to be established.

In the more affluent sectors of society the Victorian dinner party was at its height, featuring French style cooking and a change from French service to Russian service. The latter featured a succession of dishes served one at a time by waiters or butlers from the sideboard. At the same time there was a large reduction in the number of dishes. This style

of service encouraged the production of freshly cooked dishes and allowed chefs to demonstrate their skills.

Towards the end of the nineteenth century, the development of the great hotels of London began. The Ritz, the Carlton, the Savoy, the Cecil and the Langham were built and operated in this period.

Auguste Escoffier, through his work in the kitchens of the Ritz and the Savoy, converted the cookery of gentlemen's clubs into a product which was more suitable for the hotel dining room. In order to do this, he refined and simplified the classical cuisine. Equally importantly he had a profound influence on the organization of the kitchen through the development of the partie system.

During this time there was a reduction in the number of dishes, a decrease in the number of meat courses and an increase in the use of vegetables. This was partly because of improved knowledge about nutrition.

The development of the partie system

The partie system, which evolved during the Edwardian era and particularly under the influence of Escoffier, revolutionized the way in which kitchen staff (or brigades) were organized. Many twentieth-century developments in the design and organization of the kitchen can be traced back to the partie system. The system developed because of:

● Changes in the menu.
● Changes in cooking equipment, outlined above.

The demand for more freshly cooked food caused a change in the methods of operation, with a greater need for the pre-preparation of many items. In order to accomplish this, the work of the kitchen was subdivided into working groups, or parties.

Overall control of the kitchen was in the hands of the head chef or chef de cuisine, aided by one or more assistants (sous chefs). Each partie was under the control of a chef de partie, who functioned both as a supervisor as well as a craft specialist. Typical divisions might be:

- The storage of commodities, both perishable and non-perishable.
- The preparation of meat, fish and poultry, etc. (larder work).
- The preparation and cooking of pastry and desserts (the pastry).
- The preparation of vegetables.
- The general stove section at which prepared foods were assembled and cooked.

The partie system (or 'corner' as it is known in many British establishments), as perfected by Escoffier, was the result of analysing the work behind a collection of recipes and allocating tasks to the different specialists so as to help produce even the most complex dishes regularly, efficiently and swiftly. This meant breaking down processes and allocating different tasks, even in one dish, to different sections so that a veal escalope, for example, might be initially cut by the butcher, flattened and breadcrumbed by the larder cook, sautéed (shallow fried) and garnished by the sauce cook, using garnishes which might well have come from other corners of the kitchen.

In the kind of kitchen that Escoffier and his colleagues organized, the partie system reached the height of complexity because the end products had to be of the highest finish and yet be completed to order in rapid sequence for a substantial number of customers.

In addition to the organizational hierarchy which the partie system introduced into the kitchen, the other important but related aspect was communication. With the need

for fresh cooking and the prompt service of orders to tables, clear and accurate communication, both within the kitchen and between kitchen and restaurant, became essential. The servery became the focal point of this communication, since it was the place at which waiting staff placed orders and received cooked dishes. In the partie system, a member of the kitchen staff would stand at the hotplate and call out the requirements from the order chits of waiting staff.

The appropriate partie(s) would then acknowledge this order. The chit would then be placed on a hook, where it would remain until the order had been collected by the waiter. At the end of the service period, the chits would act as a control of all the dishes which had been produced by the kitchen.

The twentieth century

Dining in hotels and restaurants became fashionable as a family activity at the turn of the century. The standard of catering in the best hotels and restaurants was now starting to match that of the clubs.

After the First World War there was a general growth in eating out among all groups of society other than the poorest, where there were still signs of malnutrition. The years between the wars saw the start of popular catering, through the growth of operations such as Lyons corner houses, milk bars, and road houses. The cafeteria was also developed during this period.

During the Second World War legislation was introduced which made canteens mandatory for factories employing more than 250 staff. Legislation was introduced for the provision of meals to school children as a part of the 1944 Education Act. During the war and post-war years, the nutritional level of the population was improved because of the increased and publicized knowledge of nutrition coupled with food rationing.

Improved knowledge of nutrition lead to the increased awareness of the importance of food in hospital catering. Although hospital catering can be traced back to the sixteenth century, its therapeutic value was not fully recognized until the twentieth century.

During the twentieth century, there was increased concern with food hygiene. This led to legal regulations covering catering premises being introduced in 1955 (see Chapter 5). Despite this increased knowledge of hygiene, a growing number of cases of food poisoning are attributed to catering, and hygiene is still a major issue.

Since the war the average family size has become smaller and the increased employment of married women is changing domestic cooking and leading to a growth in eating out. Fewer people are employed in heavy manual work and because of this the energy requirements of food have decreased, leading to both fewer and lighter meals.

The last few years have seen a growing awareness of the nutritional value of food and an increased demand for healthy menus. This has included concern about empty calories because of the increase in obesity. Current nutritional guidelines have led to a demand for food which is high in fibre, but low in sugar, salt and animal fats. There has also been a demand for pure food which is free from additives and contaminants.

Particularly during the last half of this century, the tastes of the British consumer have changed dramatically. This is partly attributed to the development of foreign holidays and also to better food supplies. The eating out habits of the British have also been strongly influenced by the growth of ethnic restaurants. However, the number of courses consumed at any one meal has continued to decline.

In the second half of the twentieth century, culinary pioneering has moved away from the kitchens of the luxury hotels to the province of the chef-patron. Developments by Michel Guérard and Paul Bocuse, such as cuisine minceur and nouvelle cuisine, were more in tune with the growing health consciousness of caterer and customer.

Technological developments in the distribution of fresh foods has caused a decrease in the importance of seasonality in the work of the chef. Food processing through freezing and chilling in particular has led both to an increase in the range of foods available but also to a diminishing role for vegetable preparation in the kitchen.

In addition to technological developments by the food processing industry, chefs themselves have also exploited scientific knowledge and equipment developments. An example of this is the development of cuisine sous-vide by Georges Pralus (see Chapter 5). Sometimes these technology developments have strongly affected a particular sector of the industry. For example, cook-chill has had its major impact on the welfare sector of the industry. In popular commercial catering the development of fast-food and call order food production methods have been especially significant. These changes have been largely caused by American influences.

Sectors of the catering industry

Traditionally, analysis of the catering market divides catering into the two major areas: commercial (private) sector; and welfare (public) sector. Historically this division was justified on the basis that:

- The commercial sector is profit-orientated and market-orientated whereas the welfare sector is either subsidized or required to run at cost.
- The welfare sector has a clearly defined captive or restrictive market such as a school or a hospital, whereas the commercial sector must attract its own market from the general public.

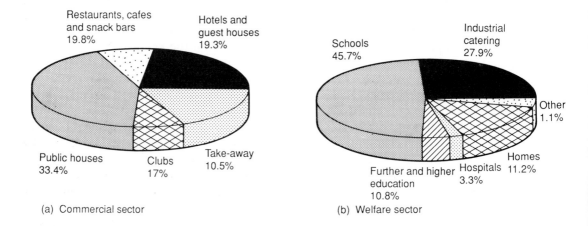

Figure 1.3   *Composition of businesses within hotel and catering*

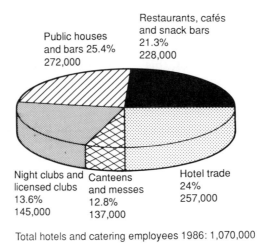

Total hotels and catering employees 1986: 1,070,000
(Department of Employment 1988)

Figure 1.4   *Hotel and catering employees*

However, these distinctions are much less clear cut than would at first appear to be the case and there is now considerable overlap between them. For example, contract caterers are profit-orientated private companies operating in the traditional welfare sectors of catering. At the same time, subsidies to welfare caterers have been gradually reduced and, in many cases, welfare caterers are now required to contribute a profit. Examples of this can be found in public sector operations such as transport and leisure facilities.

Faced with these changes, welfare caterers are now adopting marketing strategies similar to those of commercial caterers in order to attract new customers or offer new products and services.

In terms of size, the commercial catering market is much greater than the non-commercial catering market. Glew (1980) indicates that of the total catering market, some 85 per cent is commercial and 15 per cent non-commercial. A breakdown of businesses within these two sections is given in Figure 1.3. An indication of the size of the hotel and catering industry is given in Figure 1.4, which shows that the number of employees in each sector of the hotel and catering industry provide over 5 per cent of all employment in the UK.

Over the last few years the public sector catering market has been declining, particularly the consumption of meals at the place of work or in schools, where the decline is of the order of 4 or 5 per cent a year. At the same time there has been a slow but steady growth in eating out in commercial restaurants (1 per cent growth in meal occasions a year). Over the same period the actual expenditure on meals away from home has increased at a rate greater than that of inflation.

References and further reading

Baker R. (1983). From coals and spits to foil and microwaves. *Caterer and Hotelkeeper*, 15 September 1983, pp. 67–71.

Burnett J. (1979). *Plenty and Want: a social history of diet in England from 1815 to the present day*. London: Scolar Press.

Davis B. and Stone S. (1991). *Food and Beverage Management*, 2nd edn. Oxford: Butterworth-Heinemann.

Glew G. (1980). Advances in catering technology. *Applied Science*, pp. 3–15.

Hackwood W. (1987). *Inns, Ales and Drinking Customs of Old England*. London: Bracken Books.

Hartley D. (1954). *Food in England*. London: Macdonald and Jane.

Tannahill R. (1973). *Food in History*. New York: Stein and Day.

Tutorial topics

From reading this chapter you can see that the catering industry has developed because of changes in society and technology.

What changes in society and technology are likely to affect the catering industry in the next twenty years?

What do you think will be the effect of these changes on the industry?

2
Catering systems

Before considering the detailed aspects of catering operations it is useful to have an overview of some of the different ways of organizing catering production and service.

What is a catering system?

The term 'catering system' is often used to describe a particular method of organizing the production and service of food. Viewing the operation as a system provides a useful way of understanding and classifying operations since it reminds us that a catering system is not just a haphazard collection of parts but that these parts must work together if the system is to function effectively. It also helps when modifying existing operations and designing new ones.

A *systems approach* comprises the following:

1 *Systems concepts* is a method of describing and studying the parts of an organization, and the way in which these parts interact to fulfil the objectives of the organization.
2 *Systems analysis* is a method of problem solving and a means of designing new systems.
3 *Systems management* is a method of management which ensures that all parts of the organization function in unison.

By studying activities as a system, we can apply general theories or rules of behaviour to what on the surface may seem to be different situations but which, on closer examination, have common properties. For example, systems may be physical, such as the solar system, or they may be biological, such as the central nervous system. The same basic systems principles may be applied to sociobiological systems, such as bees in a hive, or to sociotechnical systems, such as a factory or a restaurant. (A sociotechnical system is one which involves the interaction of people with machines.)

Planning a system

At its simplest level we can consider a system as a set of parts which act together as a whole in order to perform an activity or process. The various parts of the system are linked together by having a common set of objectives. In the case of a man-made system, these objectives are determined by a *plan*, which can be seen as a way of achieving the desired objectives. We can think of the plan as taking place in three stages:

1 *Planning stage*, when the plan is developed.
2 *Implementation stage*, when the plan is put into practice.

3   *Control stage*, when the plan is checked to ensure that it is working.

When we think of a business like a chain of restaurants or hotels, planning takes place at many different levels within the organization. *Strategic plans* are those planning activities which take place at the highest level within the organization and determine the long-term growth and development of the company. The time scale of these plans is about five years. In order to achieve these long-term aims, a *tactical plan* is needed. This is carried out at a lower level within the organization and has a time span which is measured in months. Below this level, within the organization, day-to-day planning and control is required. This is known as *operational planning* and the responsibility for planning at this level is in the hands of the largest group of people. Because of the relationship between planning horizon (time scale) and the number of people involved, it is often referred to as a *planning pyramid*, as shown in Figure 2.1.

Figure 2.1 also demonstrates another important property of catering systems which is that the parts are often organized in the form of hierarchies. The way in which communication takes place between different levels of the hierarchy is an important aspect of the system.

Controlling a system

We can view a system as a means of changing or transforming a set of inputs into outputs (both desirable and undesirable), as shown in Figure 2.2. The inputs and outputs may be information or materials. In order to achieve its desired output, the system must be controlled.

A system can be controlled by using one of two methods:

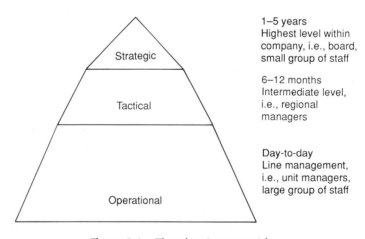

Figure 2.1   *The planning pyramid*

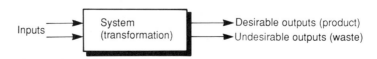

Figure 2.2   *Schematic diagram of a system*

1 *Feedback control* is the most common form of control. The output is measured or observed and the feedback is used to control the inputs (Figure 2.3). In a feedback control loop, the output of the process is measured or *monitored*, and *compared* with its desired *value*. This generates an *error signal*, which is used to *control the inputs*. The control action is such that it brings the output back to its desired value. If the output is at its desired value, there is no *error* and no control is needed. If the output is too high, the control action reduces the relevant inputs and vice versa. We can see this type of control in the operation of a thermostat on an oven (see Chapter 7).

2 *Feedforward control* is a less common form of control. If we understand a system well, or if we have observed the system for a long time, we may be able to predict the expected output from a given set of inputs. Given this knowledge, we can manipulate the inputs before they enter the process in order to achieve the desired output.

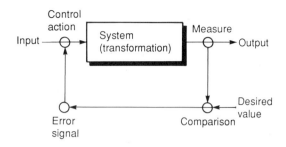

Figure 2.3   *Feedback control*

By this we mean that in a well-planned system the parts complement each other in such a way that the outcome is greater than that which might be expected from just looking at the constituent parts. Unfortunately, the reverse is equally true, where a system may not perform as well as might be expected from looking at its component parts. The aim of the caterer must be to assemble a system in such a way that the parts interact together in a positive way to produce a successful system. This positive interaction between the various parts of a system is known as *synergy*.

Components of a catering system

We cannot understand a complex operation solely by looking at its constituent parts. We have to look not only at the parts, but also at how these parts interact. For example, a menu is more than a collection of dishes. These dishes must be related by a common theme which is in harmony with the location, décor and ambience of the restaurant. The dishes must complement each other and be balanced in terms of colour, flavour and variety. They must be capable of being produced by the kitchen brigade within the constraints of space and equipment available to them.

We often express this by saying that 'the whole is different from the sum of its parts'.

Subsystems

When studying a system it is possible to define its parts in a number of different ways. There is no right or wrong way of doing this since it depends on the type of analysis which is being performed, or on the nature of the problem which is being solved. For example, when analysing the performance of a business, a traditional way of doing this is to consider that it is made up of three parts:

1 Finance.
2 Marketing.
3 Production.

Dividing the organization in this way allows us to study interactions through three of its major activities. An alternative approach might be to consider the business in terms of its major resources:

- Human resources.
- Financial resources.
- Physical resources.

From the above, it follows that it is important when looking at a system to consider how best to break it down into its constituent parts. These are often referred to as *subsystems*. We can then look not only at what goes on in the subsystem but also at the important relationships between subsystems.

It is also worth considering at this stage the nature of the interface or *boundary* between each of these subsystems. An understanding of the nature of a boundary is important in understanding the interrelationships between systems and subsystems. A boundary is important because it controls the nature of the flow of information, communication, materials and people between subsystems. In general, a boundary may be porous or non-porous. In practice most boundaries are selective, being porous to some types of flow but non-porous to others.

There are a number of ways of looking at the subsystems involved in catering. One way (see Figure 2.4) is to consider the subsystems as:

- *Physical* (facilities, technical and materials).
- *Human* (staff and customers).
- *Information* (communication and control).

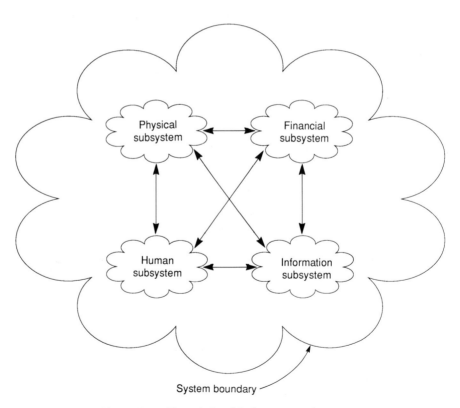

Figure 2.4   *The relationship between subsystems*

- *Financial* (capital and revenue).

Each subsystem can itself be subdivided.

The physical subsystem

Applying these ideas to a study of the physical facilities involved in the production of food we can say that there are three main physical subsystems: the *kitchen*; the *servery*; and the *restaurant*. The boundaries between kitchen, servery and restaurant are shown in Figure 2.5. We can consider the movement of the following across these boundaries:

- Material: food; dirty crockery, cutlery, etc.
- People: kitchen staff to the servery area; servery staff into the restaurant; customers into the servery area.
- Information: details of menu to customers; customer orders to the kitchen; food-ready information to waiting staff;

request for more food to the kitchen from the servery.

In addition to these types of boundary movement control, we can also control many other factors affecting our customers:

- Vision. Can customers see the servery and kitchen areas? Can food preparation staff see the customers? Is this desirable or undesirable?
- Sound. Can noises from the kitchen and wash-up areas be heard in the restaurant? (These noises can include desirable ones, such as the sizzle of a steak cooking, but can also include less desirable ones, such as the clatter of pots and pans).
- Smell. The attractive smell of freshly cooked foods can be used to attract customers into a restaurant and to whet their appetites. Other smells can be less attractive.
- Heat and humidity from the kitchen and wash-up to the restaurant.

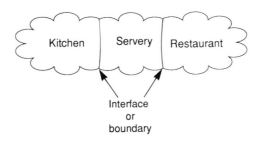

| Kitchen | Servery | Restaurant |

Interface
or
boundary

| *Kitchen*, i.e., a place where conversion of raw materials into a finished product takes place. |
| *Servery*, i.e., place for holding of the finished product and assembly of meals ready for service to customer. |
| *Restaurant*, i.e., presentation of the finished food product to the customer and location of seating area. |

Figure 2.5 *The boundaries or interfaces within a catering system*

The boundary is designed to control these flows. In designing and operating a system, we must be equally concerned about movement across the boundaries of these subsystems as we are about what goes on within them. The very presence of a boundary can lead to conflicts between subsystems. We are all familiar with stories about conflicts between kitchen and restaurant staff. A knowledge of the way in which information, people and materials interact at these interfaces can alleviate some of these problems.

The relationship of kitchen (K), servery (S) and restaurant (R) is different in each sector of the catering industry. These differences can be described in terms of the nature of the boundary between the following three physical areas:

1   Silver service restaurant

- The hotplate forms the physical boundary between K and S.
- No vision or sound barrier between K and S.
- Physical/environmental boundary between R and S.
- Flow of food by waiters from S to R.
- Flow of dirties and waste by waiters from R to K (wash-up).
- Formal communication of information via menu.
- Written orders communicated via waiter and waiter's pad.
- Verbal communication centres between K and R centres on S.
- Electronic systems sometimes replace written and verbal communication between K, S and R.

2   Self-service

- Physical barrier between K and S (not always).
- No physical or visual barrier between S and R.
- Written communication to customer via point-of-sale display in S.

- Other communication to customer by visual selection of food on display in S.
- Communication to K by S staff who predict how long stocks are going to last.
- Electronic systems sometimes replace written and verbal communication between S and K.

3   Fast food

- No physical barrier between K, S and R.
- Extraction system provides environmental barrier to prevent heat and fumes from K entering R.
- Written communication to customers via point-of-sale displays at S.
- Communication to K based on maintaining a buffer stock in servery and or electronic communication.

The process subsystem

We can usefully take the analysis of a catering production system one step further. Instead of analysing it in terms of physical locations, we can describe it in terms of *five* processes, transformations or stages:

1 Raw material acquisition.
2 Production.
3 Holding.
4 Transport.
5 Service.

For each stage or aspect of the overall system, there are a number of different methods available. Examples of these are shown in Figure 2.6.

The link between production and service

If we analyse trends in the catering industry over the last twenty years, we can see a dramatic change in the nature of the holding process. Traditionally, most foods have been cooked and held at warm temperatures. However, greater scientific knowledge has shown that warm holding causes a great loss of nutrients and the flavour and colour of the food deteriorates. Some sectors of the industry have responded either by eliminating hot food storage altogether or by minimizing it. For example, in developments such as fast food and call order service, food is produced for a specific customer order and storage times are short or non-existent (see Figure 2.7). In other areas, such as hospital or industrial catering, the food is not kept hot but is chilled or frozen and then reheated immediately before service.

This may be described in general terms as the extent of *coupling* between production and service. One of the unique features of traditional catering is the close coupling in time and physical location between the production of the food and its service. This is because the product has a short shelf life and cannot be held without the loss of quality, nutrition and the introduction of food poisoning hazards.

What we are seeing in many catering developments is one of two alternative strategies:

- A much closer coupling of production and service, with a virtual elimination of buffer stocks.
- The complete *decoupling* of production and service by the interaction of a buffer stock with a longer shelf life. This is sometimes referred to as *interrupted catering*.

Another major trend has been the removal of some or all of the preparation and cooking stages away from the catering premises to the premises of a food manufacturer. The catering premises then become concerned only with the reheating, assembling and garnishing of meals. In this way the business can concentrate on the *service* aspect of the business and can leave the *production* aspect to another organization. Some catering organizations have set up their own manufacturing units. In other cases food manufacturers produce food to the specification of the caterer.

A comparison of catering systems

We can compare existing catering systems by looking at the way in which the components in Figure 2.6 are combined.

Tutorial topic

Are there any advantages to be gained from having visual communication between kitchen and restaurant?

Is it possible to have visual communication without heat and smells from the kitchen?

The hotplate in the servery is often an area of great conflict and tension at peaks of service. How is this related to the flow of information and materials?

Draw an input–output diagram to illustrate these flows.

What can be done to reduce some of these activities?

Raw material	Production	Holding	Transport	Service
Home grown		Ready to eat Short term Long term		
Market Prepared Chilled Frozen Canned Dehydrated etc.	To-order To demand Individual Batch Schedule Continuous etc.	Ambient Hot Chilled Sous vide Frozen Plated Bulk etc.	Manual Conveyor Hot container Chilled container Refrigerated-vehicle etc.	Self-service Self-help Waiter Waitress Buffet Carvery Vended etc.

Figure 2.6   *Components of a catering system*

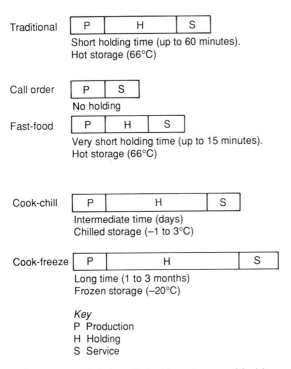

Key
P Production
H Holding
S Service

Figure 2.7   *Variations in holding times and holding temperatures*

- A *high class restaurant* would use market produce. There would be some preparation (mise-en-place) which would then be held hot or refrigerated. Most items would be produced individually and to order, with minimum holding between production and service. Transport would be manual and service by a waiter or waitress.

- A *call order service* would use mainly chilled and frozen foods with some market produce (mainly salads). Food would be cooked individually and to order, with minimal holding, and served either by a waitress or by the customer collecting an order as it is ready.

- A *cafeteria service* would use a mix of all forms of raw material. Production would be to a schedule based on a standard menu cycle. Food would be cooked in batches and held in bulk containers at ambient, hot and refrigerated temperatures. Service would be self-service or a mixture of self-help and self-service.

- A *hospital tray service* would use a mix of all forms of raw material. Production would be to a schedule based on a standard menu cycle. Food would be cooked in batches and plated, using a conveyer belt, and held hot or cold. Food would be transported using insulated trolleys.

- A *cook-chill system* would use a mix of all forms of raw material. Production would be to a schedule based on a standard menu cycle, with demand based on requirements for up to the next five days. Food would be cooked in batches, packaged into containers and rapidly chilled, either as individual plated meals or in bulk. The food would then be stored under refrigeration (-1 to $+3°C$) for up to five days. There may be a distribution stage from central kitchen to satellite kitchen, where reheating takes place.

- A *cook-freeze* system is similar to the above, except that the production schedule is based on the requirements of the next month or so. Food once cooked is rapidly frozen and held at temperatures below $-20°C$.

The quality subsystem

Quality demonstrates the importance of synergy within a system. On one level we might consider the quality of the food, as served to the customer. The customer may view quality in terms of a number of factors (Paulus, 1980) such as:

- Nutritive value.
- Health value: toxins; micro-organisms, etc.
- Sensory value.
- Convenience value: convenience; stability; yield; economic characteristics.

However, this is rather simplistic and in reality the customer will also be responding to the quality of other parts of the system such as décor, ambience, the personal service (if we are considering a silver service restaurant) or machine reliability (if we are considering a vending operation). The customer's response is therefore very complex and is based upon a whole range of subsystems. Also, the response of the customer is at a higher level in the hierarchy from these subsystems, as shown in Figure 2.8.

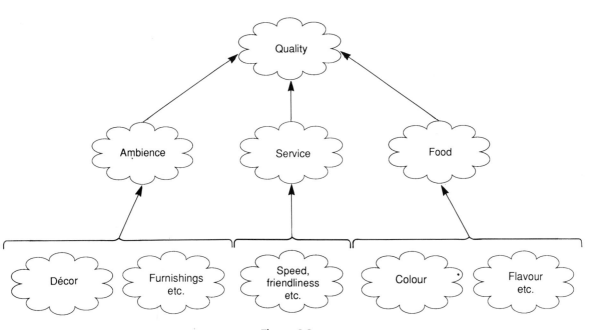

Figure 2.8

From this, it can be said that quality of food service is an *emergent property*, because it is not directly related, in a mathematical sense, to the properties from which it arises. Quality is not the sum of the service subsystems and the product subsystems. High quality depends upon a synergy between all of these properties. The catering manager cannot control quality directly, but must manipulate the lower level system variables such as décor, food presentation etc. In order to be able to do this, knowledge of the relationships between these lower level variables is required.

References and further reading

Escueta E. S., Fiedler K. M. and Reisman A. (1986). A new hospital foodservice classification system. *Journal of Foodservice Systems*, vol. 4, pp. 107-16.

Kahn M. (1987). *Foodservice Operations*, Chapter 1. Westport, Conn: AVI.

Paulus K. (1980). In *Advances in Catering Technology* (Glew, G. ed.). London: Elsevier Applied Science.

Wilson B. (1984). *Systems Concepts, Methodologies and Applications*. Chichester: Wiley.

3
The menu

Some people believe that the written bills of fare originated in Britain after the realization that dining could be more enjoyable by anticipating dishes to be served. One story attributes the origin of the menu to Henry, Duke of Brunswick, who, in 1541, had a list of dishes which enabled him to control his eating and have appetite in reserve for courses to come.

Whether a British bill of fare came before the continental menu or whether it first appeared in Chinese, Egyptian or other early cultures need not worry today's caterers. For the chef, as for the customer, the menu is now a feature of dining and is as permanent as the dish itself.

In the modern catering operation the purpose of the menu is much more complex than in the early days of catering. The menu serves many different functions which are related to both front of house and back of house activities. In reality there are two menus: the *sales menu*; and the *working menu*.

The sales menu

The sales menu informs customers about what is available and helps them to make a choice. Such a menu is marketing in action, a major step in merchandising the meal. Through the menu the caterer seeks to meet the needs of the customer that have been identified through market research and/or previous menu monitoring (Davis and Stone, 1991; Jones, 1983). The menu expresses the catering intention whether it be for one or a chain of restaurants. It also builds in merchandising as a means to help achieve these intentions.

In America the menu has long been regarded as a 'great silent salesman', as a piece of sales literature certain to be read and which inevitably produces an order. Because of this the presentation and layout of the menu is of great importance (Ninemeier, 1984).

In modern catering operations the customer does not always need to enter a restaurant in order to read the menu. The display of menus outside restaurants is now commonplace as a means of attracting customers. In these situations, the menu does not always appear in its traditional form of a bill of fare but is frequently a large (and often illuminated) display board. Great use is made of photographs of dishes and other graphic techniques. It is also now quite common for an establishment to use the menu as part of its sales literature.

The working menu

The working menu contains information about ingredients, portion sizes and yields. For a caterer the working menu arises from

and expresses catering policy. For example, it determines equipment selection, kitchen layout and staffing needs (both numbers of staff and levels of skills). Many aspects of catering management and the day-to-day operation of the kitchen are determined by the menu. It also forms the basis of the *recipe specification*, which is a central component of the management control system (see Chapter 4). A typical working menu is shown in Figure 3.1.

Food policy

As described above, the menu arises from, and is the practical implication of catering policy. Catering policy can be expressed in terms of:

● Customer profile.
● Cost and price policy.
● Service times.

Recipe number: 101
Recipe name: Beef Stroganoff

Ingredient	Quantity	Purchase unit	Cost unit £	Cost
Fillet steak	1000 g	kg	6.24	6.24
Chopped shallots	30 g	kg	1.80	0.05
Garlic	10 g	kg	2.80	0.03
Lemon juice	1/2 lemon	unit	0.85	0.43
Tarragon	5 g	100 g	2.75	0.14
Butter	120 g	kg	2.40	0.29
Double cream	125 ml	pint	1.95	0.43
Salt	1 g	kg	1.25	0.01
Pepper	0.5 g	100 g	2.35	0.01

Raw ingredients weight:	1336 g	Total costs:	7.63
Yield:	88%	Finish weight:	1179 g
Number of portions:	4	Portion/size:	250 g
Raw material cost/batch:	£7.63		
Food cost per portion:	£1.90		
Selling price:	£7.40		
Food cost (%)	25.7%		
Preparation time:	32 minutes		

Method

Cut fillet into Julienne strips.
Cook shallots to golden colour in third butter.
Sauté beef in third butter. Drain and add shallots.
Add cream and reduce.
Add tarragon, lemon and remaining butter.
Season.

Figure 3.1   *A typical working menu or recipe specification*

- Supplies.
- Kitchen staff.
- Plant and equipment.
- Balance.
- Publicity and promotional aspects.

Customer profile

The importance of consumer and marketing orientation in menu making cannot be overstressed. Market surveys and market research are essential in order to determine consumer wants and market opportunities. This information determines the nature of the type of customer who can be attracted and retained.

In some operations, menus are required to be of wide enough appeal to meet the demands of a clientele ranging from babies to octogenarians, and designed to satisfy a wide range of appetites. De luxe hotels traditionally designed menus of such great scope that they embraced all possible types of customer, with a wide margin as far as the nutritional needs and the satisfaction of hunger are concerned.

However, for most sectors of the catering market, the menu designer has more specific knowledge of a particular *market segmentation* (Lewis and Chambers, 1989). The market segment consists of those clearly identified groups of consumers to whom the menu and concept will appeal. The segmentation may be in terms of age, sex, socioeconomic group, activity (tourist, business traveller, etc.) or any relevant and measurable category. By identifying the market segment as precisely as possible it allows the caterer to have more detailed knowledge of the potential customers and of their needs.

It also helps in establishing *product differentiation*, that is, those characteristics of the operation which will distinguish it from its competitors in the same market segment. This differentiation may be in terms of

greater utility, better price value or a closer match to the needs of the market segment.

For some sectors of the catering industry, such as golf clubs, country clubs, school meals and hospital catering, the customer profile can be specifically categorized. In other sectors, market research is necessary in order to establish the market segment together with its eating out habits and needs.

In general, the menu should address three issues in order to meet the needs of the expected customer profile. It should:

1 Satisfy individual needs.
2 Meet local tastes.
3 Attract custom and promote business.

Customers have their own particular needs when they choose to eat a meal in a restaurant. As with most human needs, they can be arranged in a hierarchy, with basic physiological needs at the lowest level of the hierarchy, as shown in Figure 3.2 (Maslow, 1943). In general, people will first satisfy the lower level needs and, only when these have been met, will they consider the needs at the next level of the hierarchy.

Nutritional considerations are important in the design of a menu. The consumers of today are increasingly sophisticated in terms of their nutritional requirements. In addition to the basic nutritional needs for fat, protein, carbohydrate, fibre, vitamins and micronutrients (Harris and Robins, 1985), many customers now have specific requirements because of food allergies. Developments in medicine have shown us that there are many different food-related allergies and, because of this, customers have a right to know what ingredients are in a dish. The Food Safety Act (see Chapter 5) and EC legislation will give caterers a legal requirement to provide accurate and truthful menus.

Another aspect of the relationship between diet and health is illustrated by the findings of the 1983 NACNE (National Advisory Committee on Nutritional Education) and 1984 COMA (Committee on Medical Aspects of Food) committees. The general findings of these groups is that the risk of cardiovascular disease can be reduced by a few simple changes to the diet — less salt, less sugar, less fat in total, less saturated animal fats and more fibre. These considerations now form the basis of attitudes of many consumers to food choice, both at home and in restaurants and can easily be incorporated into menus (HCIMA, 1989). On the other hand, some customers, who normally have a strict dietary regime most of the time like to stray away from this diet when they eat out.

In the case of the captive consumer, the caterer has an important role in providing the essential nutrients as part of a balanced diet. This is particularly important where the caterer controls the total menu for a customer over a long period of time, such as a long stay patient in hospital.

In other cases the responsibility of the caterer is less specific but involves:

● Preparing food of a high nutritional quality.

● Communicating nutritional information to the customer.

Recent examples in hospital and school meal catering demonstrate that the caterer can have an important educational role in guiding customers to make sensible eating decisions.

In addition to nutritional, allergy and health requirements, many consumers have specific dietary requirements because of cultural, ethnic, religious or philosophical considerations (Eckstein, 1983). An individual's food habits are very complex. They are based on upbringing as well as physiological and psychological needs. Age, sex, race, religion, economic status and social status are all important factors.

The menu must satisfy the expectations of local clientele, and the caterer must often make a difficult decision between this and attempting to educate and broaden the expectation of customers. There are times when caterers may deplore their customer's tastes and they may wish to educate them unobtrusively and progressively. This can usually be best achieved by preparing and

Need	Example
Self-actualization	The relationship of food to the total life style. The role of food in making us the kind of person we want to be. 'We are what we eat.'
Esteem	High-levels of personal service, luxurious surroundings, exotic foods.
Belonging	Seen in response to fads and trends. The need to belong causes individuals to follow fashions and to be seen in the 'right' places.
Safety	Safe food, related to minimized danger of food poisoning by bacteria and food contaminents. Concern about use of food additives. Also related to fear of choosing unknown foods.
Physiology	Provision of basic nutritional requirements. Satisfying feelings of hunger and thirst.

Figure 3.2 *Hierarchy of needs in relation to food choice*

cooking foods known and liked by the customers, but to the highest possible quality (within constraints of time, cost etc.), gradually introducing new items only as alternatives to proven favourites. Too radical an approach may drive custom away, but too conservative an approach leaves the market open to new ventures.

Another aspect of local demand concerns the offering of local specialities, such as seafood, game, local fruit and vegetables. These can be very popular with the tourist market.

The menu planner must be sensitive to changes in consumer demand and to changes caused by competition. A successful menu can become less popular very quickly because of changing tastes and menu fatigue.

It is possible to measure food preferences using survey techniques and this information can be useful when designing menus for a specific group of consumers, such as schoolchildren. Survey techniques may be based simply on verbal descriptors, with a scaled consumer response, or they may involve food tasting. While these techniques can be very successful in ranking the popularity of dishes, it is not always easy to relate these responses to the purchasing decisions of customers. This is a particular problem with cyclic menus, where the menu planner needs to relate preference data to how often a particular meal should be offered within the cycle.

Cost and price policy

Market research, as described above, not only gives information about customer preferences but also about price expectations. Most customers have an idea of the typical or *reference price* for a particular type of restaurant. This information is vital to the menu planner since the menu dictates the two main components of cost: food and labour. Food and labour costs are linked by the food service policy and, to some extent, one can be balanced against the other. For example, labour costs can be reduced by the use of convenience foods and/or the use of labour saving and automated equipment. However, such changes must be carefully controlled to be certain that they do not have an adverse effect on customer perceptions of quality.

When labour was both abundant and cheap its significance in menu planning was less marked. Many chefs were then left free to base their menus on a food cost only. It seems unlikely that this simple, single consideration can ever determine the menu plan as it did previously. The practice of considering costs such as labour, other consumables and energy as overhead costs to be added as a percentage to food costs will not necessarily lead to a generation of the desired net profit.

The relationship between cost and price is affected by planned portion size and actual portion control. In creating a menu, the menu maker will consider food in relation to the size of portions which are to be served. The weight of cuts of meat, fish and poultry must be clearly established. Many caterers now purchase meat in ready-portioned cuts to specified weights as a means of reducing wastage and controlling costs. The portion size of even the less costly items must not only be determined but also carefully controlled. Thus, menus should be based on detailed specifications of portion size, yield, garnishes, presentation and service style of each dish. This ensures that management's decisions on portions and service are known to the kitchen and waiting staff alike.

In order to establish a sales price, costs, including ingredients of dishes served in the restaurant and for functions, must be determined as a basis for calculation. Many computer programs are now available for performing this function. Prices of items on a menu strongly influence both the choice of consumers and their idea of value. The menu

Product	Projected sales	Food cost (£)	Selling price (£)	Food cost (%)
RLL	70	2.34	7.80	30.0
PC	173	1.95	8.70	22.4
CH	151	4.22	9.00	46.8
SP	54	2.56	7.00	36.6
TA	49	3.12	10.30	30.3
VL	43	1.46	5.94	24.6

Total sales: 540   Total food cost: £1,492.27   Total revenue: £4,548.22

Overall food costs $\dfrac{\text{(total food costs} \times 100)}{\text{total revenue}}$ = 32.80%

Key

RLL	Roast leg of lamb		SP	Scampi Provençale
PC	Pork cutlet		TA	Trout with almonds
CH	Chicken suprême		VL	Vegetable lasagne

Figure 3.3   *An example of menu analysis to give food cost percentages*

planner needs to have a notion of the reference price in order to establish the final selling price, rather than to add the same percentage contribution to all items indiscriminately. In order to achieve an overall food cost percentage target, the food cost will vary for each item on the menu. The analysis of a typical menu is shown in Figure 3.3. In a similar way to that described for food costs, menus must be designed to achieve specified labour cost percentages. The food and labour percentages can then be used as a means of controlling the profitability of the operation (see Chapter 4).

and potential demand, and the menu planner should be able to answer such questions as:

- Is the market segment the same at lunch time as that for dinner or is there a need for a different menu and environment?
- Is the menu going to be the same throughout the day or will separate lunch, afternoon tea and dinner menus be needed?
- Is demand the same every day of the week or is there a need for low-cost fixed menus or specials on certain days or at certain times of the day?

Service times

The menu planner needs to know about catering policy in relation to opening hours and the nature of the food offered during these hours. Market research will have determined the expected market for various times of the day in terms of numbers of customers

Supplies

In general, food should be specified and bought for a particular purpose. While it is possible to create menu dishes using leftover items, it is unsound economics to use up high-priced surplus meat in dishes which will be sold at prices based on cheaper cuts of meat.

Seasonality of commodities such as vegetables, fruit, game and shellfish should be considered when planning the menu. While improved methods of distribution and preservation have extended the season of many commodities, high costs are associated with buying goods out of season. Over and above this consideration, however, is that of gastronomic appeal. The pattern of changing seasons forms an important aspect of lifestyle to many consumers. The wise menu maker recognizes seasonal changes in menu making for gastronomic and nutritional reasons even when factors of cost and availability are no longer so acute.

Consideration of seasons in menu making is not, therefore, simply a matter of exploiting foods that are seasonable, available and cheap, but of weaving into the fabric of the year's bill of fare a rhythm and assortment of foods that appeal because they suit the conditions of the time and the human instinct for variety. Caterers must not only be well informed and knowledgeable about the foods that are prevalent in their own locality and in their own country, but they must also know what is available from other countries. There is nothing complex about designing a menu in sympathy with the season but, simple though it is, it demands a knowledge of food and an instinct for balance.

Kitchen staff and plant and equipment

It is one thing to create a menu which reads well and, as a piece of literature, evokes a flow of gastric juices. It is quite another to actually put it into practice with the aid of staff and kitchen. When great establishments operated a full partie system they were seldom limited by considerations of craft skills. Few kitchens today can operate in this manner.

A menu must be designed to match the number of staff, the time that they have available and the skills which these staff have. It is possible to increase the productivity of kitchens (that is, produce the same

---

Tutorial topic

Set up the information contained in Figure 3.3 in the form of a *spreadsheet* on a computer. Use this spreadsheet to explore the effect of the following changes in sales and prices, on the overall food cost percentage. After each question, reset data back to their original values before going on to the next question.

1. An increase in the cost of suprêmes of chicken, increases the food cost of chicken suprême to £4.88.

2. Sales of pork cutlet fall to 125 and sales of scampi provençale increase to 102.

3. Because of the poor sales for the vegetable lasagne, it is decided to reduce its selling price to £5.10.

4. Discuss the implications for the catering manager for each of these changes.

quantity of food with less space and fewer staff) by using convenience foods and labour-saving equipment. In a similar way, the necessary level of skilled staff may be reduced by buying in ready-prepared items and by using automated equipment. The relationships between food purchasing, staff skill levels, staff numbers and equipment must be clearly defined in the food policy and carried forward into the working menu.

A further aspect of the relationship between facilities and menu is illustrated by the volume and type of storage space available. A menu must be planned around the storage space for ambient, chilled and frozen food. It is also related to frequency of delivery. In rural areas, with infrequent deliveries, the menu may be constrained by the lack of storage capacity.

Balance

The balance of a menu refers to:

- The balance of items as served on the plate.
- The balance of items selected for one meal.
- The balance of items from meal-to-meal and day-to-day in a captive situation.

The need for this balance varies from one type of menu to another. In the case of a fixed menu, the menu maker needs to produce a series of dishes which complement each other. In the case of a menu with choice, the need is to produce a menu with sufficient choice to interest all consumers within the chosen market segment.

The balance of a menu relates to harmony and variety of a number of properties of the food, such as:

- *Economics*. The balance of food and labour cost percentages over the menu to provide overall profitability.
- *Colour*. The effect of the meal experience can be spoiled by colour monotony. The appearance in sequence of dishes, for example, in which brown is the predominant colour can induce boredom in the dinner even though, individually, the dishes are good. Similarly, the presentation of food on the plate should have contrasting but harmonious colours. The method of cooking and the choice of appropriate garnishes can do much to overcome this problem.
- *Texture*. This includes descriptive terms such as crisp and colour. A menu should provide a range of food textures to prevent monotony. Texture is partly related to the choice of foods, but equally important is the method of preparation and cooking. On a menu with choice, there should be a mix of foods which are grilled or fried and foods which are stewed or casseroled. Variety can also be provided through the appropriate choice of vegetables, which may have a crisp texture, or be diced or puréed to contrast with the main dish.
- *Flavour*. This includes descriptive terms such as strong, mild, sour, spicy, sweet, astringent. The menu maker needs to be aware of flavour in a number of ways. Care is needed in the use of strong flavours such as spices. There is little point in serving a very delicately flavoured dessert after a curry or chilli con carne since the spices would remain on the palate. This is one reason for serving sorbets between courses of a banquet, since it refreshes and cleans the palate for the next course. Flavour balance is also important in choosing accompanying sauces, vegetables and garnishes. Many of the traditional accompaniments and classic compositions whether they are as simple as apple sauce and roast pork or as

refined as lamb cutlets reform often solve, or partially solve, the flavour contrast problem.

- *Kind.* In a menu which has choice, the menu planner needs to offer a variety of 'kinds' of food. These might include 'kinds' of protein item, such as seafood, a selection of meats and vegetarian items. Similarly, it could refer to 'kinds' of vegetable, such as leafy and root vegetables and pulses etc. Similarly, on a cyclic menu, there should be variety in the kinds of food from one day to the next.

Publicity and promotional aspects

The features of menu composing detailed above constitute some of the main and practical elements with which the chef or caterer has to contend. They are, on the whole, matters which involve catering staff and the kitchen. In all these elements there is, in fact, the simple concept of satisfying the customer. The menu, balanced in all the ways that have been mentioned, should reconcile the potential of the kitchen and its staff with the satisfaction of the customer. A good menu, however, can and should do more. It should function as an appetite creator, a bait for customers, a talking point and a piece of publicity. It should read well, look good and have a positive power of attraction. Some of its characteristics such as printing, style and design may be more related to corporate and marketing functions than they are to the kitchen, but the chef and/or caterer should be associated closely with the positive possibilities of the menu in promoting business.

If a menu is to be a tangible and effective expression of a marketing policy and an efficient table sales support, then *menu consciousness* must be fostered. Caterers should be constantly evaluating both their own and other menus, not as gastronomic balancing acts, but as showcases or shop windows. The menu maker should be constantly on the look-out for new ideas to incorporate both into the presentation and composition of the menu.

Composition of the menu

As part of a basic food operation plan, factors about the menu must be established ahead of any physical layout and equipment planning. These factors include:

- Style and quality of menu.
- Whether à la carte, table d'hôte or a blend of both.
- Menu range related to number, variety and standard of dishes.
- Preparation and cooking of each dish in terms of recipes, portions, quantities and service styles.
- Speciality items to be featured (for advanced planning of appropriate equipment).
- Extent of processed or convenience foods usage, that is, types and quantities of foods to be produced and served determined so that requirements, in terms of processes and equipment, can be efficiently planned.

For the person in charge of the kitchen, the menu summarizes all of his or her activities. The caterer or head chef, in composing a menu, is not only producing information about a meal for the benefit of the clientele but is evolving a blueprint or basic plan on which the kitchen operation will develop. Thus, clarity and accuracy are as important to chefs as to customers. The menu also briefs the various groups of staff or parties within the kitchen about how they should plan their work. From their point of view, as much as from the customers', it would be disastrous if its language was ambiguous or lacking in meaning.

In many operations the chef is still the menu maker. In such cases the menus should be composed according to a clear catering policy expressed by the proprietor or manager (in a large hotel through the food and beverage manager). A chef's menu composing will be within cost, pricing and profit constraints and other constraints related to purchasing and dish merchandising.

Another aim seeks to minimize the number of commodities to be purchased, received and stored and this is helped by selecting food items which can have a multiple purpose. Convenience foods, especially pre-cut, high-cost protein items to close specifications, when effectively built into menus can affect production economies.

In some situations, another objective of the menu planner may be to limit the number of items on a number of menus and to coordinate various menus used in any one operation. The coordination of menus for different rooms and functions can minimize production procedures and eliminate problems.

Types of menu

Today's menu can be one of several types or it can incorporate features from a number of types. Terms in catering change but the different styles of menu include:

- À la carte.
- Table d'hôte.
- Selective menu plan.
- Static menus.
- Cyclic menus.
- Market menus.

À la carte

The à la carte menu offers a large selection of dishes, each independently priced, from which customers can compose their own meal by choosing from 'the card'. Naturally, à la carte selection by the customer may involve waiting a short time for some of the dishes, such as grills and sautés, while they are being cooked, unless the dishes have been chosen by the customer in advance. With the reduction in size of the kitchen brigade, the number of items on an à la carte menu has been reduced. As an alternative to this, menu breadth may be maintained by the use of pre-prepared dishes, either prepared on-site or bought in chilled or frozen form.

In some à la carte menus, items such as vegetables and side salads are costed into the selling price of the dish. In other cases, these items are described and costed separately.

Many à la carte menus will also offer one or more daily specials. There are a number of ways in which information about specials can be conveyed to the customer. One method is to have a menu insert with a description of the specials, which is either loose or attached to the menu. Another method is to use a blackboard or lightboard and the special dishes are written on. A third way is to use waiting staff to describe the specials of the day.

Table d'hôte

The table d'hôte (literally the host's or hotelier's table) is a set menu at a fixed price with much less choice or even no choice at all. A restaurant may offer several table d'hôte menus, each at a different price, as in the popular French 'menu'. Another variation is to vary the price based upon the main protein item or to add an additional sum to the fixed price for certain selections.

Selective menu plan

This type of menu is a cross between table d'hôte and à la carte styles. It provides a limited number of choices within a fixed price menu and with a fixed number of courses. A selective menu plan might be formulated from items along the following lines:

- Four to six appetizers.
- Five to eight entrées.
- Three to six vegetables or salads.
- Four to eight puddings or desserts.

If some of the selections involve high-cost items, they may necessitate a supplement to the basic fixed cost menu.

Static menus

Many restaurants, particularly in popular and fast-food catering, use a menu which is largely unchanged for long periods of time. This covers many speciality restaurants such as steak houses, carveries, pizzerias, hamburger restaurants and roadside restaurants. These restaurants are usually part of large chains where a consistent and well-known product are a part of their attraction.

Although unchanging, these menus gain through public familiarity and favour. The fixed menus allow national advertising of menu items in the press and on radio and television. Narrowness of the menu range enables the production and service teams to build up expertise. But, of course, review and change must still be applied even to static menus.

Cyclic menus

This type of menu is one which is 'rotated' or repeated in a predetermined pattern. A year is divided into quarters, normally coinciding with the seasons: spring; summer; autumn; and winter. Within each quarter, a cycle's length and the number of times each cycle

runs has to be decided by the menu maker. However, it is wise not to have too long a cycle. Cycles often coincide with a fixed number of weeks, typically two, three or four weeks. In this way, within any season, a cycle would consecutively run three to four times before the next seasonal cycle begins. Popular and non-seasonal items may be carried from one season's menu cycle to the next.

Cyclic menus require careful planning. The repetition of each dish or menu item in the same context with other dishes enables a better conclusion to be reached regarding dish popularity. A menu maker can therefore forecast more accurately how much of each item to prepare for the day's business. Sales history over a period of time allows accurate forecasting of sales and enables best-selling items to be used more often and poor selling ones to be eliminated.

The planning of cyclic menus is particularly critical in the case of the captive consumer. The menu cycle must be long enough, and the dishes varied enough to prevent menu fatigue. Additionally, the menus must be nutritionally balanced to provide macro and micro nutrients. In these situations, the computer can be of great value in calculating nutrient levels.

Market menus

Market menus are those which are particularly responsive to season and availability. A new interest has been generated in market menus through the influence of chefs associated with la nouvelle cuisine. In France such chefs as Bocuse, Gúerard, the Troisgros brothers and others have stressed their belief in personal appraisal of fresh produce available and advocate market selection before completing their menus. Market menus are therefore thought to have special application in so-called gourmet operations at all price levels, from modest chef proprietor to grand restaurants. Many restaurants with a fixed or other type of menu offer daily 'specials' based on the market menu principle.

The computer and menu planning

The computer may be used in a number of ways to assist in the menu-planning process:

- To provide a recipe/menu database.
- To generate menus.
- To produce printed menus using word processors and desktop publishing.
- To analyse a menu using menu engineering.

Recipe and menu databases

A database represents an efficient and effective way of storing, recalling and editing information. A database is composed of two parts:

1 A set of files.
2 A database management program.

The database management program is used to manipulate information in the files and to relate information from one file to another. A file is a collection of information about related items. It is made up of records, one per item. The records are indexed to facilitate the retrieval of information. For example, in a menu database, we may have three files, as shown in Figure 3.4.

The database management program has options to add or edit ingredients, recipes and menus; to cost recipes and menus; and to calculate the nutritional value of recipes and menus. The value of a *receipe/menu* database is increased, when it is used as part of a catering control system, as discussed in Chapter 4.

Menu generation

The computer can play a part in the process of generating menus. With the current generation of computers it works best as an aid to the menu planner, rather than as an automatic system.

One method which has been found useful in this area is based on a technique called integer linear programming. The linear programming technique is used as a way of optimizing the use of resources, an example of which is the provision of basic nutritional needs at least cost. 'Integer' refers to the fact that we normally deal with whole portions, rather than with precisely weighed quantities.

Most research and application has been in relation to developing cyclic menus with no choice. Computer assisted menu planning (CAMP), which was developed by Balintfy (1979), is one such program. The objective of the program is to produce the lowest cost menu cycle which satisfies a number of constraints, such as nutrition, food preference and variety (colour, flavour, texture, and kind). The program has been used successfully in school and hospital catering applications.

One of the difficulties with this type of program has been relating the expressed preferences of consumers to the number of occasions that a dish should be offered in a menu cycle.

Menu preparation

Word processors and desktop publishers can be used to produce more professional menus at a lower cost and they can be updated on a regular basis (Kass, 1989).

In particular, the use of desktop publishing programs together with a laser printer can produce professional looking menus in a short period of time. This is useful for market menus and for special menus, which need to be produced quickly and in small quantities, because professional printing is very expensive.

Desktop programs can incorporate clip-art (ready-drawn artwork which can be used to decorate menus). As an alternative, artwork can be incorporated using a scanning device to capture printed pictures and photographs.

Menu engineering

Earlier in this chapter the relationship between food cost, labour cost and selling prices was discussed. When using percentages, the result can often be misleading and may cause an incorrect decision to be made. For example, it is not easy to compare a high-sales volume and low-profit item to a low-sales volume and high-profit item.

Menu engineering is a method of analysing the menu which does look at this kind of relationship. One advantage of menu engineering is that it is easy to set up on a computer spreadsheet program, thus making it simple for the caterer to constantly review the menu.

Using this technique, each item on the menu is analysed in two ways:

1 *Menu mix percentage* (MM%). This compares the sales of all items on the menu with a *menu achievement target*, which is 70 per cent of the average sales of all

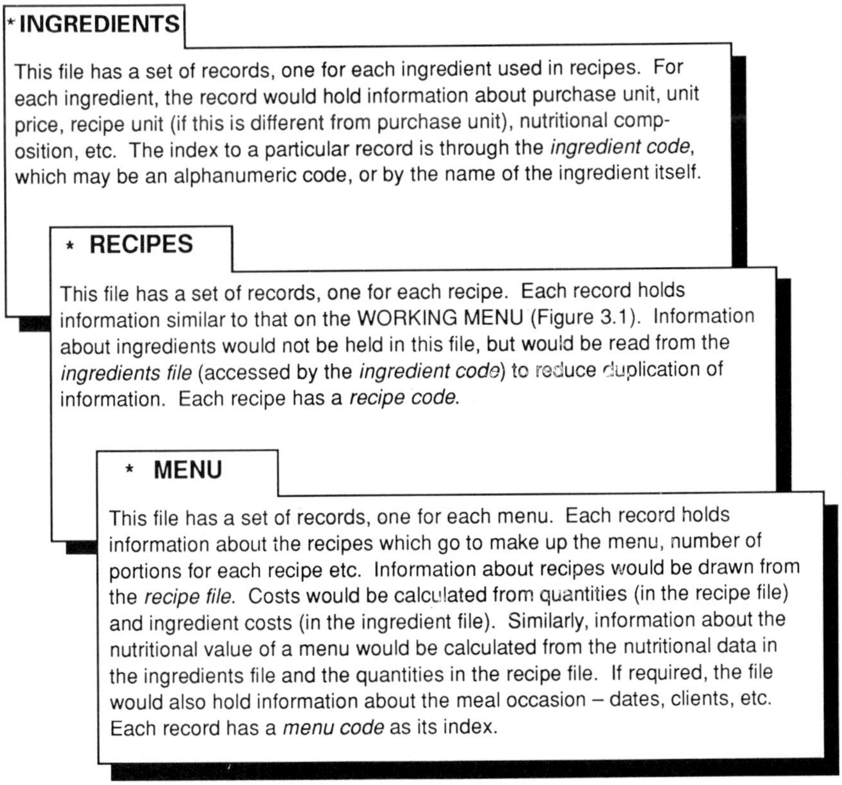

*INGREDIENTS

This file has a set of records, one for each ingredient used in recipes. For each ingredient, the record would hold information about purchase unit, unit price, recipe unit (if this is different from purchase unit), nutritional composition, etc. The index to a particular record is through the *ingredient code*, which may be an alphanumeric code, or by the name of the ingredient itself.

* RECIPES

This file has a set of records, one for each recipe. Each record holds information similar to that on the WORKING MENU (Figure 3.1). Information about ingredients would not be held in this file, but would be read from the *ingredients file* (accessed by the *ingredient code*) to reduce duplication of information. Each recipe has a *recipe code*.

* MENU

This file has a set of records, one for each menu. Each record holds information about the recipes which go to make up the menu, number of portions for each recipe etc. Information about recipes would be drawn from the *recipe file*. Costs would be calculated from quantities (in the recipe file) and ingredient costs (in the ingredient file). Similarly, information about the nutritional value of a menu would be calculated from the nutritional data in the ingredients file and the quantities in the recipe file. If required, the file would also hold information about the meal occasion – dates, clients, etc. Each record has a *menu code* as its index.

Figure 3.4 *Possible files in a recipe/menu database*

menu items. If an item's MM% is greater than the menu achievement target, it is classified as *high* (because it is among the best-selling items). Conversely, if it is less it is classified as *low*, because, compared to other menu items, its sales are relatively weak.

2   *Contribution margin* (CM). This compares the profit contribution (selling price/food cost) for each menu item with the *contribution achievement target*, which is the average contribution for all items on the menu. As with the menu mix, items are classified as *high* or *low*, depending on whether they are above or below the target.

For each menu item we have four possibilities, as shown in Figure 3.5. Based on which category a menu item is in, we can make decisions about its relative performance. It cannot help us in a situation where, for example, all menu items sell poorly or where all food costs are too high. The four menu categories have the following characteristics:

- *Stars*. These items sell well and have a high profit contribution. This means that they are subsidizing less popular and less profitable items. The caterer must

obviously look after these items and be sure to maintain quality. They should also be displayed in a prominent position on the menu.

- *Plough horses*. These sell well but have a low profit contribution. They represent good value for money on the menu and should not be strongly promoted. The costs and portion sizes should be reviewed to see if there is any way of reducing the food costs.

- *Puzzles*. These items do not sell well but provide a high profit contribution. They are more difficult to deal with than the other categories — hence their name. A number of options may be tried. For example, a decrease in the selling price may increase sales without making the item unprofitable. Alternatively, better promotion or display on the menu may increase the popularity of the dish.

- *Dogs*. Menu items which fall into this category do not sell well and have a low profit contribution. Consideration should be given to taking these items off the menu, depending upon their performance. Care is needed in making a decision about dogs since the outcome of savagely removing dogs may result in there being only one item left on the menu!

Plough horse High menu mix % Low contribution margin %	*Star* High menu mix % High contribution margin %
Dog Low menu mix % Low contribution margin %	*Puzzle* Low menu mix % High contribution margin %

Figure 3.5   *Menu engineering categories*

The method of carrying out a menu analysis is shown in Figure 3.6. An example of a menu engineering table based on the menu given in Figure 3.3 is shown in Figure 3.7. The ratios calculated can be plotted on a graph, as shown in Figure 3.8. This gives a visual indication of the relative performance of all items on the menu.

References and further reading

Balintfy J. L. (1979). The utilisation of computers in menu planning. In *Food Service Systems* (Livingstone G. E. and Chang C. M.). New York: Academic Press, pp. 155–75.

COMA (1984). Diet and cardiovascular disease. Committee on Medical Aspects of Health. Report on Health and Social Subjects 28. London: HMSO.

Davis B. and Stone S. (1991). *Food and Beverage Management*, 2nd edn. Oxford: Heinemann.

Eckstein E. F. (1983). *Menu Planning*, 3rd edn. Westport, Conn.: AVI.

Harris A. B. and Robbins G. V. (1985). *Nutrition in Catering*. Oxford: Heinemann.

HCIMA (1989). *Implementing Healthy Eating in Catering*. London: HCIMA.

Jones P. (1983). *Food Service Operations*. London: Cassell.

Kasavana M. L. (1984). *Computer Systems for Foodservice Operations*. New York: Van Nostrand Reinhold.

Kass M. (1989). Computer age menus. *Restaurants and Institutions*, June, vol. 99, no. 16, pp. 64–80.

Lewis R. C. and Chambers R. E. (1989). *Marketing Leadership in Hospitality Management*. New York: Van Nostrand Reinhold.

The method of carrying out a menu analysis is as follows:

1 For each menu item record the *number sold* (NS), the *food cost* (FC) and the *selling price* (SP).

2 Sum the NS for all menu items to give total sold (TS).

3 Record the number of items on the menu (N).

4 Multiply 100 by (1/N) x 0.7 to give *achievement ratio* (AR).

5 For each menu item, calculate number sold as a percentage of total sales to give the menu mix % (MM%) equals (NS x 100)/TS.

6 For each menu item, compare MM% with AR:
    if MM% > AR record MM% as high
    if MM% < AR record MM% as low

7 For each item, calculate SP – FC to give *contribution margin* (CM).

8 For each item calculate CM x NS to give *contribution* (CON).

9 Sum CON for all items to give *total contribution* (TC).

10 Divide TC by TS to give *contribution achievement* (CA).

11 For each item, compare CM with CA:
    if CM > CA record CM as high
    if CM < CA record CM as low

Figure 3.6 *Procedures for performing menu analysis*

Maslow A. H. (1943). A theory of human motivations: the basic needs. *Psychology Review*, vol. 50, pp. 370–96.

NACNE (1983). A discussion paper on proposals for nutritional guidelines for health educators in Britain. National Advisory Committee on Nutrition Education. London: Health Education Council.

Ninemeier J. D. (1984). *Principles of Food and Beverage Operations*. East Lansing, Michigan: Educational Institute of the American Hotel and Motel Association.

Product	Sales	MM%	Food cost	Selling price	CM	CON (£)	
RLL	70	12.96 (H)	2.34	7.80	5.46 (L)	382.20	PH
PC	173	32.04 (H)	1.95	8.70	6.75 (H)	1167.75	ST
CH	151	27.96 (H)	4.22	9.00	4.78 (L)	721.78	PH
SP	54	10.00 (L)	2.56	7.00	4.44 (L)	239.76	DG
TA	49	9.07 (L)	3.12	10.30	7.18 (H)	351.82	PU
VL	43	7.96 (L)	1.46	5.94	4.48 (L)	192.64	DG

Total sales (TS): 540   Total CON (TC) £3,055.95
AR = (100/N) x 0.7 = 11.67   CA = TC/TS 5.66

Key

RLL	Roast leg of lamb	SP	Scampi Provençale
PC	Pork cutlet	TA	Trout with almonds
CH	Chicken suprême	VL	Vegetable lasagne
PH	Plough horse	ST	Star
PU	Puzzle	DG	Dog

Figure 3.7   *An example of a menu engineering table*

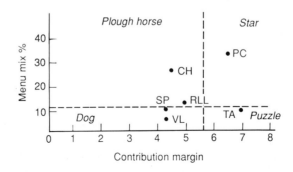

Figure   3.8 *A graph of the menu engineering example shown in Figure 3.7*

4
Production planning and control

Once a menu has been planned it must be put into operation or implemented. In this way the menu acts as a blueprint for the production and service of the menu items and the working menu acts as a basis for planning and control procedures.

Production and service systems

In general, it is possible to classify a business as being concerned with either a product or a service. In a production or manufacturing industry there is a tangible product such as a pair of shoes or a tin of peas. In a service or non-manufacturing industry there is no tangible product, the output being in the nature of advice, information, a night's sleep, or a pleasant atmosphere, etc.

However, many industries, such as the catering industry, do not fit neatly into this classification. A customer in a restaurant is receiving both a service (the atmosphere of the dining room, the personal attention and advice on food and drink) and a product (the prepared meal or drink).

This mix of products and services within one business creates some special problems. One aspect of the service industry is that it is not possible to build up or use up stock. For

example, it is not easy to smooth out the rate of arrival of customers at a cafeteria. This means that we must make the rate of production match the rate of arrival of customers. Alternatively, we may be able to *decouple* production from service, using some form of buffer stock (see Chapter 2). This allows *production smoothing*, even if service cannot be smoothed.

Before making decisions about production planning we must analyse the relationship between the placing of an order and the method of production. At the point in time when a customer places an order the food may be:

- Held as finished stock (*make-to-stock*).
- Assembled from partially finished stock (*assemble-to-order*).
- Produced from basic raw materials without any pre-preparation (*make-to-order*).

Make-to-stock

In this case we must produce food at a sufficient rate to maintain a buffer stock. We can see this in fast-food restaurants, where hamburgers and other cooked products are held on a heated display unit, visible both to production and service crews. Another example would be the holding of cooked vegetables in a self-service cafeteria. These would be cooked at a rate sufficient to maintain a buffer stock of vegetables to meet customer demand.

The quantity of buffer stock is related to:

- The shelf life of the product under the relevant storage conditions.
- The rate of demand.

For example, in many fast-food restaurants the keeping quality of a hamburger is used to determine the maximum length of time the product can be held on the display unit. Any hamburgers not sold after this period of time are discarded. This means that a close match is needed between production and service and that large stocks of finished product cannot be built up — there is only very limited decoupling of production and service.

If the buffer stock consists of pre-cooked frozen or chilled foods, which only require

reheating, the storage life may be one month (frozen) or five days (chilled). This allows a much greater decoupling of production and service. The greater the degree of decoupling of production and service, the greater the production smoothing (see Figure 4.1).

Assemble-to-order

Here sufficient stocks of the partially finished dishes must be produced to satisfy orders. One example of this is the traditional use of *mise-en-place*, by which we mean the pre-preparation of stocks, sauces and partially finished goods before the service period. In a similar way, a pizza restaurant has ready-prepared and proved pizza bases, pizza sauce and toppings so that pizzas can be quickly assembled and baked. Another example is a sandwich bar, where the sandwiches are not made in advance but are assembled from previously prepared components in response to a customer's order.

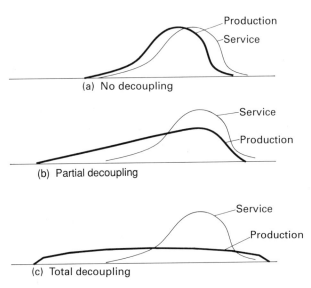

Figure 4.1   *Relationship between production and service for a catering operation with a lunchtime service*

Make-to-order

Few restaurants operate this model in its most extreme form with complete production of all dishes to order, starting with the raw materials. The nearest to this would have been the largest kitchens in the heyday of the partie system, with their armies of staff. Today, there would normally be some degree of pre-preparation or ingredients would be purchased in a partially prepared form. Many pubs and snack bars operate in this way. Meat and fish products are bought ready portioned. Vegetables are bought frozen. By doing this, a meal can be quickly cooked from its basic raw materials on receipt of an order from the kitchen.

Although we have identified three models to express the relationship between production and service rates, in practice restaurants use a combination of these models. For example, most high-class and speciality restaurants would use a combination of all three models, based upon identifying the most suitable method for each menu item. It is important to be clear which model is being used for each menu item before commencing production planning.

The catering information system

As with any other business, success in catering depends upon effective planning and control and for this we need a *management information system* (MIS). This system is designed to monitor key performance variables of an operation, to compare these performance variables with those predicted by the plan and to produce reports based on performance. From this, we can see that the MIS operates as a feedback control loop.

As we saw in Chapter 2, the plan consists of three related activities:

1 Planning.
2 Implementation.
3 Control.

These three activities are linked, as shown in Figure 4.2.

The unique features of catering, when compared with other industries, lead to particular problems of planning and control. For example, we have already discussed the mix of production and service within the same unit which differentiates catering from

---

Tutorial topic

For a restaurant that you know, analyse all the items on the menu and determine their method of production in terms of:

1 Make-to-stock.
2 Assemble-to-order.
3 Make-to-order.

For each item, what are the characteristics of the restaurant and the menu item that make this the most appropriate method?

Suggest different methods of production for those items where you think that the current method could be improved.

---

many other industries. Similarly, the fact that many dishes are produced in response to a personal customer order, with the customer visiting the place of manufacture, is quite unique, as is the short time span between placing the order and receiving the product.

The close link between production and service, both in physical terms and in time, requires special consideration and this leads to many unique features of the *catering information system* (CIS).

Another factor in catering is the short life of both the product and the service. If there is an over-production of food, it may not be possible to store a high-quality perishable product for long periods of time without obvious deteriorations in quality. At the service end, if a customer's needs cannot be met, they cannot be satisfied by a promise to 'have it ready by 3 o'clock' or 'it should be in sometime next week'. In this sense both the

product and the service have short shelf lives.

Finally, an important fact is that the stock is volatile, in the sense that once it has been consumed, it can no longer be audited. Staff can, if not effectively managed, consume food and drink without any records of this consumption being kept.

Because of these aspects of the catering operation, the management information system needs to have specialized features. In this chapter we are concerned with planning and control at the operational level. The type of catering system and the style of production and service have been fixed by the food policy and the menu has been planned, as discussed in Chapter 3.

Operational planning covers ordering of raw materials, issuing of goods from store, planning of the detailed schedule of production and service, allocation of resources, and

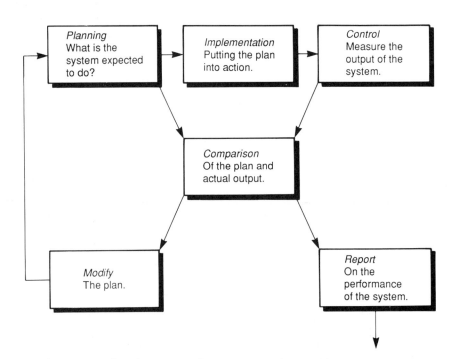

Figure 4.2   *The planning, implementation and control loop*

costing and controlling procedures to make sure that the objectives of the plan are being attained. We can consider operational planning as occurring in three stages (Kasavana, 1984), as shown in Figure 4.3.

Standard recipes amd the projected sales mix

The basic relationship between the menu and the production quantity of food is calculated from the standard recipe (see Figure 3.1) together with projected information about the sales of each item on the menu. The latter is called *the projected sales mix*.

Because of the importance of the information in the standard recipe, it is important that frequent checks are made to maintain its accuracy. These checks should include yields, portion sizes and food cost percentages. Recipes should be tested to verify portion yields and to determine losses in cooking and portioning. The cost of accompaniments such as garnishes, vegetables and salads served with the item but not priced separately on the menu must be included. Since yields for items like roast meats depends on cooking conditions, cooking times and temperatures should also be specified in the standard recipe. Similarly, the yield will depend upon the type of equipment used. It is possible to have full preparation details on the back of the recipe card or on the computer system.

Standard recipes thus precisely record ingredients and methods used for preparing each menu item and thereby help to ensure consistent quality and establish realistic costs. By using a standard format, recipe cards build up to constitute a card index system which can be used both in planning and control.

In order to purchase, issue and prepare foods for a particular meal, it is necessary to determine the *projected sales mix*. This is the number of portions or *covers* which are to be produced for each menu item. The projected sales mix should also have a breakdown of sales through the hours of opening. For an existing operation which uses a cyclic or

---

Pre-production stage
- Calculation of quantities and costs.
- Purchasing and receiving.
- Scheduling of equipment and staff.

Production stage
- Issuing of stock.
- Pre-preparation.
- Order taking.
- Production.
- Service.
- Billing.
- Quality control.

Post-production stage
- Cash control.
- Sales analysis.
- Stock control.
- Management reports.

Figure 4.3 *Stages of operational planning and control*

fixed menu we can use previous sales history to make these estimates. Where no previous information is available, caterers must use market research data or their knowledge of the market.

The next stage is to determine basic production quantities from a knowledge of portion sizes and sales mix analysis. This information can then be collated to determine the total amount of food which is to be produced and it can also be used for purchasing, stock control, goods issuing and production planning.

Portion sizes

The portion size for each menu item needs to be carefully defined and controlled if the balance between cost, wastage and customer satisfaction is to be achieved. An indication of typical portion sizes for a 'full' meal is given in Figure 4.4. However, this needs careful interpretation in the light of trends in nutrition and diet. Scaled down values may be required when catering for children or the elderly.

Whatever portion size is decided upon, the method of *portion control* must be clearly defined as a part of the standard recipe. Accurate portioning cannot be maintained by forms and paper work alone but also demands physical control. This implies the need for:

- Workable standard recipes.
- Visual guides to plate and dish layouts.
- Suitably sized implements: ladles; scoops; serving spoons; serving dishes, etc.
- Meat and fish cuts (steak, chops, escalopes, chicken, etc.) to be accurately weighed to pre-cooked specifications, either purchased pre-portioned or cut to the required size in the larder department.
- Skill in carving or using slicing machines.
- Differentiation in portion sizes for the same dish when used in different ways: buffet; starter; table d'hôte; à la carte.

Recipe explosion

The *recipe explosion* used to calculate purchase quantities and production quantities from the standard recipe and the projected sales mix (Figure 4.5).

The explosion of a menu consists of taking each ingredient and calculating its quantity as follows:

Production quantity = recipe quantity (per cover) × number of covers

If the standard recipe is for more than one cover, the formula needs to be adjusted. For

Appetizer	50 – 75 g
Salad	50 – 75 g
Soup	175 – 200 g
Vegetable	50 – 100 g
Potato	100 – 115 g
Meat	75 – 100 g
Bread and butter	50 – 75 g
Dessert	115 – 150 g
Beverage	115 – 200 g

Figure 4.4   *Typical portion sizes*

example, if the recipe is for 100 covers, the formula is:

Production quantity =
$$\frac{\text{recipe quantity}}{100} \times \text{number of covers}$$

Purchasing

Purchasing policy

Purchase quantities are obtained directly from the information in the recipe explosion.

Once the recipe explosion has been completed for all menu items, all occurrences of the same ingredient are grouped together. For example, butter may appear in several recipes. Each time it appears the quantities are added together to give the total requirement for that ingredient.

Once this has been done, purchase quantities are compared with current stock levels taking into account other commitments. The difference between the two gives the amount which must be purchased. In practice, purchase orders will probably result from a combination of requirements for menus from

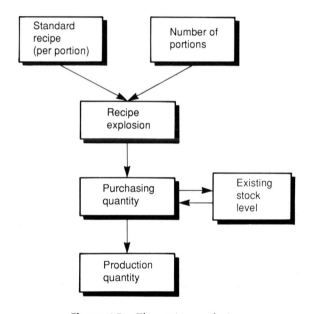

Figure 4.5   *The recipe explosion*

Tutorial topic

Using the recipe in Figure 3.1, carry out a recipe explosion for sixty-four portions.

Set up the same recipe on a spreadsheet, with the number of portions as a variable. Test the spreadsheet model to make sure that you can calculate recipe quantities for any number of portions.

several days. For example, some goods will be ordered once a week.

Some ingredients and consumables (particularly those with a long shelf life) are purchased in pre-defined purchase quantities. In these situations, the purchasing function is not directly linked to the procurement of ingredients for a single menu but is related to purchasing requirements for a period of time. In this situation, ordering may be triggered by *minimum stock levels*, rather than by specific menu requirements.

The purchase of food materials represents a major factor contributing to the success or failure of a catering operation. The quality of the buying decision affects both the market, through the perceptions of customers, and profitability, both of which are key factors to the survival and growth of a catering venture.

Buying policy and practice have to be concerned with the prevention of waste and loss. Buying commodities that, on the one hand, are not good enough or, on the other hand, too good for their purpose, represents potential loss. Over ordering can lead to a waste of perishable items or to capital being tied up in high value stock. Poor storage and stock control can result in waste.

Intelligent buying, using careful specifications, helps avoid not only direct errors but helps cooks and other staff to avoid attendant errors exacerbated by using inappropriate materials. Food which is wasted represents loss of food at its potential sale price not at its cost price. Buying procedures must be directed towards total effectiveness.

In most large organizations the responsibility for determining purchase specifications and for the actual purchasing does not come within the role of the chef or catering manager. These are increasingly determined by top management adopting firm menu and food beverage policies. In these organizations, purchasing is frequently the responsibility of specialist buyers. Kitchen responsibilities in relation to buying are increasingly those of ensuring that standards set through specifications are met.

Factors influencing food purchase

As we have seen in Chapter 3, the method of food purchasing has a major influence on the menu planning process. It also has an impact on production planning.

For example, in a kitchen which buys meat products in the form of a side, the caterer must link the menu and the production plan to use up all parts of the meat. This means that the caterer must understand the relative weights of each cut so that the utilization of the meat is as great as possible. In order to obtain the maximum value of the side of meat, the high-quality cuts should be used on high-value dishes. The economics of using a high-quality cut such as sirloin in a low-cost dish such as shepherd's pie is not sound, unless the only alternative is to discard the meat. In this situation menu planning, purchasing and production planning are closely linked.

We can contrast this situation with the catering operation for which all meat products are purchased as pre-portioned, ready-to-cook joints, with purchasing quantities related to one menu item. Here, there are no complex links in purchasing terms between the various menu items.

Another way in which there is a close link between the menu, purchasing and production is through the purchase specification. By specifying precise portion weights and/or sizes for raw materials, the control of costs and production becomes simplified. For this reason seeking uniform sized fish or pre-cut meat portions is now the rule rather than the exception.

Many companies now use nominated suppliers who are contracted to supply specific items against known specifications and quality levels. Some companies have their own supplies division for providing a large part of the requirements of the units. This is often the case with fast-food companies. This reduces the purchasing responsibility of unit management to that of deciding what quantity of food to order.

In Figure 2.6 the various forms of raw material available to the caterer were described and the nature of them will obviously influence purchasing policy and procedures. The alternatives described affect the important properties of *shelf life* and *quality*. Shelf life will determine if a material must be ordered for a single service occasion, for a number of occasions covering several days, or even longer for shelf stable items. This decision is obviously closely linked to the nature of the menu and, in particular, whether it is fixed or cyclic.

The method of purchasing food is related to the food distribution chain, as shown in Figure 4.6. It is important that the people who are responsible for food purchase understand the nature of food supply channels and how they may change in the future. While caterers still buy direct from fresh produce

markets, they also buy fresh foods from retailers and wholesalers. Convenience food usage has increased the supply of food from food processing plants (especially frozen foods) directly to the caterer. But patterns of food supply and purchasing continue to change. Sometimes 'backlash' from consumers switches buying emphasis. For example, there has been renewed interest in traditional beer brewing, in fresh seasonal vegetables and in 'old-fashioned' crusty bread.

Purchase specifications

For many years Britain lagged behind countries such as the United States in the rigorous use of food specifications as a key part of the buying function. However, the situation has now changed and most successful catering organizations purchase to agreed specifications. A specification provides:

● Buying standards for the operation.

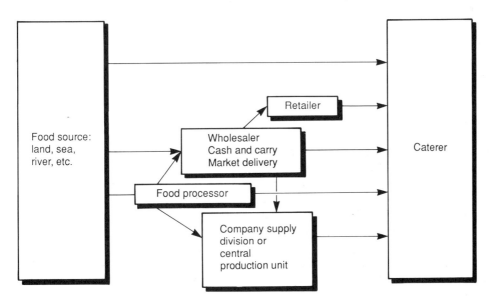

Figure 4.6   *The food distribution chain*

- Common denominator of market bidding for food buyers and sellers.
- Uniformity and consistency in purchasing and receiving.

A specification should include details regarding: quality; type or variety; quantity; characteristics; delivery time; and frequency. The definition of a 'specification' would have been reached through discussions with the appropriate staff involved in receiving, storing, preparing, cooking and serving food. In short, key catering staff need to be involved and kept informed to help maintain both food quality and food cost.

Production planning

The purpose of production planning is to ensure that the correct *dishes*, of a defined quality, are produced at the right time and with efficient use of the resources of *materials*, *staff* and *equipment*. As such, the exercise is one of working back from the required service time in order to determine the inter-related sequence of activities required to produce all foods. The detail of how this is done varies from one type of catering to another. There are two main considerations:

1   The rate of service.
2   The method of production.

The rate of service in some types of catering, such as school meals and industrial restaurants, is characterized by having large peaks of service concentrated over short periods of time, as shown in Figure 4.1. In other cases the demand is much more evenly spread over the day. The projected sales mix analysis can give us information about relative sales levels throughout the day.

As we have seen in the earlier part of this chapter, the production may be make-to-

stock, assemble-from-stock, or make-to-order.

With make-to-stock we can consider two situations, the first of which is where the stock is in the form of freshly cooked food which is kept at its service temperature for a short duration, that is, limited decoupling. The second is where the freshly cooked foods are reduced to a safe storage temperature and held (chilled or frozen) before being reheated for service.

In the first case, the object of production planning is to prepare and cook batches of food at such a rate that the stock in the hot cupboard or bain-marie is maintained. Since holding food hot causes a deterioration in sensory and nutritional properties, and introduces a risk of bacterial growth, maximum holding times should be defined for each menu item. The cooking batch size can then be related to cooking times and rate of sales.

Let us take as an example the cooking of fresh broccoli. Assume that the portion size has been fixed at 100 g and, because of nutritional and quality considerations, the maximum holding time is limited to fifteen minutes. Over the period from 12 to 2 p.m. it is expected that we will sell 240 portions at an even rate.

The broccoli is to be cooked in batches of 2 kg in containers which can be transferred straight from a convection steamer to a bain-marie. Cooking time is five minutes per batch. Using this information, we must balance the rate of production with the rate of sale.

$$240 \text{ portions in 2 hours} = 2 \text{ portions per minute}$$

$$1 \text{ batch of } 2000 \text{ g} = 20 \text{ portions}$$

Therefore:

$$1 \text{ batch will last } 20/2 = 10 \text{ minutes}$$

And we need:

100 g × 240/1000 kg broccoli in total = 24 kg

Total number of batches = 24/2 = 12

Since the cooking time is five minutes, we can start the first batch at 11.55 a.m. This will then be ready for service at 12 noon. At a rate of two customers per minute, this batch will last for ten minutes. Therefore, we must start the second batch at 12.05 p.m. This cycle will then continue throughout the lunch period, cooking a new batch every ten minutes. The relationship between production and stock is shown in Figure 4.7. In practice, this precise production schedule will be modified depending on the actual flow rate of customers. Batches can be started earlier or later to match the actual service to customers.

Where we are producing food for a long-term buffer stock, such as cook-chill or cook-freeze, the organization is similar to that shown above, except that the critical factor is

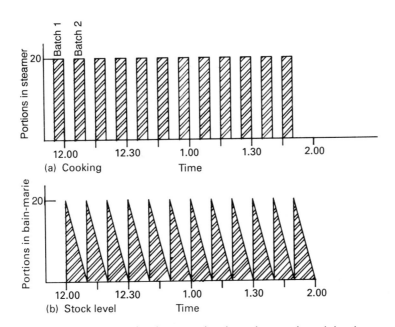

Figure 4.7   *Relationship between batch cooking and stock levels*

Tutorial topic

Using the example of the broccoli:

1   What is the maximum holding time?
2   What rate of service would lead to a holding time of longer than the required fifteen minutes?
3   What would be the maximum rate of service that this piece of equipment could satisfy?

to assemble batches for the blast-chiller or blast-freezer. The chilling or freezing process takes a maximum of ninety minutes. We must therefore organize food production so that we have a full load for chilling or freezing every ninety minutes.

Control

Control provides the necessary feedback so that the caterer can be certain that plans are being followed and targets met. The control function satisfies a number of different needs. It provides:

- Immediate feedback to the chef or food and beverage manager.
- Feedback of information to senior management about short- and long-term objectives.
- Information on which to base future planning and operational targets.
- Information for auditing and tax purposes.

The purpose of covering the topic of control in this book is not to provide a full discussion of accounting and control procedures, which is the subject of complete textbooks (Sutton, 1983). Attention here is concentrated on activities within the kitchen and its ancillary sections. Its purpose is, first, to deal only with records and aspects of control as an integral part of the work of staff within food stores and kitchen and, second, to shed light on cost, price and profit goals. Factors which could contribute to low gross profit include:

- Bad buying, particularly poor value for money.
- Over-purchasing, resulting in stock lying around and not earning money.
- Poor storage, resulting in waste.

- Poor quality control with low acceptability and customer dissatisfaction.
- Poor portion control: if too large, inadequate yield; if too small or too erratic, customer dissatisfaction;
- Poor preparation with resultant low acceptability and yield.
- Bad pricing with inadequate profit margin and loss.

Within kitchens and food stores the purpose of control records is to:

- Ensure incoming goods accord in quantity and quality with what was actually ordered and with specifications.
- Record receipt of such goods to ensure their safe custody.
- Control movement of goods, both from stores to kitchen sections and from kitchen to restaurant and other outlets.
- Enable the cost of goods consumed (food cost) to be compared with corresponding food sales figures.
- Prevent or limit losses through deterioration, carelessness and pilfering.

Although practices vary throughout the industry, the principles of control are similar for all organizations. To be effective, records should be based on daily food and payroll information because, if delayed until the end of the week or month, they become history. Food and labour costs must remain pertinent to the volume of food and beverage sales. Daily information aids management in identifying current performance and in forecasting future performance. One reason that computers have become so important in catering is that management reports can be produced very quickly, allowing faster identification of, and response to, problems.

Recording orders, receipts, stock and issues

Goods ordered from suppliers use a printed, serially numbered, multipart *order form* —

usually one copy for the supplier, one for stores in order to authorize reception and one for the control or accounts office (see Figure 4.8). Where orders are placed by telephone, a written confirmation order is also required.

It is important that a designated member of staff is given responsibility for goods reception. This may be the owner, the manager, the storekeeper (in operations large enough to employ one full-time), or a nominated member of the kitchen staff.

Once goods are received, the storekeeper (or member of staff with responsibility for goods reception) should check the quantity and quality of goods received against a copy of the order and the *delivery note*, using written specifications where appropriate. Commodities which do not match specifications may make kitchen production harder and reduce profits and should not be accepted.

If, on checking, goods are missing or damaged, then the supplier and carrier must be notified immediately. In most cases, supplier and carrier are one and the same person. Most contracts in catering specify the supplier as being responsible for delivering the goods to the buyer's premises. Once on the buyer's premises, ownership of the goods and responsibility for them passes to the buyer. To avoid deliveries when no one is on duty for checking, the order should include the time and place of delivery. This then becomes a condition of the contract with which the supplier must conform.

It is helpful to caterers if a supplier prices all delivery notes. The *goods received book* can then be used as a check against the invoice, which usually arrives after the goods.

As soon as goods have been checked and accepted they should be placed in a secure place. If they are not to be used immediately, they should be placed in the appropriate

From: Name and address of catering company		Order number:			
Date: —/—/—					
To: Name and address of supplier					
Please supply on —/—/— at — a.m./p.m. the following:					
Description	Unit	Quantity	Unit cost	Cost	Received
			Signed: _____		
			Date: —/—/—		

Figure 4.8 *Specimen order form*

storage area. The store's copy of the order is sent to the control or accounts office. Details of the goods received should then be entered into the goods received book.

Invoices, when received, should be sent direct to the accounts or control office provided that the goods referred to have arrived. The accounts or control office can then marry invoices to the office copy of the order and the certified delivery note from the storekeeper. Prices as well as the calculations on the invoices can be checked. Normally invoices are summarized on a daily basis by the accounts office and, when checked, entered into the account of the respective supplier. Payment is usually on a monthly basis.

Goods taken into the various stores may be controlled through independent *bin cards* (Figure 4.9) or tally cards for each item, in a *stock book* or by a computer. Bin cards are attached to the appropriate bin, shelf or drawer where the goods are stored. Their use necessitates a neat arrangement of commodities in storage and adequate storage space. As well as the bin cards, a *stock record system* which may be in the form of a loose leaf book (with one page for each commodity) or a set of file cards, may be used. The information recorded on a stock record is similar to that recorded on the bin card, but with the addition of costs of receipts, issues and balance.

Bin cards, or whatever stock record arrangement is used, must be written up at the time that the goods are issued or received. The card may contain information about minimum and maximum stock levels for common and long shelf life stock items. This information is useful to the storekeeper

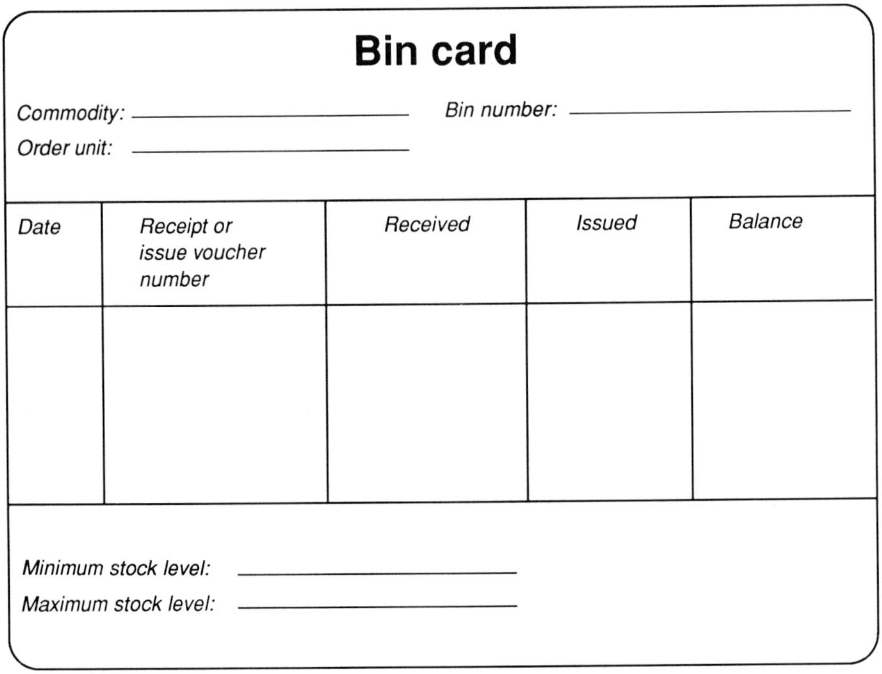

Figure 4.9   *Typical layout of bin card*

(or whoever is responsible for ordering goods). The minimum level is based on a combination of rate of usage and delivery lead times (the time interval between placing an order and receiving delivery). Maximum levels are there to prevent too much capital and space being tied up in stock.

In order to control stock usage effectively, control is required over *stock issue*. This is always a problem for the small unit which cannot afford to employ a full-time store-keeper. Whatever system is used, responsibility for and access to the stores should be assigned to a named person. If unauthorized access to stores is allowed then it is unrealistic to expect any one person to accept responsibility for stores control.

A simple *internal requisition* or chit system is desirable. Requisitions should only be issued by authorized staff and issues, other than for emergencies, should take place only at fixed times in the day. As soon as goods have been issued, the stock record should be updated to give an accurate balance. Account may also need to be taken of goods returned to the stores from the kitchen, using a stores return form.

As an alternative, or in addition to the internal requisition, each department drawing stock may keep a *departmental requisition book*, into which all requests are entered. The advantage with this system is that prices can also be entered into this book, allowing departmental heads to calculate food costs on a regular basis.

Correct stock-taking and accurate inventories are important. For each item, the quantity of issues should be equal to commencing stock plus stores received less final stock. If a deviation is allowed to occur between physical (actual) stock levels and theoretical (recorded) stock levels, this may lead to over- or under-stocking. The frequency of stock-taking is normally determined by the operating policy of the organization. Stock-taking helps to reveal losses from the store due to pilfering, deterioration or negligence.

Production control

Production control is designed to monitor the relationship between the cost and amount of food issued and the number of meals sold. Standardized recipes are the basis of control because the cost of each menu item can be based on a firm foundation. The standardized recipe can be costed, based on current prices so that the portion cost of each menu item can be calculated.

The control takes place in a number of stages:

1   Goods issued from stores are checked against kitchen production records.
2   Food production cost are compared with costs based on standard recipes.
3   Kitchen production is checked against the information from the check pads of waiters, to measure discrepancies between portions produced and portions sold (with allowances for staff meals etc.).

Budgeted or estimated costs can be achieved only with strict waste control and through production efficiency. Even so, budgeted costs may need to be adjusted to practical costs by allowing a tolerance for unavoidable waste and human error. A final cost may thus be established after allowing a tolerance of between 5 and 10 per cent. This final standard cost can be used as a control measure by comparing with actual costs, based on goods issued. Variances between standard cost and actual cost may be caused by a number of factors, such as high preparation and/or cooking waste, poor portion control, over production, errors and pilferage.

A popular method of control is the use of the *gross profit percentage*. This is the difference between food cost and total sales, expressed as a percentage of sales. Percentage targets may be applied to each commodity, to a course, or to a meal or menu. These percentage targets can be compared with actual performance targets as a means of control.

As discussed in Chapter 3, it is not always sensible to use the same gross profit percentage on all menu items. It may be better to achieve higher profit margins on some items and lower margins on others, provided that over the whole sales mix the target is achieved. A typical food cost percentage is 35 per cent, giving a gross profit percentage of 65 per cent. From this must be subtracted labour costs and overheads to give the net profit, for example:

	£	£
Food cost	525	35
Labour cost	450	30
Overheads	300	20
Net profit	225	15

It is normal to allocate labour costs as a percentage of the selling price when working out the costs of an individual menu item. This does not always give a true picture, since it assumes that the amount of labour required is proportional to the selling price, which is frequently not true. Many low-cost food items require more labour than high cost items. Therefore, the labour content should be taken into account when fixing the relationship between food cost and selling price.

Computers for production planning and control

There are now many computer systems available for production planning and control within the catering industry. While these systems vary in their complexity, ease of use, storage capacity and number of users, they all perform similar functions. When considering the purchase of computer software for catering control it is important to be clear about the objectives of the system (Fowler, 1986).

The core of such a system is formed by a set of databases storing information on suppliers, stock levels, recipes and menus. These are linked together by a database management program, as shown in Figure 4.10, which performs a number of functions, as shown in Figure 4.11.

The fundamental part of a catering management information system is the ingredient file, which contains information about each stock item. Information held includes unit size, issue size, who supplies it, how much is in stock, how much is on order, how much is already committed and minimum stock levels. It also contains a price for each ingredient which may be the average price paid for the stock or it may be based on the price of the latest delivery. Additionally, some systems allow the storing of a recipe price for dish-costing purposes. In many catering operations, the stock file may contain thousands of items.

Ingredients go to make up recipes which are held in a recipe file. The recipe is a list of ingredients and quantities required to make up a standard number of portions. The recipe file is likely to contain information about yields, cost prices and selling prices. The recipe may also contain information about preparation time, cooking time and method of preparation. For operations such as cook-chill it may also contain information about chilling packaging quantities, chiller capacity and chilling time (Plumb, 1986). The system needs to be able to handle the situation where a recipe may itself be an ingredient. For example, we may have a recipe for brown stock, which itself is an ingredient in a number of dishes.

These recipes are linked to a menu file. In a cyclic menu, a database may be held for a periodic menu cycle of three, four or five weeks. These menus form the basis of the production planning process. The production plan consists of the menus for one meal, for one day, or for a period of time, together with estimated sales for each menu item.

With this information, all of the menu plans for the defined period of time can be 'exploded', as discussed earlier in this chapter in relation to manual systems.

The trend over the last few years has been towards the development of integrated computer systems which act as a management information system for the whole cycle. This has lead to the need to integrate food production systems with point of sale (POS) terminals or electronic cash registers (ECR) in a restaurant and with front office systems in a hotel. The use of price look up (PLU) tables on the above devices has allowed much more sophisticated control, together with a more detailed sales mix analysis which, as we have seen, is very useful at the planning stage. In a POS terminal system or ECR with price look-up, keys on the terminal are labelled with the name of a menu item, and the key entry is

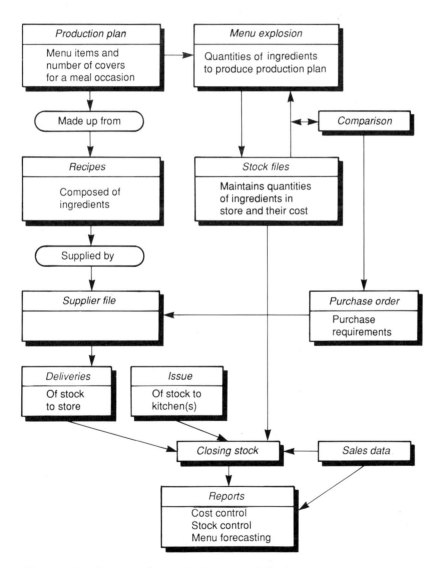

Figure 4.10 *Features of a production control database management system*

programmed with information on the price of the dish. This information can also be linked into stock usage calculations and to accounting software.

A further development has been the use of *hand-held* computer terminals, which are used by waiting staff for taking orders. This means that an order goes directly into the system at the moment the order is taken.

A number of systems are now available to ease the communication between kitchen and restaurant. The interface between kitchen staff and waiting staff is often problematic. The pressures of service time leads to friction between the two groups of staff. Simple communication systems allow waiting staff to pass orders through to the kitchen at the same time as they are entering the order on to a point of sale terminal. The order may either be printed out on to one or more kitchen/bar printers or display terminals. When the order is ready, the waiting staff can be paged, so that they know when to come to the hotplate to collect their order. This paging may be done by discreetly placed monitors or printers, or by using personal pagers. This type of system can link into a food and beverage management system, to give total integration, as shown in Figure 4.12.

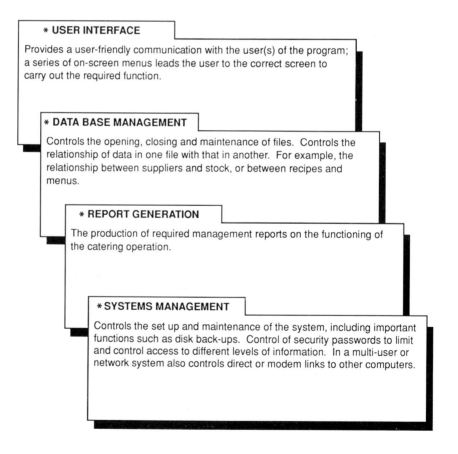

Figure 4.11 *Attributes of a database management system*

Another example of an application is the use of automated systems for recording patient menu choices in hospitals. In a hospital food service system which provides a plated service and patient choice, the collecting and recording of patient choices is a lengthy and costly process. This means that the process has to be carried out a long time ahead of production and service. This in turn leads to errors because of patient admissions and discharges. In order to speed up the process of collating patient information, a number of devices such as card readers and digitizers have been used to semi-automate the process. This means that the collation of information can take place much nearer to the time of production and service.

Quality control

The *quality* of a service industry is much harder to define than is the case with production industries. We can define quality as being the totality of all of the attributes which go to make up a product or service and determine to what extent it measures up to the consumer's expectations. We can consider quality in terms of (Dilworth, 1989):

- Quality of design.
- Quality of conformance.
- Quality of performance or service.

Attitudes towards quality and the control of quality have changed in recent years,

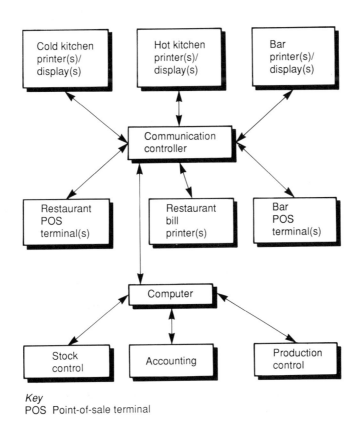

Figure 4.12 *An integrated food and beverage system*

Key
POS Point-of-sale terminal

under the influence of the Japanese 'just in time' manufacturing concept. The traditional view has always been that of quality control as an external and monitoring function of production and service. Nowadays, it is realized that quality is the responsibility of everyone within the company and that it covers all functions from interior design, menu planning, purchasing, stores, production, service, cleaning and maintenance.

Another important feature is that every department is responsible for the quality of goods or service which it passes on to the next department, that is, every department should see the next department as its customer and should only pass on goods without defects. This means, for example, that stores should not send out low grade or deteriorating goods to the kitchen. Similarly, the kitchen should not hand over defective meals to the serving staff.

By making everyone in the organization responsible for the quality of their own work, we reduce the importance of external monitoring of quality. Groups of workers (five to twelve workers are ideal) should meet on a regular basis to identify and solve problems, a technique often referred to as *quality circles*. Data collection and analysis, problem solving and brainstorming are just a few of the techniques the groups should be taught.

In a production industry the emphasis of quality control is on the establishment of numerical standards for a product and the checking of products against these standards, using statistical sampling techniques. These techniques are hard to apply in a service industry. We can, and should, define and measure quantifiable aspects such as portion sizes, service temperatures, maximum holding times and other conformance standards (Thorner and Manning, 1983), but we should

also be able to measure performance of the service element (Merricks and Jones, 1986). Here the danger is that we may concentrate on aspects of service performance which we can measure, such as customers/minute served by cafeteria lines, covers per hour by waiting staff. In doing this, we exclude large elements of the service component such as helpfulness, advice and friendliness.

Too often, complaints are used as an index of quality. This is not satisfactory for a number of reasons. First, for every customer who complains there will be many customers who will not even though they are dissatisfied with some aspect of the product or service. Second, the nature of the complaint, as expressed by the customer may not reflect the true problem area. As we saw in Chapter 2, quality and customer satisfaction is a complex outcome of the total system. The customer may be dissatisfied with the atmosphere or ambience but complain about the food.

One technique for measuring quality aspects of the service element of catering is the use of customer surveys, administered on a regular basis and covering areas such as quality of the food and service, cleanliness of the restaurant and other public areas. Another technique is to use a checklist incorporating key control points, such as the time customers wait in a queue, the time they wait at the table before their orders are taken, the friendliness of service, the helpfulness of service, the temperature of the food, the appearance of the food on the plate and so on. This checklist can cover both quantifiable data and subjective responses and it can be used on a regular basis using test customers or management. It can also be used by staff for self-appraisal.

Tutorial topic

For a restaurant that you know, make out a quality control checklist.

Use this checklist to evaluate service in the restaurant.

Suggest ways in which the quality of service could be improved, based on problem areas you have identified using your checklist.

References and further reading

Braham B. (1989). *Computer Systems in the Hotel and Catering Industry*. London: Cassells.

Dilworth J. B. (1989). *Production and Operations Management: Manufacturing and Non-manufacturing*. New York: Random House.

Fowler K. D. (1986). Evaluating foodservice software: a suggested approach. *Journal of American Dietetic Assocation*, vol. 86, no. 9, pp. 1224-7.

Kasavana M. L. (1984). *Computer Systems for Foodservice Operations*. New York: Van Nostrand Reinhold.

Merricks P. and Jones P. (1986). *Management of Catering Operations*. Eastbourne: Holt Rinehart and Winston, pp. 74-91.

Plumb R. (1988). Cook-chill Control. In *HCIMA Yearbook, 1986-7*. London: HCIMA, pp. 177-8.

Sutton D. F. (1983). *Financial Management in Hotel and Catering Operations*, 2nd edn. Oxford: Heinemann.

Thorner M. E. and Manning P. B. (1983). *Quality Control in Foodservice*. Westport, Conn.: AVI.

Whitehall B. (1988). Taking stock. *Caterer and Hotelkeeper*, 8 September, pp. 75 and 78.

5
Kitchen hygiene

Because of the biological nature of food it is likely that it will often be accompanied by microorganisms, such as viruses, bacteria, yeasts and moulds. Additionally, since food contains many nutrients, microorganisms (which may either be naturally present in the food or which may get into it by some other means), may survive or even multiply. Some of these microorganisms have beneficial effects on the food or the people who consume it, while others have no effect at all. However, some microorganisms cause spoilage of the food and a minority can cause food poisoning.

The importance of hygiene

The importance of hygiene for anyone involved with food is illustrated by Figure 5.1, which shows the growth in reported cases of food poisoning cases in England and Wales from 1981 to 1989. Some of this increase can be attributed to increased knowledge and vigilance, but the general upward trend in reported cases is clear (Gilbert, 1987).

Legislation and control

As a result of the grave dangers attendant on negligent handling, preparation, cooking and service of foods, legislation exists to reduce and control risks. This legislation covers not only the catering industry, but also markets, dairies, slaughter houses, goods vehicles and so on. The legislation arises from a number of Acts of Parliament, including:

- Food and Drugs Act 1955. Revised in 1984 as the Food Act.
- Food Hygiene (General) Regulations 1970. Revised in 1990 as Food Hygiene (Amendment) Regulations.
- Food Hygiene (Control of Premises) Act 1976.
- NHS (Amendment) Act 1986.
- Food Safety Act 1990.

In addition to the legislation which covers the caterer directly, there are a number of

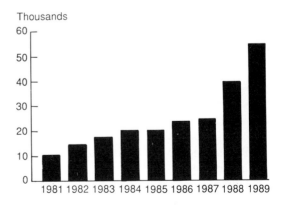

Figure 5.1 *Bacterial food poisoning and Salmonella infections in England and Wales from 1981 to 1989*

other provisions affecting the hygiene of a catering business. For example, medical practitioners are required to notify the community physician should they become aware of or suspect a case of food poisoning and they must provide their local authority with full details.

There are a number of general points which may be made regarding the Food Act 1984. Under these regulations it is illegal to sell food which is not of the:

- *Nature* demanded by the customer. For example, crab sticks are served when crabs are advertised.
- *Substance* demanded by the customer. For example, serving contaminated food.
- *Quality* demanded by the customer. For example, frozen vegetables are served when advertised as fresh.

Additionally, any premises used in connection with the sale, preparation and manufacture of food for sale must be registered with the local authority. This does not include catering premises used for the preparation of food for immediate sale and consumption.

Subject to the provisions of the Act, a local authority may make by-laws to ensure clean food or clean methods of preparation. It must be stressed, therefore, that caterers require not only to learn the main provisions under the Act of Parliament but also the local requirements of their own authority.

Under the Food Safety Act 1990, legislation covering food production and service changes in a number of ways. The regulations include a number of measures which will affect caterers:

1 Registration of premises with local authorities.
2 Compulsory training of food handlers.
3 Tighter control over 'unfit' food.
4 The requirement for anyone selling food products to demonstrate 'due diligence'.

5 Emergency powers to confiscate unfit food and to stop imports of contaminated food.
6 Simplified procedures for closing establishments.

In addition to the Food Act and Food Safety Act, other statutory requirements are outlined in the Food Hygiene (General Regulations) 1970, which came into effect on 1 March 1971. Similar legislation affects Scotland and Northern Ireland. The law has been further reinforced by the introduction of the Food and Drugs (Control of Food Premises) Act 1976 which gives the environmental health department of a local council the power to completely close down a catering operation which presents a serious risk to the public health.

A revision of the Food Hygiene Regulations has also been passed by Parliament. The most significant change is a reduction in the maximum storage temperature for chilled food. Under the 1970 regulations, a temperature of 10°C is specified for a wide range of susceptible foods. Under the 1990 Act, the temperature for the storage of cooked foods is reduced to a maximum of 5°C for:

- Soft cheeses which have been ripened by mould or microorganisms and which have been separated from the whole cheese.
- Cooked products (ready for consumption without further heating) comprising or containing meat, fish, substances used as substitutes for meat, fish, egg, cheese, cereals, pulses or vegetables.
- Smoked or cured fish.
- Smoked or cured meat which has been sliced or cut after smoking or curing.
- Sandwiches containing any of the above ingredients, unless they are sold within twenty-four hours.

For other foods, the proposed maximum temperature is 8°C. These foods include:

- Whole soft cheeses.
- Yoghurt and desserts with a pH of 4.5 or more.
- Prepared vegetable salads (except those containing mayonnaise).
- Sandwiches (other than those indicated under the 5°C list).
- Cooked pies and pasties containing meat, meat substitute, fish or vegetables in pastry, sausage rolls.
- Cooked pies and pasties containing meat, meat substitute, fish or vegetables in pastry, sausage rolls.
- Uncooked or partly cooked dough or pastry products containing meat, fish or substitutes.
- Cream cakes.

However, these requirements are introduced in two stages. From 1 April 1991, all of the foods on both lists must be kept at or below 8°C. From 1 April 1993 the 5°C requirement is introduced for those foods on the first list.

From 1 April 1992, delivery vehicles will have to deliver foods controlled by the regulations at a maximum of 8°C. From 1 April 1993, large delivery vehicles will have to comply with the 5°C requirement for relevant foods.

Exemptions to these regulations will include any product which is to be served within two hours of preparation, or within twenty-four hours of manufacture.

The minimum temperature for hot food storage remains at 63°C.

The proposed new regulations also include a requirement to prevent birds entering all food premises.

Initially, certain areas of public service catering, such as the National Health Service, did not come under food legislation because of what was known as Crown immunity. However, this immunity was removed in 1986 with the NHS (Amendment) Act, requiring all health authority premises in which foods are stored, prepared or consumed to comply with the Food Act and the Food Hygiene Regulations (Wadley, 1987). Crown immunity still remains for prisons, but the immunity will cease in April 1992.

The Chief Environmental Health Officer and his/her staff, including health inspectors and food inspectors, represents a local authority in all matters relating to clean food. The Chief Environmental Health Officer of a district has powers to take samples of food, to stop the sale of food until tests have been made and to condemn food. The authority's authorized officers have a right to enter premises at any reasonable hour to carry out their duty. It is clearly important for hoteliers, caterers and their senior staff to seek help and advice from the officers of the authority and to cooperate with them in every way possible to promote public health. Under the Food Safety Act, they can seize consignments of food which they consider to be unfit.

number of essentials procedures to be followed for the preparation and storage of food. Failure to obey these regulations can lead to prosecution with penalties of fines, imprisonment or both. Under the Food Hygiene (Control of Premises) Act, which does not apply to Scotland or Northern Ireland, an order can be obtained prohibiting the preparation, storage and sale of food from premises until a local authority certifies that the danger to health has been removed.

When applying this closure order, the local authority must give fourteen days' notice and must specify in writing what measures should be taken to remove any danger to health. Following a closure order, the owner of the premises or person wishing to carry on a food business at the premises can apply to the local authority who will issue a certificate that the danger to health has been removed, if they are satisfied that this is so.

In situations of imminent danger, the Act allows an emergency closure of the premises. In this situation, notice of three clear days must be given of the intention to apply for a closure order. As with the case above, the written notice must indicate what measures must be taken to remove the risk to health. If it can be proved that an emergency order was wrongly obtained, and that as a result the business suffered a financial loss, compensation may be sought.

Under the Food Safety Act, the above regulations are replaced by the following:

- An *improvement notice*, which gives the proprietor fourteen days to comply with the specified requirements.
- A *prohibition order*, issued by the court, which can stop a process or close a premises, if the proprietor has been convicted of a related offence.
- A *prohibition notice*, served by an authorized officer in cases where there is an imminent risk of injury to health. This is only a temporary measure and must be followed by application to the court for an *emergency prohibition order* within three days of placing the prohibition notice.

In any of the above cases, the proprietor may receive compensation if the food which was seized was uncontaminated, or if the court does not grant an order.

Causes of food poisoning

Food poisoning may be caused by chemical, physical or biological agents. However, the largest number of cases of food poisoning are caused by microorganisms: bacteria; fungi (yeasts and moulds); and viruses. Of these, bacteria are responsible for the greatest problem.

Bacteria

Bacteria are a type of microorganism which grow as a single-celled organism and they are so small that they can only be seen with the aid of powerful magnification. Bacteria occur everywhere in our environment and are frequently associated with animals and plants. While some bacteria are harmful, most are harmless or even helpful. Of the harmful kind (known as *pathogens*), some gain direct entrance to the human body through, for example, the air or water, while others invade food or live in it.

In order to be able to prevent food poisoning, it is necessary to understand something about bacteria, how they grow and how they are affected by their environment. With this knowledge we can control their survival and growth.

Tutorial topic

Over the last twenty to thirty years there has been increased knowledge about the causes of food poisoning and a higher level of education of food handlers about food hygiene. And yet, over this period, we have seen a rise in the number of outbreaks of food poisoning. Discuss this statement.

What effect do you think that the increasing publicity about food poisoning outbreaks will have on the public's attitude to the catering industry?

Microorganisms in food can be controlled in a number of ways. They can be excluded from the food in the first place or removed from the food. However, in terms of control which can be exercised by the caterer, inhibition of growth or destruction is much more effective (ICMSF, 1988a).

The increase in numbers of a colony of bacteria follows a distinct growth curve, as shown in Figure 5.2. Initially, when the organisms are introduced into a new environment, they do not start reproducing immediately, but have to go through a *lag* phase. This can be of the order of two to three hours for foods removed from chilled or frozen storage and warmed to ambient temperature. Once the organisms start to multiply, they enter a phase of rapid growth, as one cell divides into two, two into four, four into eight and so on. This stage is known as the *log* phase. As cells are being created by division, older cells are dying and eventually a *stationary* phase stage is reached where the rate of creation and the rate of death balance. Later, more organisms die than are being created and the bacterial population declines.

Bacteria need water, nutrients, appropriate temperatures and the correct pH (acidity/alkalinity) to grow. Thus, the nature of the food (its composition, water content and pH) and the way it is stored (temperature, humidity, atmosphere and packaging) determine which, if any, of the microorganisms present will grow.

In particular, temperature has a profound effect on the growth and survival of bacteria and therefore is one of the most effective methods of control. Basically, in terms of their response to temperature, there are four groups of bacteria (ICMS, 1988a):

> *Thermophiles* grow from 40–45°C up to 60–90°C. Optimum 55–75°C.
> *Mespohiles* grown from 5–15°C up to 35–47°C. Optimum 30–45°C.
> *Psychrophiles* grow from − 5–+ 5°C up to 15–20. Optimum 12–15°C.
> *Psychrotrophs* grow from − 5–+ 5°C up to 30–35°C. Optimum 25–30°C.

Most food poisoning bacteria are *mesophiles*, which grow rapidly at the temperature

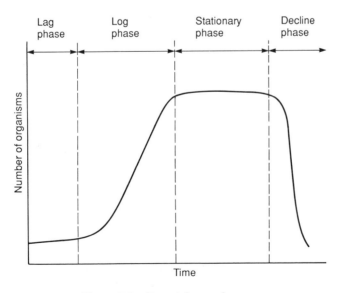

Figure 5.2 *Bacterial growth curve*

of a warm kitchen (21–25°C) and grow at their fastest at body temperature (37°C), a temperature often found in food being improperly kept hot before and during service. The rate of growth of vegetative cells is affected by temperature, as shown in Figure 5.3. The cells of bacteria cannot survive high temperatures. For example, many are killed by heating at a temperature as low as 65°C for ten minutes. However, the spores of some spore-forming bacteria can survive heating at boiling temperatures for several hours.

At the other end of the temperature scale, low temperatures can also be used to inhibit the growth of microorganisms. Storage at chilled temperatures of between − 1 and 8°C is common in the catering industry. In particular, storage at 3°C or below will prevent the growth of food poisoning bacteria, but will not destroy them.

Freezing does not necessarily destroy all bacteria. Some bacteria will be killed by the freezing process, but the rest will be held in suspended animation. The number of organisms will gradually decline during extended frozen storage.

The amount of water and the pH of a food can also be used to control the growth of microorganisms. The amount of water can be controlled not only by the removal of water (such as the process of dehydration), but also by the addition of salt and/sugar, as we see in many of the traditional curing processes. The food poisoning bacteria will not grow at pHs below 5 (mildly acidic).

The presence or absence of oxygen also affects the growth of bacteria. For example, some microorganisms will only grow in the presence of oxygen (*aerobes*), while others will only grow in the absence of oxygen (*anaerobes*). A third group are not influenced by the presence or absence of oxygen (*facultative*). It is possible to control the atmosphere in order to inhibit the growth of the various spoilage and food poisoning bacteria. Most food poisoning microorganisms are aerobes, with the exception of Clostridium species. The use of vacuum sealing is one way of removing oxygen from foods and can be used to control the growth of many organisms.

The use of irradiation with gamma rays has been suggested as another way of controlling the micro-microorganisms found in food (Goodburn, 1989). Depending on the dose of radiation used, the shelf life of foods

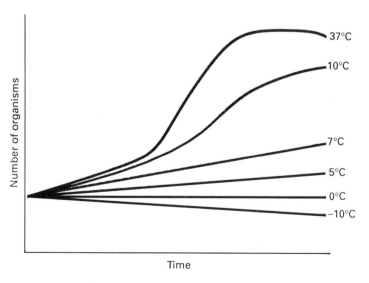

Figure 5.3   *Effect of temperature on the growth of mesophiles*

can be increased by controlling spoilage fungi and bacteria. It can also be used to produce a similar effect to thermal pasteurization by killing of food poisoning bacteria such as Salmonella. There is concern that it is possible for unfit foods to be treated and made apparently safe. This could be dangerous in the case of microorganisms where food poisoning is caused by toxins. The radiation would kill the microorganism, but any toxin in the food would survive.

The Food (Control of Irradiation) Regulations 1990 permits the radiation of food. The premises used for irradiation must be licensed and application must be made to irradiate any food, specifying the purpose and level of radiation and any treated foods must be labelled (excluding catering sales). Currently, within the EC, irradiation is permitted in various countries for a wide range of food products including herbs, spices, poultry, shrimps, prawns, dried fruit and vegetables, potatoes, onions and strawberries.

Bacterial food poisoning organisms

There are three types of bacterial food poisoning, although the distinctions are not always clear cut:

1 Intoxification by toxins produced as the organism grows in the food before ingestion.
2 Intoxification by toxins produced by the organism as it grows in the human gut.
3 Infection by bacteria which invade the tissues of the human body.

The first type of intoxification is caused by a group of microorganisms which cause illness because of toxins produced by the microorganisms as they grow on the food before ingestion. These toxins may remain in the food even if the microorganism is destroyed.

In the case of the second type of intoxification, bacteria are able to multiply in suitable foodstuffs and reach such numbers that they cause illness soon after the food has been eaten, and almost always within twenty-four hours. The illness is caused by enterotoxins produced by the bacteria as they grow in the intestinal tract.

The third group of microorganisms cause food-borne infections. Here, the microorganisms invade and multiply within the tissues of the intestines and are responsible for illnesses. In practice, the distinction between these latter two types of bacterial food poisoning is not always absolutely clear.

Salmonellae

Members of this bacterial type cause food-borne infections if consumed in large numbers, when they can multiply in the gut. They have been associated with outbreaks of food poisoning for decades and are associated with a wide range of foods. Food poisoning by members of Salmonella is often referred to as *Salmonellosis*.

The bacteria cause classical food poisoning symptoms of diarrhoea, headache and vomiting, possibly with some fever. Salmonella are principally associated with the bowel of animals. During the slaughter of animals, bacteria are frequently spread from the intestine to the surface of the meat. If the temperature conditions are suitable, the microorganism will multiply and, if present in large numbers, will cause illness. The bacteria are easily killed by heat, and adequate cooking at temperatures over 60°C will eliminate the hazard, providing the product is not reinfected from raw meats after cooking. Foods usually implicated are sliced cooked meats, meat and poultry, sausages, salads, synthetic cream and eggs.

Of particular recent concern is the growth in cases of *Salmonella enteritidis*, which is particularly associated with chickens and eggs. Recently, this organism has been identified as being responsible for 44 per cent of all cases of salmonellosis.

Salmonella typhi and typhimurium

These organisms cause the bacterial infections typhoid and paratyphoid. The source of the bacteria is the bowels. The symptoms of diarrhoea, vomiting, fever etc. are characteristic of typhoid. The incubation period is from seven to twenty-one days and the duration of the illness is four to six weeks. Foods usually implicated are raw milk and other dairy products, salads, 'warmed-up' foods, synthetic cream, ice-cream and shellfish. In addition to foods, contaminated water is often the source of infection. *Salmonella typhimurium* is responsible for 21 per cent of all cases of Salmonellosis.

Human carriers are often implicated, exclusively so in the case of typhoid. Known carriers of the bacteria cannot be permitted to work as food handlers, and one has to rely upon adequate sewage disposal and purification of water supplies to prevent the bacteria entering the kitchen. Para-typhoid microorganisms may be present on fresh meat, however.

Staphylococcus aureus

These organisms are found in the nose, throat and on the skin of humans. Between 5 and 20 per cent of the population are carriers of the bacteria. Of the Staphylococci, only 30 per cent are types which can cause food poisoning. There is a particular danger of food being contaminated during handling, particularly if personal hygiene is low.

If food becomes contaminated and is left to stand overnight in a warm kitchen a number of toxins are produced by the growing Staphylococci. Some of these toxins are heat resistant. Dangers can be reduced by:

- Reducing the amount of handling.

- Making full use of refrigeration for cooked foods.
- Ensuring that food is consumed immediately after preparation.
- Strict personal hygiene — washing hands, not touching nose and lips during food preparation, etc.

There are special dangers in foods which have to be handled after cooking such as dishes which have to be decorated and left to set. Since the organism is not heat resistant and will not grow at refrigerated temperatures, it is relatively easy to control.

Foods which are frequently involved include custard, pastries, pies, cooked meats and hams, gravies, dressings, synthetic cream, ice-cream and improperly processed canned foods.

Staphylococcus aureus causes intoxification. The incubation period is from two to six hours and the symptoms of severe abdominal pain, diarrhoea, headache and vomiting usually occur about four hours after eating the contaminated food. The illness lasts from six to twenty-four hours.

Clostridium perfringens

This microorganism produces heat resistant spores which can survive light cooking processes. The spores may survive at boiling temperatures for several hours. Pressure cooking may kill the spores in fifteen minutes. These spores are also resistant to dry conditions and high salt concentrations. If the food containing the spores is not eaten immediately after cooking, rapidly chilled or kept above 63°C, the spores will germinate to produce actively growing bacteria. These actively growing bacteria produce a toxin in the stomach.

The bacteria is found in the soil as well as the bowels and faeces of man and animals. Because of cross-contamination in slaughter houses, the bacteria can get into meat products.

The incubation period for the bacteria is from eight to twenty-two hours and the symptoms occur from ten to twelve hours after the contaminated food has been ingested. The symptoms are severe stomach pains with accompanying diarrhoea and nausea.

Campylobacter jejuni

This microorganism is becoming increasingly implicated in cases of food poisoning, particularly as a cause of gastroenteritis in the young, where it is now more commonly isolated than Salmonella, following a sudden increase in the number of cases between 1975 and 1985. In 1980 there were 9600 cases, but this had risen to 28,714 cases by 1988 (Public Health Laboratory Service, 1988).

The organism has been isolated from unpasteurized milk and undercooked poultry and meat. It does not multiply in foods but only requires a low dose to cause illness. It can survive, but not multiply, at refrigerated temperatures. The result of ingestion is a food-borne infection, with symptoms of abdominal cramps and blood in the faeces, after an incubation period of three to five days (although sometimes as long as ten days).

Listeria monocytogenes

Occurrence of this microorganism has increased in the last fifteen years. It is a very common microorganism in the soil, water and vegetation, and in the faeces of animals. It has been isolated from uncooked meats, poultry, raw milk, soft cheeses, salads such as coleslaw, and chilled cooked foods. Unlike many of the other food poisoning microorganisms, it is a psychrotroph and can proliferate in refrigerated foods at temperatures above 4°C and can grow slowly down to 2°C. It can also grow at temperatures up to 42°C.

Listeria monocytogenes causes a food-borne infection. Once ingested, it becomes an intracellular parasite. In most people it causes flu-like symptoms, but in the very young, elderly or people with a suppressed immune system, the illness can be much more serious, causing septicaemia and meningitis. In these groups it is fatal in 30 per cent of cases.

Bacillus cereus

Like *Clostridium perfringens*, this is also a spore-forming bacteria but it is aerobic rather than anaerobic. It is much slower growing than *Clostridium perfringens* and it has to be present in large numbers before causing problems. It is found in cereal products and has in particular been implicated with outbreaks associated with the consumption of boiled rice. Boiled rice, which has been cooked in bulk and then left at room temperature for a considerable length of time provides an ideal condition for the growth of *Bacillus cereus*. Stir-frying or merely warming rice before serving may not be enough to eliminate the microorganism and food poisoning results. It can produce a toxin when growing in foods, but also, if sufficient numbers of cells are ingested, produce a toxin in the gut. The incubation period may be one to six hours or six to sixteen hours and it causes symptoms of nausea, diarrhoea and vomiting.

Vibrio parahaemolyticus

This bacteria is particularly associated with uncooked shellfish and is a common cause of food poisoning in the Far East. Several cases of poisoning due to this bacteria have recently been experienced in the UK and it is suspected that the bacteria may become established in coastal waters. Particular care over temperature control during the holding of seafood dishes is required together with precautions to prevent cross-contamination during preparation from uncooked shellfish to the cooked and cooled product.

Clostridium botulinum

This is fortunately a rare type of food poisoning in the UK. It is associated with improperly processed canned foods, particularly home processed low acid foods, and occasionally with vacuum packed foods, such as smoked trout. Recent cases in the UK were found in hazelnut yoghurt, resulting from underprocessed tins of hazelnuts. The bacteria originates from soil or from the sea and lake sources. It will only grow in the absence of oxygen and thus it is not associated with fresh foods prepared by usual kitchen practices for immediate consumption. The bacteria produces a very powerful toxin in the food in which it is growing. The toxin itself is not heat resistant. Outbreaks of botulism have a high mortality rate. It is usually associated with canned meat products, pastes, soups and with vacuum packaged smoked fish. In general, *Clostridium botulinum* cannot grow below 7°C. The exception to this is Type E *Clostridium botulinum*, which can grow down to 4°C. It is found in fish and marine products.

Yersinia enterocolitia

This microorganism causes a food-borne infection, with symptoms of diarrhoea and severe abdominal pain. It has been isolated from milk (both raw and pasteurized), cream, synthetic cream, seafood and meat products. It can grow down to 4°C.

Shigella species

Bacteria of this group cause the disease dysentery, which produces symptoms of diarrhoea and vomiting, sometimes with mucus or even blood in the faeces and, possibly, with some fever. Dysentery bacteria take some eighteen hours to incubate.

The spread of these microorganisms is not necessarily through foodstuffs. It can be due to poor personal hygiene, and contamination can spread from person to person through, for example, a towel. Infected employees need to be excluded from food-related duties until they are clear of the organisms.

Other types of food poisoning associated with foods include:

Brucellosis or 'undulant' fever

This disease originates from cattle and can be transmitted to man through milk supplies. Pasteurization of milk destroys the bacteria as it does the tuberculosis bacteria. Drinking raw milk, unless it is from tuberculosis- and brucellosis-free herds, can lead to infection.

Infectious hepatitis

This is a virus illness, one type of which (Hepatitis A) can be spread through foodstuffs as a result of faecal pollution. The disease is associated primarily with tropical and semi-tropical regions and is more likely to occur where environmental hygiene is poor. Hepatitis A may be spread by foods and has been associated with cockles, oysters, mussels, milk and cream. It can also be spread by food handlers, who should be excluded from food areas until they are cleared of the organism.

Virus-related food poisoning

There is a suggestion that certain viruses originating in the bowel can cause mild food poisoning symptoms, including diarrhoea and vomiting. Though no virus has actually been isolated, the disease has been traced to faecal contamination, particularly of seafood. Viruses cannot replicate in food.

The role of viruses in this type of sickness has not yet been fully clarified. Evidence of virus involvement in food poisoning was strengthened following the illness of 797 people in the period 1976–77 and 650 people in the period 1985–86. These outbreaks were caused by cockles and, in the absence of any bacterial cause, virus particles were looked for and shown to be present in a high proportion of those studied. However, no viruses could be found in the cockles (Cruickshank, 1987).

Mixed infections

In addition to cases of food poisoning which can be traced to specific toxin-type contamination, there are infections where, because of inadequate storage conditions, large numbers of bacteria have multiplied and produced their toxins. Where there are no specific microorganisms involved, the symptoms are usually more vague. Diarrhoea and vomiting may occur at any time between eight and twenty-four hours from the time of consumption of the food.

Relative frequency of types of bacteriological food poisoning

The frequency of outbreaks of caused by specific microorganisms are indicated in Figure 5.4. (Gilbert, 1987). When interpreting these data, it must be remembered that gastroenteritis caused by organisms such as *Camplyobacter jejuni* are not recorded.

Insects and vermin

Insects and vermin can often play a significant part in the spread of food poisoning. This can either be because they are carriers of organisms, such as Salmonella, or because they cause cross-contamination.

Cockroaches

These insects belong to a group which includes crickets, grasshoppers and locusts. They are a class of pests described as 'visitors' because they live in crevices in the structure of buildings or other harbourages (even in the ground outside) and make journeys within to obtain their food.

Three kinds of domestic cockroaches are found in Britain:

1 The German cockroach (*Blattella germanica*) which is also called the steamfly or 'croton bug'. This is a yellowish-brown insect, growing in length to about 12 mm, with large wings. It commonly infests large buildings especially those warmed by central heating.

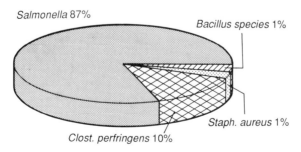

Figure 5.4 *Relative proportions (%) of organisms implicated in cases of food poisoning for England and Wales, 1981–89*

2   The oriental cockroach (*Blattella orienta-lis*) or 'black beetle' grows to 25 mm and is a shiny, dark brown colour. The male has wings covering two-thirds of its abdomen but the female has much fore-shortened ones. Though once very common, they are now less frequently found in modern buildings. However, this type of cockroach is still encountered in kitchens and bakeries of older construction.

3   The American cockroach (*Perplaneta americana*) or 'Bombay canary' is reddish brown in colour with a margin of yellow on the thoracic shield. The insect grows to 38 mm and both sexes have large wings.

Because of their size and nocturnal activity, cockroaches are generally easy to detect. Moreover, an unpleasant 'roachy', fetid smell is associated with them. Their flat bodies enable them to lie concealed in cracks and crevices during the day, but they emerge at night to feed. They will eat almost anything (wool, leather, book covers, etc., as well as food) and they leave their smell wherever they have been. They are difficult to control because of their rapid rate of reproduction and because of their ability to develop resistance to insecticides.

It is relatively unusual for cockroaches to act as carriers or transmitters of disease through having eaten contaminated material. It is obviously important to eradicate them because of the smell, the soiling by excrement, the destruction and spoilage of food and packaging and the general revulsion they cause.

Flies

There are several types of housefly and blowfly. Their ability to spread disease is nowadays generally accepted. When flies feed on food, they both regurgitate and defecate on the food which allows the ready transmission of pathogenic bacteria.

Ants

While ants are normally found out of doors, they do, on occasion, invade food stores and are particularly attracted by sugar products. Pharaoh's ants can act as carriers of pathogenic bacteria.

Other insect pests

There is a vast range of insect pests which can invade foodstuffs, or which may be found in supplies. Purchasing from reliable suppliers should minimize the danger from the latter. Weevils and mites are associated with a wide range of foodstuffs and once a storeroom becomes infested, destruction of the insects can be quite difficult, requiring fumigation. Wasps and bees are more of a nuisance than a health hazard.

Mice and rats

Rodents are not only a health hazard, but also cause damage to stored foods. The house mouse and the long-tailed field mouse are both associated with buildings, particularly where food is stored. They are a particular nuisance and hazard because they contaminate much more food than they consume. They also damage packaging, increasing the rate of food spoilage, and create fire hazards because of their habit of gnawing through electrical cables.

The brown rat is the most common species of rat in the UK. Like the mouse, it damages food packaging and contaminates food with pathogens.

Birds

Birds such as sparrows, feral pigeons and starlings can cause contamination of food with pathogenic bacteria via their droppings.

Breaking the food poisoning chain: hazard analysis

Food poisoning is usually caused, at least in part, by negligence or ignorance on the part of the person preparing the food. Certainly it never happens without a reason. All kitchen staff should be aware of the causes, dangers and results of food poisoning. An analysis of cases of food poisoning in England and Wales (Figure 5.5), shows that effective time temperature control, together with the elimination of cross-contamination, could have prevented most outbreaks (Gilbert, 1987).

In general, a case of food poisoning does not result from a single lapse in hygiene, but from a sequence of mistakes. The microorganism must gain access to susceptible food materials on which it can grow. It must then be left at suitable temperatures for growth to take place, and for a suitable period of time. Control can arise by preventing any of the stages shown in Figure 5.6. One technique which is of great value in identifying and eliminating bacteriological growth is known as *hazard analysis*.

The technique of *hazard analysis and critical control points* (HACCP) can be used to minimize the risk of food poisoning in any catering organization. It consists of six stages, as shown in Figure 5.7. In carrying out this technique, it is useful to draw a flow diagram of the stages in the processing of each dish, which can be used to identify hazards, determine critical control points and establish control criteria, as shown in Figure 5.8.

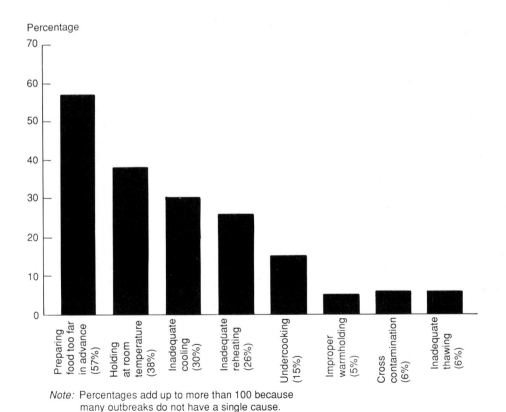

Note: Percentages add up to more than 100 because many outbreaks do not have a single cause.

Figure 5.5 *Analysis of the causes of food poisoning outbreaks in England and Wales between 1970 and 1982*

Hygienic catering

The source of infection

From the foregoing, it will be apparent that although it is possible for some of the dangerous organisms to be transmitted from, say, the soil, it is more usual for infections to be spread by human or animal carriers. Staphylococci, for example, are found in the noses of most humans and are also commonly found on the skin and clothes. Similarly, *Clostridium perfringens* are found in the excreta of animals. Shigella and Salmonella species are carried in humans and animals.

Of particular importance is the incidence of 'carriers' within the population (Cruikshank, 1987). Employees who are found to be carriers of Salmonella and Shigella species, Hepatitis A and *Staphylococcus aureus* should

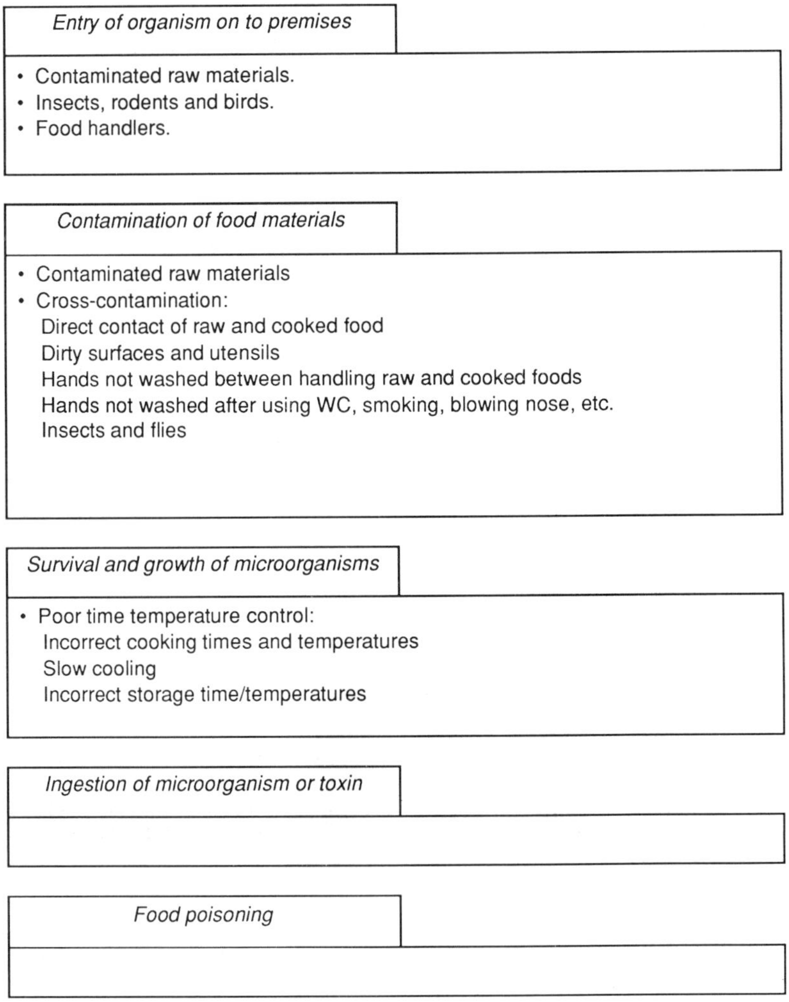

Entry of organism on to premises

- Contaminated raw materials.
- Insects, rodents and birds.
- Food handlers.

Contamination of food materials

- Contaminated raw materials
- Cross-contamination:
  Direct contact of raw and cooked food
  Dirty surfaces and utensils
  Hands not washed between handling raw and cooked foods
  Hands not washed after using WC, smoking, blowing nose, etc.
  Insects and flies

Survival and growth of microorganisms

- Poor time temperature control:
  Incorrect cooking times and temperatures
  Slow cooling
  Incorrect storage time/temperatures

Ingestion of microorganism or toxin

Food poisoning

Figure 5.6   *Stages in food poisoning*

be excluded from food production and service, until they are shown to be medically clear.

Meat and poultry are a particular problem as a source of pathogenic organisms, due to the high rates of Salmonella contamination which can occur on intensively reared and factory slaughtered products. In addition to the ease of infection being transmitted from one animal to another, infection can arise from contaminated feedstuffs.

Domestic pets are also known carriers of Salmonella, as are rodents. Some insects, particularly flies, can transfer bacteria from a location outside the kitchen to food inside. A strenuous effort should be made to exclude all animals and insects from food production areas because of the potential health risk.

Contamination can be further spread within the kitchen by poor food storage conditions, poor preparation practices and poor personal hygiene. Because of the high level of manual manipulation of food in the catering industry, it is very easy for bacteria to get from the hands, fingernails and noses of catering staff on to food. As a result of this, personal hygiene is critical.

Clothing, kitchen cloths and similar materials can become contaminated with food poisoning bacteria, as can kitchen surfaces,

---

Step 1: Identification of hazard

For all stages of storage production and service, identify all hazards – the risk of contaminated raw material, cross-contamination with pathogenic bacteria and the potential for their growth or survival.

Step 2: Determine critical control points (CCP)

For each hazard, identify the location at which control can be exercised to either (a) eliminate the hazard (CCP1) or (b) minimize the risk (CCP2). The control should be aimed at preventing a potential hazard becoming an actual hazard.

Step 3: Specify criteria for control

This may be physical, such as time/temperature conditions, water content etc., chemical, such as pH, salt content etc., or biological and should be designed to ensure that control is effective.

Step 4: Establish and implement a procedure to monitor criteria for every critical control point

A system for the regular checking of control criteria should be implemented to monitor the avoidance of risks.

Step 5: Take necessary control action to ensure that criteria are being achieved

If control criteria are not being achieved, the process must be modified to bring it back under control. Foods which are at risk must not be passed on to the consumer.

Step 6: Verification

Use of supplementary information such as microbiological testing to ensure that the system is working.

Figure 5.7 *Hazard analysis and critical control points*

equipment and chopping boards. Every effort must be made to prevent the cross-contamination from any of these sources to cooked or finished food. Ideally, the pre-cooking preparation of food and the post cooking activities should be totally separated, using a different physical location, different staff, different sets of clothing and equipment, different storage facilities. While this is not practicable in many operations, the

Control point		*Criteria*
● Thawing raw frozen chicken	CCP2	Absence of ice in deep thigh muscle – no part less than 0°C.
Cooking	CCP2	74°C in coldest part.
Chilling	CCP1	70°C to 3°C in 90 minutes.
● Carving and portioning	CCP2	Temperature should not rise above 10°C.
Chilled holding	CCP2	Temperature 0°C to 3°C. 5 days maximum storage.
Reheating	CCP1	Temperature above 70°C.
Warm holding	CCP1	Temperature above 70°C, time less than 15 minutes.
● Serving	CCP1	Any food not consumed to be discarded.

Key

●   Risk of contamination
CCP1 Eliminate hazard
CCP2 Minimize risk of hazard

Figure 5.8 *Typical HACCP flow diagram*

Tutorial topic

Draw a flow chart for a food dish, as shown in Figure 5.8.

Identify the hazards and determine the control points.

Establish control criteria.

planning of facilities and the organization of staff, equipment and laundry should be done in such a way as to minimize these risks of cross-contamination.

The promotion of hygiene

If the causes of food poisoning as outlined earlier are thoroughly understood by catering managers, supervisors and operatives, the risk of food poisoning can be minimized. All those concerned with food should be ready to take the necessary precautions to prevent contamination and growth of food poisoning microorganisms (HCIMA, 1989), and to comply with food hygiene legislation.

Positive measures that are required to promote hygiene in the kitchen can best be considered under the three following headings:

1 The proper handling and storage of foods before, during and after cooking.
2 The proper maintenance of premises, tools and equipment used for the storage, preparation, cooking and holding of foods.
3 Personal cleanliness on the part of the food handler, including the provision of clean uniforms and adequate hand washing and changing facilities.

Receipt and storage of foods

Using the principles of hazard analysis as described above, susceptible foods should be identified and subject to appropriate controls and inspections. However, it must be said that contaminated foods may not show any visual sign of contamination. Thus, while the chef or storekeeper may reject foods which are tainted or do not look fresh, there is no guarantee that other food is free from contamination. This vigilance is still of obvious importance in terms of food quality control and these quality factors will often form a part of purchase specifications, as described in Chapter 4.

Meat, fish and poultry

Any meat which shows discolouration, off-odours or decomposition should be rejected.

Eggs

Particularly when catering for the young, elderly and sick, pasteurized eggs (frozen, liquid or dried) should be used as a replacement for raw shell eggs when either no cooking or only a light cooking is to follow. Eggs which have cracked shells should be discarded.

Vegetables and fruit

Vegetables which may be contaminated with soil-borne microorganisms should be isolated from other raw materials and cooked foods until they have been washed or prepared. A different sink and preparation area should be used for vegetables. For hygiene reasons as well as culinary and aesthetic ones, bruised, damaged or rotting vegetables should be rejected.

Dry goods

Dirty and damaged bread should be rejected, as should musty smelling or weevily flour. If any packaging shows obvious rodent damage, these foods should also be rejected. Wrappings and packaging should be intact and tins should not show signs of rust or corrosion. A 'blown' can (a can in which gas production by bacteria causes a swelling of the ends of the can) should be rejected, as should any cans with signs of seam damage.

Provided that dry goods are purchased in sound containers, they will remain relatively safe until they are opened. At this point it is easy for them to become contaminated. For example, dried eggs may have been pasteurized during their manufacture to remove Salmonella, but the eggs may easily be recontaminated by dirty utensils or other ingredients. Because other microorganisms have been removed by pasteurization, any contaminating bacteria may grow quickly under the right temperature conditions.

During storage every effort should be made to:

● Minimize the growth of any potential food poisoning.
● Prevent the risk of cross-contamination of susceptible foods at any stage, but particularly at the stage when the foods are fully processed and awaiting service.

In particular, refrigerated storage should be frequently checked to make certain that:

● Correct storage temperatures are being maintained.
● That there is no risk of cross-contamination from raw to cooked foods.
● That appropriate storage temperatures are used for all foods.
● That refrigerators and freezers are not overloaded.

The recommended temperatures for a variety of products are given in Figure 5.9. Most food poisoning bacteria cannot grow at temperatures below 7°C and above 63°C (note the exception to this in the case of Listeria at low temperatures and spore formers at high temperatures). The *danger zone* (Figure 5.10) represents those temperatures at which food should not be held. When heating and cooling foods, they should pass through this danger zone as quickly as possible.

All store areas should be checked frequently for old stock. Strict principles of *first in first out'* should be adhered to and 'Sell by' and 'Use by' dates should be observed.

Preparation and cooking of foods

If the HACCP system has been used, all hazards and necessary controls will have been established. The simplest control of the growth of food poisoning is adequate time temperature control, together with the elimination of contamination from raw foods and handlers.

Because of problems with Salmonella, raw egg products should not be used in catering, particularly when feeding young, elderly or sick people.

If the cooking process is designed to destroy vegetative cells of microorganisms, check temperatures with a thermometer. There are now excellent portable electronic thermometers, complete with a metal probe, which can be used to measure the centre temperatures of foods. It is not sufficient to follow recipes which state that x minutes at y degrees will cook a food. Because of the variation in shape size and composition of foods, these guides can be out by several minutes which can mean the survival of microorganisms. Temperature measurements at the centre of cooked meats and poultry are much more reliable. Susceptible foods must be cooked in such a way that all parts achieve a temperature of at least 63°C (poultry 70°C). Care should be taken with large joints of meat.

Another possible danger results from the use of microwave ovens with chilled foods. For a number of reasons microwaves do not always heat uniformly and therefore all parts of the food may not reach a safe temperature, particularly in relation to *Listeria monocytogenes*.

There are particular problems when low-powered domestic microwave ovens are used in catering operations. The power output is too low to heat foods uniformly and the power output can fall after a period of continuous use. Domestic microwave ovens should not be used in catering operations.

Thawing of frozen products needs careful control, particularly in the case of large joints of meat and poultry. These products should be thoroughly thawed before cooking. Poultry should be thawed at temperatures below 15°C.

Similarly, the temperatures of ovens and particularly refrigerators and freezers should be checked with an accurate thermometer. The loading of a piece of equipment can affect its temperature. For example, overloaded refrigerators and freezers may operate at a temperature above the designed maximum.

Separate colour coded utensils, knives and chopping boards should be used for raw foods and cooked foods (see Chapter 8).

Temperature	Types of food
−18°C to −21°C	Frozen foods
−1°C to +1°C	Fresh fish
−1°C to +2°C	Fresh meat poultry, offals and sausages Cured raw and cooked hams, bacon and sausages Cooked meats for slicing
−1°C to +3°C	Cook-chill and sous vide products

+2°C to +5°C	Cooked meats
	Pasties
	Raw and pasteurized dairy products – milk,
	  cream, yoghurts, soft cheeses, cut hard
	  cheeses, butter
	Eggs
	Margarines and fats
	Flour confectionery containing cream,
	  artificial cream, custard, jam
	Raw pastry, dough and pizzas

+3°C to +8°C	Meat pies
	Whole hard cheeses
	Salad vegetables and fruit (except those
	  damaged by low temperatures)
	Prepared salads
	  (except those containing mayonnaise)

+13°C	Wines
+5°C to +10°C +10°C to +15°C	Vegetable store Dry store

Figure 5.9 *Recommended food storage temperatures*

Different work surfaces should be used for raw and cooked foods. Staff should not touch cooked foods which are capable of supporting growth of pathogens. Instead, clean implements should be used, or staff should wear disposable plastic gloves.

Holding of food prior to service

Strict time temperature control should be maintained over food which is being kept hot prior to service. In order to satisfy the requirements of the Food Hygiene Regulations, susceptible foods which are being kept hot for immediate service, must be stored at a temperature above 63°C, preferably 70. If the food falls below this temperature it must be quickly and hygienically cooled to at least 5°C.

Frequent checks should be made to ensure that hot-cupboards, bains-marie and refrigerated service units are operating at a safe temperature. Food which is not to be consumed immediately should be rapidly chilled to 5°C or below. For large items of food, the only way that this can be done rapidly enough is to use a blast chiller.

This temperature control is particularly important with food which has been prepared previously and then reheated for service. Foods should not be reheated in appliances designed for the storage of hot foods, as the rate of heating will be too slow. Any reheated food which is not consumed straight away should not be chilled down again but should be discarded.

Cafeteria and self-service counters should be fitted with effective 'sneeze guards'. Refrigerated counters should always be used for cold buffets and desserts. Sweet trolleys at ambient temperatures represent a real hazard if used with dairy-based products. Similarly, 'cold buffets' which contain cooked meats, poultry and seafood and which are at ambient temperatures form a serious risk.

Great care should be used with foods containing or covered in aspic jelly or similar aspic-based foods. When these materials are used as part of a cold buffet very strict temperature control is required. These gelatin-based jellies are a favourable medium for the growth of bacteria. If foods covered in aspic are left in a function room without adequate refrigeration, there is a risk that any food poisoning bacteria will grow. Where it is impossible to provide refrigeration, susceptible foods should not be used as part of a buffet.

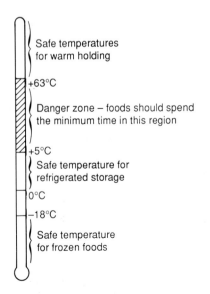

Figure 5.10   *The temperature danger zone*

Premises, tools and equipment

It is obvious from other sections of this chapter that the design and equipment of the kitchen and the ancillary departments are strongly influenced by the need for the highest standards of cleanliness.

The Food Hygiene Regulations indicate that no food business must take place in unsanitary premises or any place which would expose food to the risk of contamination.

Facilities for washing food, equipment and utensils must be provided. This must be in addition to hand washbasins. Sinks for washing equipment must receive an adequate supply of hot water. Sinks that are designed only for rinsing vegetables, fruit and fish can be supplied with cold water only.

Food rooms must be properly lit and ventilated. They must not be used for sleeping purposes and they should not be adjacent to a sleeping place.

Food premises including walls, floors, doors, windows, ceilings, woodwork and other parts of the structure must be kept in sufficiently good repair and condition as to enable them to be effectively cleaned. They must prevent infestation by rodents and insects and prevent the entry of birds.

Proper provision must be made for the removal of refuse and neither solid nor liquid refuse nor filth must be allowed to accumulate in food rooms.

Surfaces of walls and floors should be sound and washable and kept clean. Scrupulous cleanliness should be observed in the case of food shelves and preparation tables. Surfaces on which food is prepared should be made of an impervious material such as stainless steel. Sinks and tanks in which food is rinsed, soaked and stored should be also of a non-corroding metal or of undamaged porcelain.

Articles or equipment used in connection with a food business must be clean. They must be made of such materials and in such a way as to:

- Enable them to be thoroughly cleaned.
- Prevent, in so far as is reasonably practicable, matter being absorbed by them.
- Prevent, in so far as is reasonably practicable, any risk of contamination of the food.

No foods should be stored on the floor and storage areas should be designed to prevent cross-contamination.

Suitable and sufficient first aid materials must be provided in an accessible position for food handlers and must include bandages and dressings.

Hand washing

Food premises must comply with the statutory requirements with regard to hand washing facilities. The minimum requirements are a hand washbasin with adequate hot water, soap, a nail brush and some method of hand drying. These facilities must be used exclusively for hand washing.

Washing with soap is often ineffective at removing pathogenic bacteria and a bar of soap can actually pass on bacteria. A liquid soap dispenser is more hygienic (providing it is regularly filled) and bactericidal gel soaps are more likely to remove bacteria from the hands.

There is little point washing hands if the method of drying recontaminates them. Pull-down roller towels are satisfactory, provided that the machine works correctly (that is, it does not jam), and provided that the towel is replaced when it reaches the end. Alternatives are paper towel dispensers, continuous tear-off paper rolls and electric, warm air hand-drying machines.

Staff should be trained in the correct hand washing procedures. They should wash their hands not only when entering the kitchen, but also after handling potentially hazardous food and when transferring from preparation work to servery duties, after handling waste and refuse, and after touching their mouth or blowing their nose. Preparation sinks should not be used for hand washing.

Wash-up

The provision of proper facilities for washing-up is vital. Separate facilities are required for washing cooking vessels and utensils (the pan wash or plonge) and for crockery and cutlery. The latter must be sterilized following washing, using either heat alone (at a temperature of 77°C for two minutes or a higher temperature for a shorter period of time) or using a combination of heat and chemical sterilizing agents. Where washing-up is done by hand, a separate sterilizing sink is required into which crockery and cutlery can be immersed.

Staff facilities

Toilets in food premises must be provided in sufficient numbers for the staff employed. They must be kept clean and sited so that no offensive odours can reach food rooms. Toilets must be well lit and ventilated. No room containing a toilet can be used for food purposes. No room directly communicating with a room containing a sanitary convenience can be used for either handling open food or even for the cleaning of equipment used in connection with the handling of open food. Near every sanitary convenience and toilet in a food premise, there must be a clear notice display reminding users to wash their hands after they have used the toilet. The drainage system connected to sanitary conveniences must be isolated from food rooms, as must air inlets and water supplies to sanitary conveniences. There must be isolation between water supplies to sanitary conveniences and to food preparation equipment. Water supplies must be sufficient to cope with the requirements of the Food Hygiene Regulations and must be clean and wholesome.

Lockers or similar suitable accommodation facilities for the storage of clothing must be provided.

Disposal of waste

A most important feature of the kitchen premises are the facilities for the disposal of waste food. It forms a hazard on two counts:

1 There is the danger of cross-contamination of other foodstuffs directly from the waste.
2 Waste food materials will attract flies, insects, rodents and birds.

Ideally, waste food materials should leave the kitchen area at a different location from that where goods are received. However, this is not always practically possible. It is important to have clean food-waste bins (with tightly fitting lids) standing on a hard surface outside the kitchen. It should be possible to clean, disinfect and deodorize both the bins and the area in which they are located. Food refuse bins should be washed out internally as well as externally at regular intervals.

With the increasing difficulty of disposing of food waste, and because of the smell and hygiene risks associated with stored waste, more use is being made of electrical waste disposal units. Because of the increased use of disposables and packaged foods, waste compactors are also becoming much more common. Electrically operated compactors both reduce the volume of waste and bind it into neat bales.

Cleaning and the use of disinfectants

Care should be taken in the selection of cleaning materials and disinfectants for the cleaning of kitchen surfaces and utensils (ICMSF, 1987c). Separate detergents and disinfectants may be used or, alternatively, a combined detergent/disinfectant can be used.

Whichever of these methods is chosen, the chemicals must be suitable for the material of construction of the surface being cleaned, they must not be hazardous to the operative, they must be effective at removing soil and they must sterilize the surface. These disinfectants are only effective if used as directed by the manufacturer. It is important to check that the proper concentration of solution is used.

The cleaning agent chosen depends both on the nature of the soil and on the type of surface. Sugars, starchy foods, fats, fruit and vegetable residues require a mildly alkaline detergent, while high protein soil requires a chlorinated alkaline detergent (Thorpe, 1987). Rough surfaces and absorbent surfaces are more difficult to clean than smooth and impervious ones.

Hot water (above 80°C) is an effective sterilizing agent in locations where it can be easily used. Some modern kitchens are designed to be cleaned by high pressure hose. However, this can add considerably to the cost of the building because of the need to protect electrical equipment. Similarly, steam cleaning can be effective in a kitchen which has been specifically designed for this.

Chemical disinfectants should have the following properties:

- They should act rapidly on as many types of microorganism as possible.
- They should have an effective degree of penetration (this will vary according to the surface tension).
- They should be active and efficient at low concentration because of the cost factor.
- They should be active in the presence of organic matter.
- They should be stable for storage purposes.
- They should be safe under the conditions

of use. For this reason, stronger detergents can be used for mechanised cleaning than is the case for manual cleaning.

Many disinfectants are based on *chlorine* or *chlorine-based compounds*, such as sodium hypochlorite. These disinfectants may be unstable and hence lead to storage problems. They may also produce odours and taints in food. Their effectiveness is inhibited in the presence of organic matter as is found in the solid debris left in washing-up soil.

Derivatives of coal tar, such as carbolic acid, lysol and some alcohols, can cause tainting of the food which makes them unacceptable.

Chemicals based on quaternary ammonium compounds (QUACs or QUATs) can be extremely effective for dealing with swabs, knives, preparation tables and utensils. They are stable and least affected by the presence of organic matter. However, they are not equally effective against all pathogens.

Iodophors are stable and effective against a wide range of pathogens. They are not stable in solution, are affected by the presence of organic matter, and are expensive.

Detergent/sanitizers are combinations of suitable detergents and biocides which can be used in a single stage application.

Whatever disinfectant is used, the manufacturer's directions in terms of concentration, temperature and protective clothing should be followed explicitly. On no account should detergents be mixed, as there is a danger of the production of highly toxic chemicals. A cleaning guide and cleaning audit should be developed (DHSS, 1988). This can be one way of demonstrating 'due diligence' under the new Food Safety Act.

A useful technique is to provide charts or racks, on which are listed all daily and weekly cleaning schedules. In the case of a chart, the cleaning duty can be signed and dated (with a washable marking pen) once the job has been completed. When using racks, cards describing each cleaning job can be held in a *'to do'* rack and moved to a *'done'* rack once the job has been completed.

Personal hygiene

The caterer, the chef and all kitchen staff must be concerned to see that all measures to promote hygiene are observed effectively. Among these is the observation of simple rules about personal hygiene. Contamination is often caused by food operatives, which could be eliminated by raising the awareness of the necessity for care and attention with personal hygiene.

We have seen above that the caterer has a responsibility to provide changing facilities and sanitary facilities, to provide notices to instruct operatives to wash their hands after using the toilet and to provide clean protective clothing. Posters and visual displays are available from a number of organizations.

Hygiene rules, such as the *'ten point code'* shown in Figure 5.11 (DHSS, 1988), should be incorporated into training programmes.

In addition to providing safer food, it should also be made clear to all staff that personal hygiene improves the comfort and well being of staff. Frequent bathing or showering and the frequent changing of clothing eliminates both body odours and cooking odours from the skin and clothing of individuals. Care with the feet can reduce fatigue. Short hair is preferable as it is easier to protect. Too often kitchen headwear does not fully cover the hair and therefore does not provide adequate protection.

Staff should be instructed in the importance of personal health and what to do in the case of stomach or bowel upsets. They must be instructed to report any relevant illnesses, including diarrhoea, vomiting, gastroenteritis, sores, boils, discharges and skin infections. In the case of specified illnesses, exclusion is required until cleared by a doctor or environmental health officer. Similarly, staff must inform employers if they aware that they are carriers of any infections

---

1 Always wash your hands before touching foods and *always* after using the toilet.

2 Tell your supervisor at once of any skin, nose, throat or bowel trouble.

3 Cover cuts and sores with waterproof dressings.

4 Wear clean clothing and be clean.

5 Remember than smoking in a food room is illegal and dangerous. Never cough or sneeze over food.

6 Clean as you go in food rooms. Keep kitchen equipment and utensils clean.

7 Keep food clean, covered and either cold or piping hot.

8 Keep your hands off food as far as possible.

9 Keep the lid on the dustbin.

10 Do not break the law – tell your supervisor if you cannot follow the rules.

Figure 5.11   *The ten point code*

likely to cause food poisoning. Employers or proprietors must notify this information to the medical officer of health. Infections specifically mentioned in the regulations are: typhoid fever; paratyphoid fever or any other Salmonella infection or dysentery or any Staphyloccocal infection. Staff should also report any illness at home, of the types associated with food poisoning.

All food handlers, other than waiting staff, are required to wear clean and washable overclothing and full hair covering. Outdoor clothing must not be stored in kitchen or food store areas.

Anyone engaged in the handling of food must:

- Keep all parts of their person liable to come into contact with the food clean.
- Keep clothing and overalls clean.
- Cover any open cut or abrasion with a suitable waterproof dressing which is easily visible (that is, blue).
- Refrain from spitting.
- Refrain from smoking not only while handling food but while in any room in which there is open food.

Staff should be shown how to taste food in a hygienic way: to avoid the use of fingers; not to put a spoon which has been used for tasting back into a cooking vessel; and not to eat in the kitchen.

Precautions against contamination by insects, vermin and birds

Expert advice should be sought on all aspects of insect and vermin control from the appropriate officers of the local authority. Within the scope of this book it is only possible to indicate the normal precautions that the caterer and catering staff should take in the kitchen to combat the possibility of infestation. Usually, once a building has become infested, destruction is best left to the expert. Treatments against rodents and cockroaches may require treatment over a long period of time because insects and eggs are usually well protected. Fumigation may be required for heavy infestations.

The first stage in dealing with insects and vermin lies in preventing access to food rooms:

- Holes made through walls for cables, gas pipes, drains, etc., should be filled. The filling must be rat and insect proof. Concrete to which glass has been added is often used.
- Airbricks, gulleys and manhole covers should be inspected regularly and broken fittings renewed.
- Accessible windows to stores and food rooms that may be left open at night should be covered with fly, rodent and bird proof material.
- Wooden doors and frames to kitchen areas should be protected against gnawing by metal kicking plates. Any gaps caused by worn steps should be attended to.
- Drains and sewer connections should be checked since these are frequently entry passages for rats.
- All areas in a kitchen, such as service ducts and the space behind and beneath equipment, should either be sealed or capable of easy and frequent inspection and cleaning. Much use is now being made of mobile equipment in order to allow thorough cleaning.
- Electric flying insect killers should be installed in kitchens where flies are a problem.

The second stage is to discourage insects and rodents through good management:

- Materials such as rubbish and cartons should not be left against walls where it can act as a cover.

- Food should not be left out in the kitchen at night, but should be held in appropriate vermin proof storage rooms or cabinets.
- Food debris should be removed from floors at regular intervals and definitely not left overnight.
- Waste storage should be well away from points of access to the kitchen (doors, windows, cracks in the fabric of the building etc.); swill bins should stand on hard washable surfaces.
- Waste bins should be frequently emptied and cleaned.

The third stage is to recognize the evidence of infestation so that control measures can be taken and to know when expert advice and treatment is required:

- Rodents often leave hole and scrape marks and small piles of debris. Similarly, smear traces are often left on walls. Often, when rodents use the same route in a building, they leave a track or runway. Another tell-tale sign is the presence of droppings.
- Rodents can often be detected by damage caused by gnawing, not just of foodstuffs, but also packaging materials, wood, etc.
- Where infestation is suspected, bait may be left, which should not be poisoned. The bait should be inspected for signs that it has been eaten.

Hygienic aspects of specific catering systems

Cook-freeze and cook-chill

These two processes were developed to eliminate warm holding of foods by providing a buffer between production and service. The buffer stock can be held at −20°C for one to three months in the case of cook-freeze, or 0°C to +3°C for up to five days (including the day of production and the day of service) in the case of cook-chill. Freezing provides complete control over the growth of pathogens (though they will survive if present in large numbers), but it has a marked effect on the food and is not suitable for many foods. Cook-chill does not provide the same safety margin over pathogens and hence requires much stricter control (DHSS, 1989). However, chilling does not have the same effect on food as does freezing and therefore a wider range of food products can be handled by this process. The stages in the processes are shown in Figure 5.12.

Safety is a major area of concern with cook-chill (Sheppard, 1987). Provided that the above time temperature conditions are adhered to (based on DHSS guidelines) there is no hazard. In order to ensure rapid chilling, care must be taken to ensure that food in their trays is of a controlled depth. If the depth of food varies some may freeze and some may not be fully chilled. If the ninety-

---

Tutorial topic

Prepare a hygiene checklist based on the points in this section.

Use this checklist to carry out a hygiene audit on a kitchen to which you have access.

Write a hygiene report for the manager of this kitchen.

minute chilling time is exceeded, bacteria may spend too long in the temperature danger zone and may actively start growing.

Where foods are plated after chilling or before reheating, as in many hospital systems, strict control is needed over environmental temperature and over stock control. If the environmental temperature is high (above 10°C) and if food spends a long time above 3°C, bacteria may start to multiply. Similar problems may arise during the distribution stage.

The DHSS guidelines state that chilled and frozen foods which are to be reheated centrally must be distributed and eaten within fifteen minutes.

Cook-freeze	Cook-chill
Purchasing All raw materials of good microbiological quality.	
Preparation Strict conditions of hygiene. High-quality raw materials. Cooking to at least 70°C for 2 minutes.	
Packing No time delays. Strict conditions of hygiene. No cross contamination.	
Freezing Use a blast freezer. Chilling must start within 30 minutes of cooking. Foods must be reduced from 70°C to –20°C in a maximum of 90 minutes.	*Chilling* Use a blast chiller, or immersion chiller. Chilling must start within 30 minutes of cooking. Foods must be reduced from 70°C to 3°C in a maximum of 90 minutes.
Storage Must be below –18°C. Storage life 1 to 3 months depending on the product.	*Storage* Must be between 0°C and 3°C. Purpose-built store not used for other foods. Maximum storage life 5 days.
(Distribution)* Under same temperature control as for storage. Insulated containers for short transport. Refrigerated vans for long distribution.	
Reheating Hot foods must achieve at least 70°C Cold foods must be thawed in refrigerator. Reheating in forced convection oven.	*Reheating* Hot foods must achieve at least 70°C for 2 minutes. Cold foods must be consumed within 30 minutes of removal from storage. Reheating by microwave, forced convection, infra-red oven or combination oven.
Service Minimum delay between reheating and service (15 minutes). Holding temperatures outside the danger zone Any foods not consumed must be discarded	

* Distribution is not always a part of cook-freeze or cook-chill.

Figure 5.12 *The cook-freeze and cook-chill processes*

Sous vide

In recent catering developments, the combination of vacuum packaging, pasteurization and low temperature has been used to control the growth of both spoilage and food poisoning bacteria. A particular application is the sous vide process. A flow diagram for the sous vide process is shown in Figure 5.13. Sous vide carries many of the risks associated with cook-chill. Effective vacuum packing together with in-pack pasteurization will remove the risks of the growth of most pathogens, other than spore formers. The low temperature of storage (0 to 3°C) will also inhibit growth of all pathogens, including spore formers − there is a risk of the growth of *Clostridium botulinum* type E if temperatures rise above 4°C. Strict control is needed over the level of vacuum, the quality of the heat seal on the package, together with full monitoring of temperature histories in order to ensure safety.

There are a number of variants of the sous vide process. Some of these involve a heat

---

Purchasing
All raw materials of good microbiological quality.

Preparation
Strict conditions of hygiene.
High-quality raw materials.
Uniform thickness.

Vacuum packaging
Oxygen impermeable plastic bags.
Leak-proof seam.
Effective removal of air.

In-pouch cooking
Strict temperature control to kill all vegetative cells
  (70°C for 2 minutes at coldest point).
Use of convection steamers or combination ovens.

Rapid chilling
To comply with cook-chill guidelines.
Blast chiller, iced water bath or conduction chiller.

Refrigerated storage
Time and temperature to comply with cook-chill guidelines.

*(Distribution)**
As for cook-chill.

Reheating
Rapid heating to at least 70°C at coldest point,
  and maintained for 2 minutes.
Use of convection steamer or combination ovens.

Service
Immediately following reheating.
Any foods not consumed must be discarded.

---

* Distribution is not always a part of sous vide.

Figure 5.13   *The sous vide process*

treatment followed by aseptic vacuum packaging such as the CapKold and ChillVac systems.

References and further reading

Cruickshank J. C. (1987). The Problem of the 'Carrier' Food Handler. Conference on Microbiological and Environmental Health Problems Relevant to the Food and Catering Industries, Campden Food Preservation Research Association, 19–21 January.

DHSS (1986). *Health Service Catering Hygiene.* London: HMSO.

DHSS (1988). *Chilled and Frozen: Guidelines on Cook-Chill and Cook-Freeze Catering Systems.* London: HMSO.

Electricity Council (1987). *Planning for Cook-Chill.* London: Electricity Council.

Gilbert R. J. (1987). Foodborne Infections and Intoxifications – Recent Problems and New Organisms. Conference on Microbiological and Environmental Health Problems Relevant to the Food and Catering Industries. Campden Food Preservation Research Association, 19–21 January.

Glanfield P. (1980). *Applied Cook-Freezing.* London: Applied Science Publishers.

Goodburn K. (1989). Irradiation – Just a Matter of Time. *Caterer and Hotelkeeper,* 8 June.

HCIMA (1989a). *Technical Brief 4, Keeping Pests Out by Design.* London: HCIMA.

HCIMA (1989b). *Technical Brief 5, HACCP – The Effective Approach to Food Hygiene Safety.* London: HCIMA.

HCIMA (1989c). *Technical Brief 12, Preventing Food Poisoning.* London: HCIMA.

ICMSF (1988a). Microbiological Control of Foods, Chapter 1. In *Microorganisms in Foods – 4: Applications of the Hazard Analysis and Critical Control (HACCP) System to Ensure Microbiological Safety and Quality.* Oxford: Blackwell.

ICMSF (1988b). The Hazard Analysis Critical Control Point Approach, Chapter 2. In *Microorganisms in Foods – 4: Applications of the Hazard Analysis and Critical Control (HACCP) System to Ensure Microbiological Safety and Quality.* Oxford: Blackwell.

ICMSF (1988c). Cleaning and Disinfection, Chapter 6. In *Microorgansims in Foods – 4: Applications of the Hazard Analysis and Critical Control (HACCP) System to Ensure Microbiological Safety and Quality.* Oxford: Blackwell.

ICMSF (1988d). Food Service, Chapter 12. In *Microorgansims in Foods – 4: Applications of the Hazard Analysis and Critical Control (HACCP) System to Ensure Microbiological Safety and Quality.* Oxford: Blackwell.

MAFF (1988). *Food Hygiene – Report of a Consumer Survey.* London: HMSO.

Public Health Laboratory Service (1988). *Communicable Diseases.* Report Number 88/152.

Roberts D. (1982). Factors Contributing to Outbreaks of Food Poisoning in England and Wales 1970–79. *Journal of Hygiene,* 89, pp. 491–8.

Shepperd J. (1987). *The Big Chill: a report on the implications of cook-chill for the public service.* London: London Food Commission.

Social Services Committee (1989). *Food Poisoning – Listeria and Listeriosis.* Response of the Government to the 6th Report (1988–9), November 1989. London: HMSO.

Thorpe R. H. (1987). Factors Affecting the Use of Biocides.

Conference on Microbiological and Environmental Health Problems Relevant to the Food and Catering Industries. Campden Food Preservation Research Association, 19–21 January.

Wadey C. J. (1987). Standards of Food Hygiene in NHS Hospitals – Are They Improving. 94th Environmental Health Congress, Brighton 7–10 September.

6
Accidents and their prevention

Kitchens are inherently dangerous places. The combination of a high level of manual work, sharp cutting appliances, hot surfaces together with hot fats and oils leads to a high risk of cuts and burns. Slippery floor surfaces cause slips and falls. Open flames and hot fats are fire risks. These risks are increased by the tempo of activity in the kitchen and the high tension at service time.

As well as the danger to employees, caterers also have a responsibility to their customers. The effects of injuries to customers is damaging both because it affects the image of the restaurant, but also because of the cost of damages and the cost of insurance to cover injury liability.

It should also be understood that the word accident does not just cover human injury. It can also relate to financial loss caused by damage to equipment and facilities.

According to the Royal Society for the Prevention of Accidents, 16 per cent of all accidents requiring hospital treatment were caused at work (see Figure 6.1).

Of those accidents which occur at the place of work, the majority are within the manufacturing and construction industries. Accidents which occurred within catering are reported to the local authority. For the year 1985, there were 209 major accidents within catering, of which four were fatal. Of the major accidents, 87 per cent were to employees and 13 per cent to members of the public. Over the period from 1981 to 1985, there was a fall of 5 per cent in the

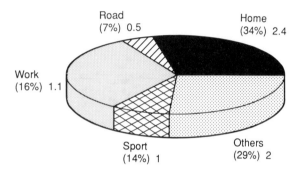

Number of hospital cases resulting from accidents (millions)

Figure 6.1 *Location of accidents for Great Britain, 1987*

number of major accidents associated with catering, despite the increase in the number of establishments over this period.

Statutory safety requirements

The Health and Safety at Work Act 1974

Apart from the natural concern to eliminate hazards and prevent accidents, hoteliers and caterers, as do all employers, now have specific responsibilities under the Health and Safety at Work Act (HSWA) 1974. The Act covers ways of maintaining the health, safety and welfare of people at work, the control of dangerous substances and the control of the discharge of noxious or offensive substances into the environment. The primary responsibility for these safety measures rests with the employer. However, all employees also have a responsibility to work safely and to cooperate with their employer on matters of safety.

The legislation comes under the supervision of the Health and Safety Commission and its Executive. However, in the case of catering, enforcement is normally by the environmental health department of the local authority. In addition to legal penalties, inspectors can serve improvement notices (requiring a person to remedy a contravention of the Act within a stipulated time period) or a prohibition notice (requiring the cessation of a process or activity). In both cases the inspector must provide reasons for this action.

Under the legislation, it is obligatory for employers to prepare, and keep revised, a written safety policy, together with organizational arrangements for its execution. This safety policy must be brought to the attention of all employees.

The sole exception to this requirement is for operations employing less than five people, including any part-time employees. But even small establishments with less than five employees can grow, for example in the high season. It is therefore prudent for the smallest operator to be ready with a safety policy statement.

Enforcement officers with wide powers are responsible for ensuring that the Act's provisions are met. Neglect of its provisions makes employers and employees open to personal and corporate criminal prosecution, with the possibility of severe penalties. Officers are authorized to inspect premises. They can enforce the act by improvement notices where there are unsafe conditions or by prohibition notice (that is, immediate stoppage) when the risk of serious injury arises.

Although the Act provides for enforcement and penalties, it stresses self-regulation and aims to involve employers and employees alike in a realization of the importance of safety. In focusing attention on personal and collective responsibility, the Act chiefly outlines what employers must do; but it stresses, too, that employees must be aware of their responsibilities for their own safety, that of their works and of the general public. Those responsible for kitchen management must be involved with their employers in the preparation of the safety policy statement and its application to the kitchen.

Guidance notes are available from the Health and Safety Executive and its local officers to help in the preparation of a firm's health and safety at work policy statements (Health and Safety Executive, 1989a). These notes are in general terms to cover all industries. Specific aspects relating to catering operations are discussed in the following sections.

Safety policy document drafting

The safety policy document must result from careful consideration of activities and possible hazards in all sections of an operation.

Aims: The safety policy document should be prefaced by a brief statement in general terms covering the health and safety at work of employees. This general statement would include something of the nature of Figure 6.2.

This general statement of *aims* should be followed by details of *responsibilities* for implementing the policy, including ways in which responsibilities will be assigned. These details must take into account the specific circumstances of each operation. In a multiple unit company, details may vary from branch to branch. Rules, regulations and codes of practice covered within the document must deal with both general hazards and the particular hazards encountered in the operation to which they relate.

In a multiple company, responsibilities for safety are split between headquarters and branch managers. Headquarters have overall responsibility for policy implementation. Area managers usually are responsible for local arrangements and advising top management on safety action. Nevertheless, a safety policy document must relate to each particular operation. The document must be made readily accessible to every member of staff, so that everyone is aware of possible dangers and appropriate precautions.

This part of the document must also give the name and business address of the person responsible for implementing the policy in a particular workplace. For example, an executive chef may well be assigned responsibility

---

General statement of policy

Health and Safety at Work Act 1974

Health and Safety policy of:

_____

_____

_____

'...........................'s' (name of company) policy aims to provide and maintain safe and healthy working conditions, equipment and systems of work for all our employees, and to provide such information, training and supervision as they need for this purpose. We also accept responsibility for the health and safety of other people who may be affected by our activities.

The allocation of duties for safety matters and the particular arrangements which we will make to implement the policy are set out below.

The policy will be kept up-to-date, particularly as the business changes in nature and size. To ensure this, the policy and the way in which it has operated will be reviewed every year.

The policy objectives include:

1 Compliance with the Health and Safety at Work Action 1974 and other relevant legislation in achieving standards of safety, health and welfare.

2 Maintenance of a safe and healthy workplace, procedures and work methods.

3 Protection both of employees and members of the public from work hazards.

4 Information, training, instruction and supervision of employees to ensure their safe working.

5 Promotion of vigilance and awareness of safety among employees, collectively and as individuals.

6 Consultation with staff and creation of conditions of cooperation between staff and management in safety matters.

Figure 6.2 *Outline safety policy: aims and objectives*

for the kitchen and ancillary departments. It must also indicate the method of consultation through the use of safety representatives, a safety committee or whatever method is appropriate.

In particular, named individuals must be identified who are responsible for:

- Ensuring that working conditions and staff accommodation comply with the HSWA and other relevant statutory provision.
- Receiving reports on structural faults.
- Acquainting staff with fire procedures, organizing fire drills, taking necessary precautions regarding storing flammable materials in order to minimize fire risks.
- Ensuring that entrances and exits are not obstructed and that staff and public have adequate means of escape from the premises in the event of fire or other hazard.
- Receiving reports on personal injury to staff or public.
- Training staff in necessary procedures.
- Organizing first aid and maintaining first aid boxes.

The second part of the policy statement should cover *general arrangements*. In this section specific responsibility for accidents, fire safety, advice and consultancy and training is detailed, together with details of rules for contractors and visitors.

The final part of the policy statement covers the identification of hazards which are specific to an operation, including housekeeping, premises, electrical equipment, dangerous substances and fluids under pressure.

Many or all of the specific points which relate to a particular operation of the type identified later in this chapter should be incorporated into the rules, regulations and code of practice accompanying or linked

with the policy statement. Other measures of safety peculiar to a particular operation must be added.

The written policy statement must be communicated to all employees but additionally, under Section 2(2) (c) of the HSWA, employers are obliged to provide any information, instruction, training and supervision which is necessary in order to ensure the health and safety of their employees. This includes codes of practice and safety manuals. Even in kitchens, the written policy statement may not be the appropriate way of covering detailed rules for, say, handling knives or treating wet floors. But it would be appropriate for the statement to refer to additional rules, codes or manuals.

The Act also covers the safety of all persons on the premises who are not employees of the company. This includes customers, visitors, suppliers and maintenance engineers.

There is a requirement, under the Health and Safety Information for Employees Regulations 1989, to either display a poster or to give each employee a leaflet. These posters or leaflets give information about the Health and Safety at Work Act and of the need for a safety policy.

Employee involvement

A fundamental element in safety at work and one recognized by the HSW Act is communication to, and involvement of, staff. Employers cannot pass their responsibility for safety on to employees or their representatives but it is sensible management to consult employees. A safety committee with appointed or elected employee representatives is the recommended medium for such consultations under the Safety Representatives and Safety Committees Regulations 1977 (Health and Safety Commission, 1988).

In catering operations where unions with recognized negotiating rights exist, safety representatives may be appointed by a union and such representatives may request that a joint safety committee be formed. In non-unionized operations, and where such a committee is not obligatory, the Health and Safety Commission recommend that employers should create a committee on their own initiative. If two or more employees make a written request for the establishment of a safety committee, the employer is obliged to comply with this request. The safety committee should help draw up, revise and implement the safety policy document, study the pattern of accidents and perform safety audits. Nevertheless, employers must recognize, as must all at management level, that safety responsibility still rests with them as employers.

Code of practice

A code of practice should be available as part of the safety policy statement of the HSWA. Moreover, a catering operation can use the code of practice as part of its training programme. The code of practice should be based on a thorough and on-going analysis of hazards which relate to the specific operation. Techniques available include:

- Safety inspections.
- Job safety analysis.
- Safety sampling.
- Hazard and operability studies.
- Safety tours.

A policy of regular safety inspections should be incorporated into the code of practice so that hazards can be continuously identified and eliminated. These inspections may be on a daily, weekly or monthly basis.

Checklists should be constructed, based on the agreed code of practice for a catering operation. The survey should look at:

- The design and structure of the facility.
- The location of equipment.
- The functioning of equipment.
- Working methods and practices.

The code of practice should start with a general preamble, which could include the points indicated in Figure 6.3.

Recording and reporting accidents

Accidents involving staff and equipment can become the subject of insurance claims, compensation demands and of litigation in the courts. Because of this, an immediate and accurate written report of the accident is necessary. The report should be made by the member of staff involved and signed by a designated member of staff. This report should provide information regarding:

- The person involved and/or machine damaged.
- Where the accident occurred.
- What supervision was in force.
- Names of any witnesses of the accident.

As necessary, the chef or departmental manager should attach a confidential note giving any supplementary information about the accident and why it occurred.

There is also a statutory requirement under the Social Security Act 1975 for business premises to keep an *accident book* (Form B I 510). This book is available from HMSO. It must be made readily accessible at all reasonable times to any injured employees and any bona fide person acting on their behalf. In order to comply with this Act, an entry in the accident book has to be made, as soon as is practicable, after an accident. Particulars of an accident may be entered into the book either by the injured person, or by someone on his/her behalf. The book provides for the following information to be entered:

● Full name, address and occupation of the injured person.
● Signature of the injured person, or of the person making the entry.
● Where the entry is not made by the injured person, the name, address and occupation of the person making the entry should be entered.
● Date when the entry was made.
● Date and time of the accident.
● Room or place where accident occurred.
● Cause and nature of injury (with clear information about the work or process being performed at the time of the accident).

In addition to giving notice of the accident to his/her employer (through entry in the accident book) an injured person wishing to obtain *industrial injuries benefit* must ensure that a claim is lodged within twenty-one days at a local office of the Department of Health and Social Security.

Under the Reporting of Injuries, Diseases and Dangerous Occurrences Regulations 1985 (RIDDOR), an employer must give written notice to the local authority, when an accident:

● Causes loss of life to a person employed; or
● Disables any such person for more than three days from earning full wages at the work at which he/she was employed.

A statement of general conduct, covering statutory duties under the HSWA.

Specific requirements for clothing and/or uniforms, including footware.

Instructions to prevent recognized hazards, based on an accident hazard survey and covering prevention of:

Falls and collisions.

Cuts and machinery injury:
Handtools and knives
Sharp debris
Machines
Gas equipment

Avoidance of strains.

Fires, burns and scalds.

Poisons and allergies.

The method of *reporting faults* should also be covered by the Code of Practice.

Figure 6.3   *Outline of points covered in safety code of practice*

Major injuries include:

- Fractures of skull, spine, pelvis, major bone of arm or leg.
- Amputation of hand or foot.
- Loss of sight of an eye.
- Any injury resulting in hospitalization.

A form is available for this notification (F2508). An accident resulting in death or serious personal injury must be notified to the local authority as quickly as is practicable, that is, by phone.

Notification alerts enforcement agencies to serious accidents and provides an opportunity to identify patterns of accidents. Enforcement agencies can decide whether to investigate, using their powers under the HSWA.

Additionally, employers must alert enforcement agencies following certain statutorily identified dangerous occurrences. These are injuries which may occur frequently and could potentially cause serious injury, although no such injury may result in a given instance. The type of mishaps which must be notified include those involving lifts, hoists, cranes, pressure vessels, boilers, electrical incidents and certain explosions.

In any policy statement required by the HSWA, the employer's intent to keep accident records should be expressed. Also included should be the method of maintaining the record and a named person (with his/her post) charged with responsibility for keeping records and investigating accidents. Information recorded should include:

- Date and time of the accident or dangerous occurrence.
- In the case of an accident, particulars of the person injured:

- Name.
- Address.
- Sex.
- Age.

- Occupation.
- Nature of injury.
- The place where the accident or dangerous occurrence took place.
- A brief description of the circumstances.

Enforcement authorities are authorized to see such records or have them sent to their offices for scrutiny. Additionally, they may also require to see the accident book. Records should be kept for a minimum of three years.

Records must also be kept of all enquiries from the DHSS regarding claims made by the employer or employees of any disease prescribed under Section 76 of the Social Security Act 1975. This record must include the name, address, sex, age, occupation, nature of the disease for which the claim was made, the date of the first absence from work.

The Social Security Act also requires a record of all notifiable accidents, which includes those which cause a person to:

- Lose his/her life immediately or contribute in a major way to his/her demise after an accident.
- To be absent from work for three days or more (the day of the accident counts as day one for the purpose of the Act, even if there is only five minutes left of it to work; the three days also include any rest day or days, that is, a weekend).

Control of Substances Hazardous to Health Regulations 1988

These regulations are designed to protect people at work against risks to their health arising from the effects (immediate or delayed) of hazardous substances. The substances are listed in the Classification, Packaging and Labelling of Dangerous

Substances Regulations 1984. The regulations also apply to microorganisms which are hazardous to health.

Although most materials used by the caterer do not come under these regulations, there are some (such as oven cleaners, bleaches, cleaning agents, detergents and sterilizing agents, etc.) which do carry a significant hazard. For any such materials the responsibilities of the employer are identified in the regulations:

Assessment

All substances used must be subjected to an assessment by the employer before use. This assessment must cover both the risks involved and measures necessary to control exposure. This would include methods of dealing with spillages, and treatments for accidental exposure.

Control

The employer must ensure that exposure is either prevented or adequately controlled. This applies whether the substance is hazardous through inhalation, ingestion, absorption through the skin or when in contact with the skin.

The employer must ensure that the above control measures are correctly used by every employee and that the control measures are properly maintained and in efficient working order.

Training

Suitable and sufficient training must be given about the risks to health from substances used and about precautions to be taken in the handling of these materials.

Other legislation involved with safety

The Offices, Shops and Railway Premises Act 1963 also covers areas of catering which are related to accidents. It specifically covers cleanliness, avoidance of overcrowding in relation to people and equipment, the maintenance of reasonable temperatures, ventilation and lighting, construction of floors and stairs and guarding of machinery.

The Health and Safety (First Aid Regulations 1981) replaces some parts of the above act. It requires an employer to provide suitable equipment and facilities for providing first aid to employees.

The Offices, Shops and Railway Premises (Hoists and Lifts) Regulations 1968 provides for the regular inspection of hoists and lifts and for the control of their use.

The Safety Signs Regulations 1980 covers the colour, shape and form of signs displayed as part of an employer's responsibility under the HSWA.

Investigation of an accident

Investigation of accidents may take place internally within a company or they may be carried out by the enforcement officer. In the case of a serious incident, a court of enquiry may be used (Socrates, 1981).

The method of operation of internal investigations should be described in the safety code of practice. Typically, an investigation might involve a team made up of:

- The safety officer.
- The relevant supervisor.
- Safety representative(s).

- Union representatives.
- Technical advisors, if required.

The purpose of the enquiry should be to determine:

- Why the accident occurred.
- How similar occurrences could be prevented.
- If there were any lapses in safety procedures.
- If the accident indicated any training needs.

The investigation can include interviews with relevant staff. However, staff are under no legal obligation to answer questions other than to the enforcement officer or a court of enquiry. Even in the latter two cases, witnesses need not answer questions which will incriminate themselves.

Basic causes of accidents

Accidents are usually caused by a combination of factors, including inattention, thoughtlessness or bad planning. The basic remedies involve care, thought and intelligent anticipation. Before dealing with specific dangers in kitchens or food preparation rooms it as well to note three general factors which encourage accidents:

1 Excessive haste.
2 Use of heat and hot equipment.
3 Use of machinery.

Particularly at service times, kitchens are places of intensive activity. Because of this pressure, emphasis is often placed on speed of performance. Proper training in the use of all utensils can both increase speed and reduce the risk of accidents. For example, correct handling and use of knives both increases efficiency and speed and reduces the possibility of mishaps. The tag 'more haste less speed' is hackneyed but appropriate, as is the rider 'more haste more accidents'.

Food preparation and cooking, like other kinds of work, constitutes controlled activity. If control is lost, accidents can arise. Pressure of profit and speed must not obscure this.

It is well known that conditions of discomfort can lead to an increase in the number of errors. Many kitchens have environmental conditions which are far from optimal for human activity. In particular, high temperatures, high humidities and poor lighting levels are common in many kitchens. Conditions of discomfort can reduce levels of concentration, so that even experienced and well-trained staff can be involved in accidents.

Structural/building faults

Accidents due to faults in the fabric and structure of kitchens, adjacent corridors and ancillary departments are common. Under the requirements of the HSWA, it is the employer's responsibility to maintain plant, as well as processes, in a safe condition. Some of the common structural and building faults associated with accidents are indicated below.

Floors

Faulty floors are hazardous. Accidents from tripping particularly when carrying vessels containing foods and liquids can be serious. A frequent cause is the deterioration of floor coverings, such as a broken or displaced tiles or displaced or broken gutter and gully covers. Floors should be kept free from loose objects, such as turned up mat edges and loose or broken boards. Racks, boxes and trolleys should not be left in areas where staff walk.

A major problem with kitchen floors is slipping when the floors are wet or greasy. Many floor surfaces lose their friction when they are covered in water, oil or a combination of the two. Where slippery floors are a problem, wet cleaning should be done as far as is possible outside kitchen production periods, and mobile signs should be used, indicating that the floor is slippery. Spillages of water, fat, oil and food should be cleaned up immediately. The use of sensible footwear by employees can also reduce slips.

Walls, ceilings, windows and stairs

Structural defects of walls and ceilings are less common in causing kitchen accidents but faulty doors, unfamiliar projections from walls or damage to windows affecting lighting are items which should be checked. Stairs should be checked for defects, such as lifting treads, and for other potential tripping hazards.

Lighting

Care should be taken to avoid obscuring natural lighting. Some kitchens are entirely lit by artificial means. In all cases, illumination levels should be measured to ensure that they conform with recommended levels for all areas. This should include all passages and storerooms. Switches for these lights should be placed in convenient positions, so that staff do not have to grope around in the dark.

Prevention of accidents

Catering design

Good catering design can contribute to safety. A kitchen and restaurant should be designed to provide minimum cross flows, adequate aisle spaces (see Chapter 9) and the sensible use of vertical space. Clearance must be allowed in front of appliance doors to allow for safe loading and unloading.

In traditional ovens, heavy containers of hot food must be raised from floor level to worktop level. This is hazardous on two counts: employees can strain their backs; and there is the risk of burns and scalds. The use of ovens which have shelves at a natural lifting height, or which can be unloaded on to trolleys, is much more satisfactory.

The facility should be designed to avoid cross flows of traffic. 'In' and 'out' doors should be used in areas where two-way flow occurs.

Equipment and activities

Many pieces of equipment and activities within the kitchen and ancillary departments are potential accident hazards. These should be identified and controlled.

Equipment

Care should be taken in the maintenance and use of:

- Food machinery: choppers; mixers; mincers; slicers; etc.
- Cooking equipment: identification of hot surfaces; steam, hot oil and hot water.
- Stillroom equipment: coffee urns; boilers.

Activities

Training in the correct use of these activities should be given and followed up by supervisors and management:

- Knife, chopper and other sharp hand tool usage.
- Handling hot objects.

- Moving food or equipment trolleys.
- Lifting or moving heavy objects.
- Spillages on floor (grease, water and other materials).
- Climbing: ladder usage; steps; mounting boxes.

Manufacturers' instructions should be used as the basis of staff training, as should HMSO publications on health and safety of specific catering equipment.

All dangerous appliances should be provided with guards which prevent the operator or any other person from coming into contact with, or getting clothing caught in, any part of a machine which might do them harm.

Machines should be operated with all safety guards in place. The practice of disabling safety guards and interlocks introduces a serious safety hazard. Safety warnings should be clearly displayed in an obvious position adjoining the machine to which they relate.

All appliances should be maintained on a routine basis (see Chapter 10). Checks of wiring, pilot lights, flame failure devices, thermostats and other safety features should be included in preventative maintenance schedules.

Frequent checks should be made of electric plugs, sockets and cables. The correct functioning of equipment earthing should also be checked. Power-driven machinery should have a switch within arm's length of the operator. Machinery should be isolated from the electrical supply before it is stripped down for cleaning.

Taps, pipes and flexible hoses on gas appliances should be checked on a routine basis. Gas burners should be kept clean and free from debris.

Steps or ladders should be provided to allow staff to reach high-level storage cupboards and racks. Trolleys and hoists should be provided where it is necessary to move and lift heavy weights.

Staff and staff training

Many kitchen perils are due to human error. Climbing on to an unsteady structure of boxes to reach an otherwise inaccessible object or attempting to lift too heavy a load rather than make two journeys, exemplifies human folly, error or misplaced zeal which causes accidents. Running in corridors, leaving pan handles projecting from the stove or over burners all contribute to accidents.

Machinery causes a most dramatic kind of accident because of its suddenness and often swiftly mutilating effect. It is difficult to effectively guard many mechanical appliances such as mixers. Kitchen staff use many small but hazardous appliances such as knives and mandolins.

The only effective control of accidents in these situations is effective staff training and rigorous attention by the chef or supervisor. New staff should be fully trained in the correct use of all appliances they need to use. This training should be reinforced at regular intervals.

Staff should be trained in the correct method of lifting and carrying heavy loads and should be encouraged to use hoists and trolleys where practicable.

The proper use of oven clothes, insulated gloves and pot holders should be included in the training programme – all these aids should only be used when completely dry. Personal clothing and dish cloths should not be used for handling hot objects.

Care should be taken when lifting lids on pans and when opening the doors of steaming equipment. Steam frequently causes burning of the hands and/or face.

Surefootedness is needed in and around kitchens. The incidence of heavy objects being dropped on to feet and toes is common. Hence the choice of footwear is important. Staff should not be permitted to wear thin soled or open-toed shoes nor, from a hygiene point of view, should they be allowed to wear their outdoor shoes. There are several types of safety shoe suitable for the catering industry — safety shoes do not have to be of the heavy industrial type.

Many of the materials used in cleaning and disinfection are toxic or cause skin allergies. All supplies should carry clear labels — this may need to be symbolic and/or in several languages in some situations. Manufacturers now must mark all containers with information about hazardous chemicals. The danger lies when these chemicals are poured into smaller containers for use. All cleaning materials should be stored in a separate area from food stores. Rubber gloves should be used by staff handling detergents and other materials which might cause skin allergies.

Fire and its prevention

Designing for fire safety encompasses safeguarding life (especially dangers from toxic fumes), safe buildings, safe contents (rapid smoke and heat generation) and involves a building's structure, its services, systems of communication (alarm and emergency services, extinguishment) and fire brigade facilities (access and control). Expert guidance is needed by the caterer on the detailed fire precautions required for a specific operation.

The Fire Precautions Act 1971 and the Designating Order for Hotels and Boarding Houses, together with local authority regulations, indicate the precautions to be taken in planning against fire. The HSWA also clarifies a number of issues, such as overlap of responsibilities between the fire service and the factory inspectorate.

Under the Fire Precautions Act, a fire certificate is required for most hotels and for large restaurants, particularly those above ground level.

To obtain a fire certificate a plan of the building is required which shows such details as doors, alarm points and emergency lighting. It is also vital to incorporate a schedule of conditions for use. The schedule may specify an executive chef or a caterer by name as having responsibility for firefighting requirements in specified parts of the premises. Fire certificates are specific to each operation. They usually lay down maintenance schedules for fire alarms and firefighting equipment to ensure that positions chosen and operating conditions are not changed.

Fire risks within a kitchen are enhanced because of the nature of the cooking process. All heating presents a fire hazard and many forms of it abound in the kitchen — in particular the use of hot fat poses specific problems. Electrical machinery and cables, together with possible wiring faults, must be regarded as an added fire risk. Careless or dangerous practices and failure to take elementary precautions can turn a kitchen into a fire trap.

Tutorial topic

For a kitchen to which you have access:

1 Prepare a safety checklist.

2 Carry out a safety audit using this checklist.

3 Write a management report on possible safety hazards and training needs.

Types of fire

There are three types of fire:

Type 1 *Simple combustion*: wood; paper; textiles. Extinguished by lowering the temperature and quenching with water.
Type 2 *Flammable liquids*: oil; grease, etc. Extinguished by smothering.
Type 3 *Live electrical equipment*. Extinguished by a non-conducting agent.

In addition to the above, it should be remembered that the major hazard with a fire is not the flame, but smoke. This is particularly the case with items such as upholstery, which can give off toxic gases when ignited.

Fire hazards in kitchens include range surfaces, fryers, ductwork, hoods, grease-traps, ovens and grills. Ventilation systems over grills and fryers should have grease filters to prevent grease deposits building up in the ductwork. Both the filters and the ductwork should be cleaned on a regular basis.

A common cause of outbreaks of fire is from the ignition of frying fats. Fryers should be operated in accordance with the manufacturer's instructions. Frying equipment and extraction canopies may be fitted with automatic fire control systems.

Cloths and clothing can catch fire when open-flame cooking appliances are used. Oven fires from foods igniting during baking are also by no means infrequent.

Fire emergency action

Fire alarms should be located at appropriate places. These may be manual or automatic, the latter being linked to fire detection systems. These are activated by smoke or heat detectors. Some of these systems may also be linked to the fire station.

Emergency lighting should also be provided to cover illumination of routes of exits and exit signs. These systems should either be activated automatically if the main electrical supply fails or, alternatively, they should be on all of the time when there is insufficient daylight.

A kitchen must be properly equipped with emergency fire-fighting equipment. Staff must be drilled in action to be taken in the event of a fire. In accordance with the responsibility as allocated by management, designated staff have specific duties or procedures to follow. These procedures will have been agreed by the local authority. Whether outbreaks such as oven fires or clothing fires spread and cause a major fire and injury may largely depend on action taken before and during the accident by the caterer or chef and their staff. Hence, everyone in the kitchen must be instructed in the use of the available fire-fighting equipment such as fire blankets, sand, chemical and foam extinguishers.

As with other aspects of safety, fire precaution involves management and staff awareness, incentives for fire risk consciousness, good housekeeping and effective routine drill procedures. Training and information should be simple and practical. Many kitchens employ staff for whom English is not their first language. Fire procedures and extinguisher operating instructions should, where possible, be given in several different languages.

Fire-fighting equipment

Choosing the wrong fire-fighting apparatus and extinguishing agent can cause as much damage to kitchen equipment as the fire itself and may actually make the fire worse. Additionally, it can be a human hazard. For example, water is an excellent extinguisher for type 1 fires, but spreads type 2 fires and is extremely dangerous with type 3 fires because of its electrical conductivity. Carbon dioxide, dry chemical vaporizing liquid or foam can all be used on fires of types 2 and 3. All-purpose dry powders are effective in fighting all three types of fires, but are not recommended for kitchen use because they contaminate food. Vaporizing liquids (halons) should only be used outside on fires of types 2 and 3.

All extinguishers should be red in colour, with their type identified by a colour code:

Water	red
Foam	cream
Dry powder	blue
Carbon dioxide	black
Halon	green

Portable extinguishers should be located near to doors or other easily accessible locations in hazard areas. They should never be installed in a corner, the middle of a corridor or other hard-to-reach locations. Extinguishers should be easy to see, that is, red coloured fire-fighting appliances should be kept against a white wall.

When selecting an extinguisher, it is necessary to determine whether or not it is light enough to be carried by staff and whether its size will be adequate to fight a fire likely to occur in an operation. If larger extinguishers are required it may be worth considering mounting them on trolleys which, in the event of fire, can be easily wheeled to the point of use.

An effective safe medium for fighting a kitchen fire, available both as built-in and portable systems, is carbon dioxide. It provides safe, non-toxic protection by smothering flames without tainting food or damaging equipment. Upon expulsion it expands 450 times and reaches into every crevice. After the fire is extinguished, the carbon dioxide quickly disappears leaving no trace and no fire mess to clean up.

In the event of an oil or fat fire, the power should first be turned off before using a fire blanket, foam or a carbon dioxide extinguisher.

First aid

Despite taking all of the precautions possible, accidents will still happen. Cuts, burns, fainting and other personal mishaps must be anticipated even in the best ordered kitchens. These accidents necessitate the provision and organization of first aid.

One or more *first aid boxes* must be conveniently sited, kept fully stocked and checked frequently by a responsible person. All who work in the kitchen must be made aware of where first aid boxes are sited. The content of the first aid box, which must be marked with a white cross on a green background, is covered under the Health and Safety (First Aid) Regulations 1981. The content of the first aid box depends upon the number of employees. These regulations do not however cover guests, customers and members of the public.

First aid training should be included in organized training programmes, using a reputable organization such as the St John's Ambulance Association or the British Red Cross, and with the approval of the Health and Safety Executive. A staff member qualified and able to render first aid should also be available on any shift. All who work in the kitchen should be aware of who the qualified first aid staff are. People without knowledge of first aid, should seek immediate assistance rather than risk doing anything which could make injuries worse. Where more than 150 people are employed, it is a requirement of the above Act that a trained first aider is always on duty.

References and further reading

Health and Safety Commission (1988). *Safety Representatives and Safety Committees*. London: HMSO.

Health and Safety Executive (1988). *Safety in Meat Preparation*. London: HMSO.

Health and Safety Executive (1989a). *Writing your Health and Safety Policy Statement*. London: HMSO.

Health and Safety Executive (1989b). *Review Your Occupational Health Needs: Employer's Guide*. London: HMSO.

Home Office (1972). Guides to the Fire Precautions Act 1971. *1 — Hotels and Boarding Houses*. London: HMSO.

Socrates G. (1981). Investigating Accidents. *Hospitality*, January, pp. 15–17.

7
Kitchen equipment principles

Equipment selection

The selection of equipment for a catering operation depends upon a large number of factors:

1 Capital cost.
2 Life/duty.
3 Maintenance cost.
4 Energy cost.
5 Menu.
6 Production quantity.
7 Line balancing.
8 Staff numbers/skills.
9 Space available.
10 Ergonomics.

Capital cost

The capital cost of equipment must be depreciated over the life of the appliance and therefore must be related to turnover, food cost and labour cost. Operations which use a lot of sophisticated/high cost equipment require high gross profits to pay for them. This can be achieved by using a number of possible measures:

- High mark up (gross profit).
- High sales volume.
- Lower labour costs (less staff or less skill).
- Lower food cost.

Whichever of the above measures, or combination of measures, is used, the balance of capital cost against the savings can be made using standard pay-back techniques.

Life/duty

Catering equipment is available in various strengths, using different methods of manufacture and differing materials of construction. All of these factors affect the durability of an appliance and its life.

In general terms, equipment may be defined as being:

- Light duty (suitable for coffee shops and snack bars).
- Medium duty for non-commercial and light institutional catering).
- Heavy duty (for heavy institutional catering, restaurants and hotels).

Maintenance cost

These are related to the duty of the appliance and the level of use. Too few operators include preventative maintenance as a part of their expenditure (see Chapter 10). This is shortsighted because preventative maintenance can lengthen the life of equipment and reduce the cost of breakdown (which can lose revenue in some cases).

Energy cost

There are often different ways of cooking the same dish — some use significantly more energy than others. Some typical figures for energy consumption (kWh/kg of food) are given in Figure 7.1.

Menu

In general, a fixed menu uses specialized equipment while a cyclic or market menu uses general-purpose equipment. For example, a fast-food restaurant might use a chain broiler which can only cook a limited number of food items, whereas an à la carte restaurant would rely much more on the oven and range top. A kitchen which has to perform several functions must also use general-purpose equipment. For example, a small hotel which does not have specialized kitchens will need to use general-purpose equipment in order to handle the various types of catering activities of breakfast, lunch, dinner, room service, functions and banqueting.

Production quantity

It is important to select an appliance with the correct capacity to match the needs of the operation. A sales mix analysis gives the basic production quantities:

menu quantity/portion × number of portions

For example, soup production may require a 200 ml portion by 500 sales per day:

$$\text{production quantity} = 200 \times 500 \text{ ml}$$
$$= 100,000 \text{ ml}$$
$$= 100 \text{ litres}$$

Before we can use this information to estimate the equipment required, we need to know something about the method of production. There are three basic methods of production, as described in Chapter 3.

Tutorial topic

A fast-food fryer is available either as a basic model or with the addition of an automatic basket lift and computer. Assume that the cost of these fryers is as follows:

Fryer: capital cost   £1000
        with basket lift   £1500
        with basket lift and computer   £2000

Assume a life of five years and a usage of six days per week.

How much labour would you have to save a day to make the additional investment in the computer and basket lift worthwhile?

- Make-to-order.
- Assemble-to-order.
- Make-to-demand (buffer stock).

In the case of make-to-order we need to have sufficient equipment capacity to cope with the peak period. For example, a restaurant specializing in grills must have sufficient broiler/grill capacity to cope with peak demand, measured in terms of maximum number of steaks per hour.

Where we are using short-term buffer stock, we must have sufficient capacity to replenish buffer stock at the rate it is used – it is common to use batch cooking in this situation, to produce buffer stock such as vegetables for the bain-marie.

In situations where we are preparing long-term buffer stock, we need sufficient production capacity to produce food at a rate of average sales per hour. For example, a central cook-chill kitchen must have a weekly production rate to match the weekly rate of consumption. However, the production hours can be less than the service hours. For example, a cook-chill kitchen may operate an eight hour day, five days a week, to produce food for a twenty-four hour day, seven days a week restaurant.

Another aspect of capacity is the question of how to achieve this calculated production volume. If batch cooking, the appliance should be chosen to match the batch size, making full use of the equipment capacity. If making to demand or short-term buffer, it is

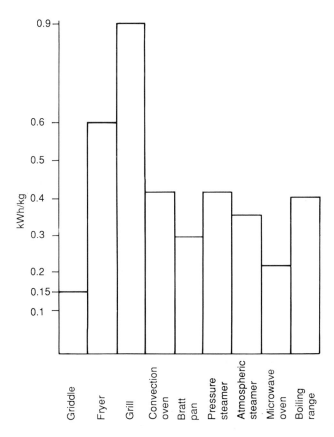

Figure 7.1 *Energy usage of electric catering equipment* (Pine, 1989)

often better to have two or three small appliances rather than one large one, particularly in situations where there is a large fluctuation in demand. In this way, during slack periods only one appliance need be used.

There are various ways of carrying out capacity calculations:

- Volume, that is, pots, pans, bratt pans, kettles, water boilers, beverage machines (litres/hour).
- Content of standard containers, that is, ovens, steaming ovens, holding equipment (number of portions per standard container).
- Cooking area, that is, broilers, grills, griddles (square metres of cooking surface).
- Weight, that is, deep fat fryers (kilograms/hour).

Calculation by volume

The total volume can be calculated, using the following relationship:

$$\text{total volume (litres)} = \frac{\text{portion size (ml)} \times \text{number of portions}}{1000}$$

This figure can then be related to the volume of the appliance, depending on the method of production. For example, if batch cooking, this volume can be decreased by dividing by the number of batches.

Calculation by standard gastronorm pans

A standard pan measures 530 mm by 325 mm and comes in several depths. The capacity of the pan depends upon both the depth of pan and the density of the food. The pan can have a solid base for ovens, or a perforated base for steamers. The capacity of ovens and steamers is often expressed in terms of:

- The number of pans per shelf.
- The number of shelves per oven.

The other important factor is the cooking time, since this determines how many pans per shelf can be cooked in a given production time.

A similar method can be used when calculating stores volume for cook-freeze and cook-chill operations.

Cooking area

For appliances with a flat cooking surface, the important parameter is the effective area of this cooking surface. For example, for a griddle, the required area is equal to:

$$\text{total area (m}^2\text{)} = \text{portions per hour} \times \text{area of portion (m}^2\text{)} \times \text{cooking time (hours)}$$

Calculation by weight

Many appliances such as fryers are specified by the manufacturer in terms of the output in kilograms per hour. The required capacity (average rate of production or peak rate of production) can be estimated from the portion size and the number of portions per hour.

Line balancing

When the food production requires the use of a succession of processes, each appliance must be matched in capacity to the next appliance in the process. This is known as *line balancing*. For example, if a mixing machine is used to make the dough for pastries, the capacity of this machine should be related to the capacity of the oven in which the pastries are to be baked. As another example, in a cook-chill system, the batch size of the cooking equipment must be matched to the capacity of the chilling equipment.

Staff numbers/skills

The choice of equipment must match the type and level of staff available. For example, we can reduce labour levels by using more automatic equipment – we have already seen the example of the basket lifts on fryers. For similar reasons, continuous cookers have been used in some large-scale catering situations.

Another example is the reduction of skill levels required by staff, through the use of equipment with more sophisticated controls,

---

Tutorial topic

Calculation by volume

Example: You are required to estimate the total volume and select an appropriate piece of equipment for producing a batch of bolognese sauce. You need to produce enough sauce for 400 by 200 ml portions.

A manufacturer produces four tilting bratt pans, with the following capacities:

Model A   40 litres
Model B   70 litres
Model C   120 litres
Model D   160 litres

Which model would you choose, if you have to cook all the sauce in a single batch?

Calculation by standard gastronorm pans

Example: A convection steamer is being used to cook vegetables. It has three shelves, each of which can hold a single standard pan.

What is the capacity of this steamer (portions/hour) if one pan holds 2 kg of broccoli, the cooking time is 5 minutes and a portion of broccoli is 100 g?

Calculation by weight

Example: A manufacturer produces three fryers which can produce 15, 30 or 40 kg of French fries per hour from frozen to cooked. One portion is 150 g.

Given the following sales analysis per hour for a typical day, which fryer, or combination of fryers, would you choose?

	AM				*PM*			
Time	9–10	10–11	11–12	12–1	1–2	2–3	3–4	4–5
Portions	25	50	100	200	200	100	50	100

such as meat temperature probes in roasting ovens and the use of computers on deep fat fryers.

On the other hand, if we are using highly qualified staff, we might prefer to use flexible, easy-to-control appliances to aid the experience and skill of these staff.

Space available

Where space is limited, choice of equipment can alleviate this problem:

- We can utilize high output equipment to give us maximum rates of production per floor area (for example, convection ovens, convection steamers, combination ovens, bratt pans, etc.).
- We can use stacked equipment to make use of vertical space.
- Multipurpose equipment can be used in order to reduce the number of appliances (for example, combination ovens, bratt pans etc.).

Ergonomics

Ergonomics is a study of the relationship between people and their environment. In relation to equipment, this is particularly important in terms of:

- Equipment dimensions, height of working areas, reach required to operate, etc.
- Ease of use of equipment, including clarity of controls, ease of cleaning and safety.
- Environmental hazards associated with the use of the appliance such as fatigue caused by high temperatures and high humidities.

Human beings vary in size and reach. This makes the design of working areas difficult, since they must either be based on average data, or work spaces must be adjustable, to allow for these differences. For example, preparation tables are available which can be easily adjusted in height. However, this tends to be an expensive solution.

Recommended heights for preparation tables used for light and/or skilled work are (Grandjean, 1973):

850 mm to 900 mm for women.
900 mm to 950 mm for men.

Equivalent values for heavy work are:

700 mm to 850 mm for women.
850 mm to 900 mm for men.

The length of horizontal work space for one person is about 1200 mm, but this figure must be increased if bench top equipment or trays are needed. Depths of tables should be between 600 and 750 mm, unless the table has to accommodate containers or other material at the back, in which case a depth of 900 mm is more appropriate.

All of these figures should be regarded more as indicative of the types of data used, rather than as definitive.

Standards and specifications

Specifications are of great value in the purchase of equipment. There are a number of types of specification:

Performance specifications

This is useful when sizing an appliance, since it tells us the capacity of an appliance under standardized conditions. For example cooking output:

- Fryer: kilograms per hour.
- Broiler: number of hamburgers per hour.
- Dishwasher: number of dinner plates per hour.
- Beverage machine: number of cups per hour.

Descriptive specifications

These are of particular value when specifying custom manufactured equipment, since they state what the equipment will be made from and how it will be made. For example, material of construction:

- 18:8 stainless steel.

Or method of construction:

- No sharp edges, no exposed screws or rivets.
- No joints where food can collect.

Reference specifications

Reference specifications are produced by official organizations, for example those produced by the British Standards Institute. Another aspect of reference specifications is testing for compliance. For this, manufacturers send a sample of an appliance to a testing laboratory, where it is tested for compliance with the relevant standards. If the appliance passes these standards, it can be sold as an approved appliance.

European and international standards are being introduced to replace the national standards. An example of this is the use of CENELEC standards for electrical catering equipment and CEN standards for gas equipment.

Another type of reference specification is one produced by a trade organization, such as the National Sanitation Foundation (NSF) standards for hygienic design of food service equipment, used in the USA.

Dimensional specifications

This sort of specification is really a type of reference specification since it needs the agreement of manufacturers and industry. Of particular importance to the caterer is the standardization of container sizes. In order to reduce materials handling, wherever possible the same container should be used for more than one purpose. For example, it should not be necessary to move food from one container to another when transferring it from a cooking appliance on to the bain-marie. To make this possible, containers of uniformly standard size should be available which can be used for storage, cooking and service.

As large scale cooking and meal production has become more systematic, multipurpose containers to aid in rationalizing operations are increasingly introduced. These containers provide the ability to store, cook, freeze, chill, reheat and hold, all in the same sized compact modular container.

The dimensions of these containers are based on the *gastronorm* modular dimension of 530 mm by 325 mm. This is now the basis of BSI standards and European standards, although it is not yet an international standard. Obviously one container size cannot suit all purposes and therefore a number of container size variations are possible:

1   *Multiple and fractional container sizes* allow greater or smaller amounts of food to be used, as shown in Figure 7.2.

2   *Container depths* are available from 20 mm up to 150 mm to suit different types of food and processes.
3   *Container bases* are available with either a solid or a perforated base.

A modular system for container sizes confers several other advantages:

● Uncomplicated flow from section to section.

● Increased stacking space within smaller areas.
● Optimum use both of space and kitchen installations.
● Simplified layout and methods leading to shorter walking paths and work simplification.
● Universal use of transport and storage units.
● Reduced stock of storage units and containers.

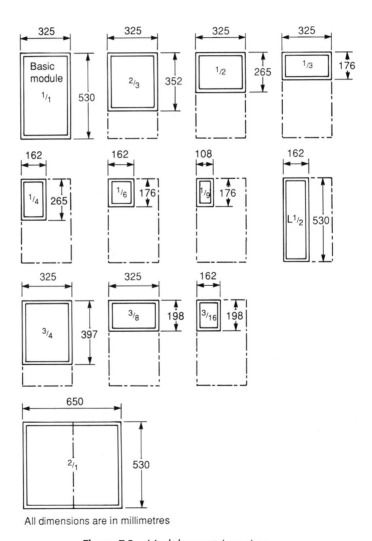

All dimensions are in millimetres

Figure 7.2   *Modular container sizes*

Equipment disposition

There are a number of ways to group equipment within a kitchen, and this has an influence on the choice of equipment, particularly in situations where equipment is to be located in a bank or suite (see Figure 7.3). Some of the possible dispositions are:

(a) Free-standing bratt pan

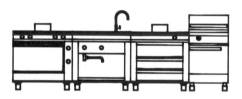

(b) Modular floor standing suite

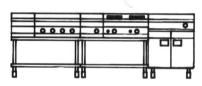

(c) Modular back bar/split units

(d) Three tier stacking bakery oven

Figure 7.3 *Equipment disposition*

Free-standing

Free-standing equipment is designed to be located with a service clearance all around it.

Modular floor-standing

Appliances are designed to fit together side by side, often with common services built in. The units have joining plates/strips to seal any gaps and they are often available with services compartments at the rear to allow the use of parallel back-to-back suites. Often the units are designed in modular widths.

Modular countertop or backbar

These units are similar to the modular floor-standing appliances in that they are designed in modular widths so that they can be linked together to form a suite but, in this case, they are mounted at worktop heights.

Modular split units

These modular units are available in a range of top units, (such as griddles, boiling tables, deep fat fryers and worktop units) and bases (such as ovens, refrigerated storage units, heated storage units and plain cupboards). They are designed in such a way that suites can be built using a combination of top and base units to suit the needs of the operation. They are often designed in modular widths, such as 300, 600, 900 and 1200 mm or 350, 700, 1050 and 1400 mm.

Stand mounted

Some appliances, such as grills and ovens,

can be supplied with a floor stand, to allow them to be used at a convenient height.

Wall mounted

As an alternative to the floor stand, some appliances can be mounted on a full- or half-height wall, using brackets. Even large production equipment is available in this form, although it may have to be cantilevered to support the weight. The advantage of this is that there is complete clearance underneath the appliance for cleaning.

Stacking

Some appliances, such as ovens, are available as units which can be stacked in order to make the design more compact and to save floor space.

Mobile equipment

Mobile equipment is becoming more popular, although it is often difficult to get the full range of services to mobile equipment (Kirk and Gladwell, 1988). Mobile equipment gives both flexibility of use and ease of cleaning.

Heat transfer

The most common physical process in catering is heat transfer since it is used in a wide range of activities such as cooking, heating, chilling and freezing.

In most situations two distinct processes are taking place:

1   Heat transfer at the surface of the food.
2   Internal heat transfer.

For example, when cooking a piece of solid food, we apply heat to the surface and this heat is then transferred to the centre (Figure 7.4). These two processes need to be in balance for efficient cooking. If too little energy is applied to the surface, internal heat transfer will also be slow, as will the rate of cooking. If too much heat is applied to the surface, the heat will accumulate at the surface faster than it can be transferred to the

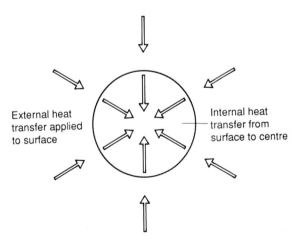

External heat transfer applied to surface

Internal heat transfer from surface to centre

Figure 7.4   *Balance of external and internal heat transfer*

centre. Since it cannot be transferred to the centre at the same rate as it is absorbed at the surface, this will cause the surface to dry out and burn.

There are three main methods of heat transfer although, in practice, most catering appliances use a mixture of all three, although one method may predominate (Milson and Kirk, 1980). These three methods are:

1   Conduction.
2   Convection.
3   Radiation.

The relationship between these three methods of heat transfer and the major methods of cooking is shown in Figure 7.5.

Conduction

Conduction is a form of heat transfer which takes place through solids. Therefore all solid foods which are required to be heated or cooled involve conduction to some degree.

Conduction heat transfer depends upon the temperature difference between a hot and cold region within a solid. The greater the temperature difference, the faster is the heating or cooling. The rate of heating or cooling also depends upon the shape of the material (food) being heated or cooled – the thinner the food and the greater its area, the faster heating or cooling will take place (see Figure 7.6). The rate of heat transfer by conduction also depends upon how well the solid material conducts heat – a property known as *thermal conductivity*. Some materials, such as metals, are good conductors. Other materials, such as glass, plastics and most foods, are not good conductors. For this reason, if we want to cook solid foods quickly, we must design dishes which have a large surface area and are not too thick. This applies to many fast-food products.

A second use of heat transfer by conduction is when we put two solids in contact. If the surface of one solid is hot and the other cold, heat will be transferred across the contact surface as shown in Figure 7.7(a). This process is used for shallow frying in pans or bratt pans, griddle plates and contact grills. We can also sandwich a solid food between two parallel surfaces (see Figure 7.7(b)), as in the contact grill.

Type of cookery	Humidity	Heat transfer method
Roasting and baking	Dry	Convection and radiation (fluid: air)
Boiling and stewing	Moist	Convection (fluid: water)
Steaming	Moist	Convection (fluid: steam at 100°C)
Pressure cooking	Moist	Convection (fluid: steam at 121°C)
Deep frying	Dry	Convection (fluid: oil)
Griddle frying	Dry	Conduction
Grilling and broiling	Dry	Radiation

Figure 7.5   *Heat transfer and cooking methods*

Convection

This method of heat transfer uses a fluid, such as air, steam, water or oil, which acts as a store of heat, allowing heat to be moved from one place to another. The fluid may move for one of two reasons (see Figure 7.8):

1   *Natural convection* using convection currents.
2   *Forced convection* using a fan or pump.

The rate of heat transfer by convection depends upon the difference between the temperature of the surface being heated or cooled and the temperature of the fluid (Figure 7.9), and the velocity of the fluid and surface area. In general, forced convection is better controlled and faster than natural convection.

The reason that fluid velocity is important is that it helps to break down the *boundary layer* surrounding materials being heated or cooled by convection (Figure 7.10). As the moving fluid gets closer to the surface, its velocity is slowed down because of friction at the surface. This leads to a layer of slowly moving fluid at the surface, through which heat must be conducted – this layer is known as the boundary layer. The higher the velocity of the fluid across the surface of a material, the thinner is this boundary layer. This in turn leads to higher rates of heat transfer.

Another way of breaking up the boundary layer is to direct the fluid directly on to the surface, as shown in Figure 7.10. This is known as *impingement*.

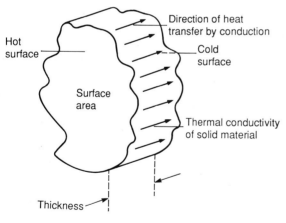

Increase in temperature difference between two surfaces *increases* rate of conduction.
Increase in area of solid *increases* rate of conduction.
Increase in thermal conductivity of material *increases* rate of conduction.
Increase in thickness of solid *decreases* rate of conduction.

Figure 7.6   *Factors affecting conductive heat transfer*

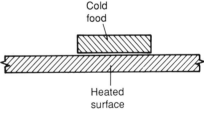

(a) Single-sided heating by conduction

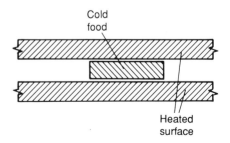

(b) Double-sided heating by conduction

Figure 7.7   *Heat transfer by conduction*

In natural convection applications, the rate of heating is often slow and, because of the presence of convection currents, there is a temperature gradient between the top of the appliance and the bottom. With forced convection, because of the mechanical movement of the fluid, the temperature gradient is much less. This means that heating is much more uniform with forced convection.

Natural convection by steam is a good method for many foods, such as vegetables and seafoods but it is a relatively slow process. One way of speeding up the process is to use high-pressure steam – this raises the temperature of the steam to 121°C. This higher temperature accelerates the rate of cooking and can reduce cooking times by as much as 75 per cent. An alternative way of improving the process is to introduce forced convection into the steamer.

Natural convection is used in general-purpose ovens, atmospheric steamers, liquids heated in pans, boiling pans, bratt pans and deep fat fryers.

Forced convection is used in convection ovens, convection steamers and combination ovens.

Radiation

Radiation, or to give it its full name *electro-magnetic radiation*, is used in a number of applications, including radio and television transmissions, radar, telecommunications and X-rays. There are three types of radiation used in catering equipment:

1   *Induction* – low-frequency radio waves.
2   *Microwaves* – high-frequency radio waves.
3   *Thermal radiation* – energy given off by hot surfaces.

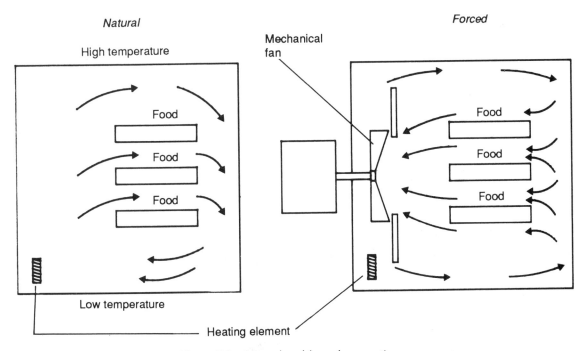

Figure 7.8 *Natural and forced convection*

Thermal radiation may be *visible* (caused by emission of red, orange, yellow or white light) or *infra-red* (dark radiation).

Induction

Induction heating uses low-frequency electromagnetic radiation to heat the base of a

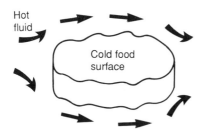

Hot fluid

Cold food surface

Increase in surface area *increases* rate of convection.
Increase in fluid velocity *increases* rate of convection.
Increase in temperature difference between fluid and food *increases* rate of convection.

Figure 7.9   *Factors affecting convective heat transfer*

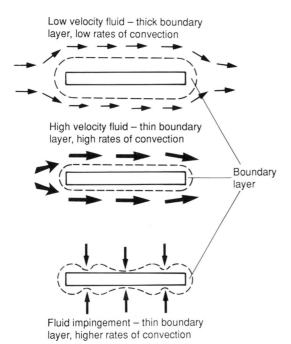

Low velocity fluid – thick boundary layer, low rates of convection

High velocity fluid – thin boundary layer, high rates of convection

Boundary layer

Fluid impingement – thin boundary layer, higher rates of convection

Figure 7.10   *The effect of fluid velocity on the boundary layer*

pan directly (see Chapter 8). The magnetic component of the electromagnetic radiation interacts with the iron in the base of the pan to produce a heating effect. Only when the pan is present does the flow of energy take place, which gives high efficiencies. Because the heat goes directly into the base of the pan, this reduces the requirement for ventilation.

Microwaves

Microwaves use electromagnetic radiation, at a frequency of 2450 MHz which is equivalent to a wavelength of 120 mm. At this frequency the energy causes heating of materials containing free water molecules, because of a rotational affect (see Figure 7.11). The high speed rotation of molecules causes a frictional heating effect.

The maximum rate of heat absorption takes place 25 to 30 mm in from the surface. This causes intense centre heating with small objects (50 to 90 mm in diameter), but means that large objects still rely on conduction to heat through to the centre (Figure 7.12). This is why when large objects are cooked, they must be left to stand (wrapped in foil) to allow heat to get through to the centre.

Microwaves may be used on their own, or in combination with forced convection or radiation.

Thermal radiation

All surfaces above absolute zero $(-273°C)$ emit electromagnetic radiation. As the temperature of the surface increase, two things happen. First, the amount of energy emitted increases and, second, there is a shift in the frequency which causes it to move into the visible region of the spectrum. Because of this we can see thermal radiation as it glows visibly. As the temperature increases, the wavelength decreases and the glow changes from red, through orange and yellow to white.

The amount of thermal radiation given off by a surface depends not only on its temperature but also on the nature of the surface. Black, matt surfaces radiate the maximum amount of energy and white shiny surfaces the least.

Thermal radiation travels in a straight line until it hits a second surface, where one of three things can happen: the radiation may be reflected by the surface; it may pass straight through (transmission); or it may be absorbed (Figure 7.13). When the energy is absorbed, it is converted into heat. Metals and shiny surfaces reflect radiation, glass transmits radiation. Materials which contain a lot of water (a group which includes most foods) absorb radiation within a few milli-metres of the surface. This causes the intense

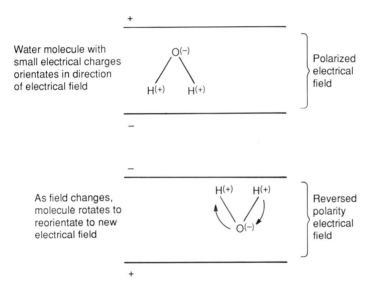

Figure 7.11   *The rotation of the water molecule caused by a microwave field*

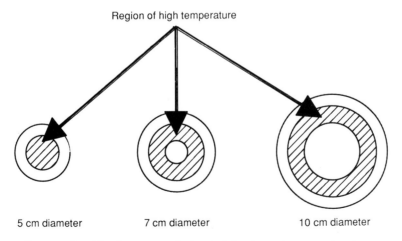

Figure 7.12   *Heating pattern in foods following microwave heating*

surface heating which we associate with grilling and toasting.

The power of heat transfer by radiation decreases as the distance between the emitter and absorber increases. Also, since radiation travels in straight lines, the two surfaces must be able to 'see' each other – any obstruction between the two surfaces will prevent heat transfer taking place. This affects radiation in ovens with several shelves of food, where shielding of the food from thermal radiation can occur.

Thermal radiation can result in a very intense source of heat because:

● It cuts straight through the boundary layer.
● It is absorbed within a few millimetres of the surface.

For these reasons, thermal radiation is normally used for the rapid cooking of foods which have a large surface area and which are relatively thin. However if lower temperature infra-red heat is used, it is less intense and can be used in reheating applications without causing surface overheating.

Radiation also has the beneficial properties of being easy to regulate and fast to respond.

Applications of thermal radiation

Thermal radiation is used in all ovens at high temperatures, such as bakery ovens and pizza ovens. It is also used in grills, broilers and toasters.

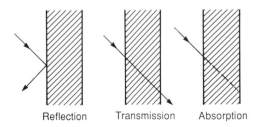

Reflection   Transmission   Absorption

Figure 7.13 *Interaction of radiation with materials*

Infra-red radiation is used to rapidly heat foods and to keep foods warm, using quartz tubes or tungsten halogen tubes.

Refrigeration

This important form of heat transfer is different from the types of radiation which have been discussed so far. In all of the examples we have seen so far of conduction, convection and radiation, heat has moved from a region of high temperature to a region of low temperature – this is a fundamental law of physics. In refrigeration we want to:

● *Extract* heat from a region at a *low temperature*.
● *Give out* that heat at a *high temperature*.

In order to do this we need a means of storing and releasing heat and one way of doing this is to use *latent heat*. When a liquid changes to a vapour as it *evaporates*, we have to supply energy, such as when we heat water to boil it (see Figure 7.14). This energy is known as the latent heat.

It is also possible to change a liquid into a vapour by reducing the pressure, such as when we release a deodorant spray into the air. The high pressure liquid in the can turns into a vapour as it passes through the valve on top of the can. As it does so, it extracts latent heat from its surroundings, causing a *cooling effect*.

The reverse is also true. When a vapour *condenses* as it changes from a vapour to a liquid, it gives out the latent heat it absorbed when it evaporated. In this way, when moist warm air comes into contact with a cold window, because heat is extracted the vapour condenses in the form of dew on the inside of the window.

If we force a vapour to change into a liquid, by increasing its pressure, the liquid becomes hot because of the released latent heat.

The above two processes are combined together in the mechanical refrigeration cycle, as shown in Figure 7.15. A liquid, known as a *refrigerant* is released through *an expansion valve* into a region of low pressure. As it passes through the valve, it is converted into a vapour and is cooled down to supply the latent heat. This heat is absorbed from the environment surrounding the *evaporator coil*, causing a cooling effect.

The vapour then passes through a pump or *compressor*, which increase the pressure of the vapour and causes it to condense into a liquid. As it does so it becomes hot because of the release of the latent heat. This heat is given out to the environment surrounding the *condenser*. The liquid then returns to the expansion valve in order to continue around the cycle.

The evaporator coil is mounted inside the refrigeration equipment, where it can extract heat from the air and food inside the cabinet. The condenser coil is located outside the cabinet in a stream of cool air. For large refrigerators, the condenser has a cooling fan and may be located some distance away from the refrigeration equipment.

In most existing refrigeration equipment the refrigerant is a *chloroflurocarbon compound* (CFC). It is thought that when these CFCs are released into the environment, such as when an appliance is serviced or scrapped at the end of its life, they cause damage to the earth's ozone layer. Plans are now being prepared to both recover CFCs from existing appliances when they are scrapped and to

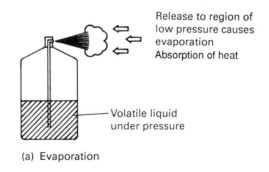

(a) Evaporation

(b) Compression

Figure 7.14   *Use of latent heat to absorb and release heat*

find long-term replacements for CFCs, which do not damage the ozone layer.

Not all CFCs are damaging to the ozone layer. The type which is currently used in refrigerators and freezers (R12) is thought to be particularly bad. This same refrigerant is also used as the blowing agent in insulants and foamed packaging. Alternatives to R12 are being developed.

Mass transfer

In addition to heat transfer, mass transfer is also important, particularly in relation to the movement of water. In Figure 7.5, cooking methods were classified as being either moist or dry.

Most foods contain large amounts of water and the movement of this water determines many characteristics of cooked foods:

- Surface texture.
- Surface colour.
- Flavour development.

As the temperature of a food material rises, water will evaporate from the surface. The rate of evaporation depends on temperature, together with the humidity and velocity of the surrounding fluid. From this it can be seen that there are many close parallels

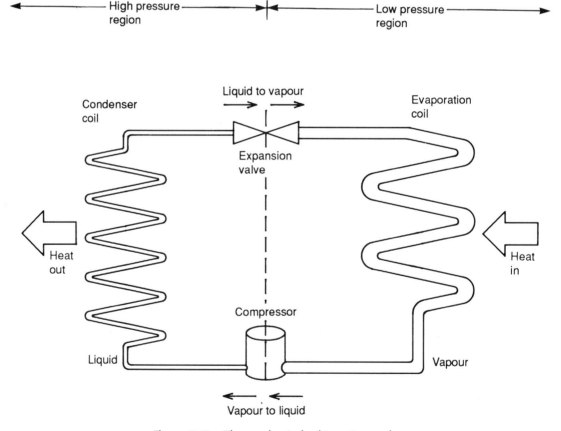

Figure 7.15 *The mechanical refrigeration cycle*

between convection heat transfer and surface evaporation.

If foods are heated in a dry atmosphere, the rate of evaporation will be at its maximum. Initially, water migrates from inside the food to replace moisture evaporated from the surface. However, if this process takes place at a lower rate than that of evaporation, the surface layer of the food will dry out, allowing crust or skin formation. The more drying out that takes place, the thicker will be the crust. Where a crust forms, the temperature of this crust can rise above the boiling point of water and, at these higher temperatures, browning reactions take place between sugars, amino acids and proteins; these reactions give rise not only to colour development at the surface of the food, but also to the characteristic aromas of roast, baked, grilled and fried foods.

On the other hand, if foods are heated in a moist environment, water will not evaporate from the surface of the food because the atmosphere is at a higher humidity than the relative humidity of the food. This means three things:

1 The surface temperature of the food will not rise above the boiling point of water (normally 100°C or 121°C in a pressure cooker at 15 p.s.i.).
2 Because of the absence of evaporation, there will be no crust or skin formation.

3 There will be no flavour development promoted by the high temperature browning reaction of proteins and sugars.

The similarity of evaporation and convection was mentioned above. The implication of this is that anything we do to improve the rate of convective heat transfer is also likely to increase the rate of mass transfer, unless humidity is increased to control the rate of evaporation. Without some form of humidity control, forced convection ovens may cause high rates of evaporation, possibly leading to large weight losses of foods and excessive surface colouration.

Energy sources

Energy is required in catering to:

- Heat and cool foods.
- Operate equipment using motors and mechanical forces.
- Provide heating and ventilation.
- Provide hot water for cooking and cleaning purposes.
- Provide artificial light.

The basic unit of energy is the joule (J), but because the joule is quite small, multiples are

Tutorial topic

For the following cooking processes, explain what is happening in terms of heat and mass transfer:

1 Frying chipped potatoes in oil held in a pan on a gas burner.

2 Pressure cooking a stew.

3 Roasting a joint of meat in a gas oven.

commonly used, such as the kilojoule (kJ), which is 1000 J and the megajoule (MJ), which is 1,000,000 J. Two other units are in common usage for energy because of their association with electricity and gas consumption data.

The unit of electricity consumption is the kilowatt hour (kWh). The relationship between this and the joule is that:

$$1 \text{ kWh} = 3{,}600{,}000 \text{ J or } 3.6 \text{ MJ}$$

The unit of gas consumption is the cubic foot or the cubic metre. This is converted into energy, using the calorific value of the fuel. In the metric system this is expressed in joules, but in the imperial system, the unit is the British thermal unit (Btu). As with the joule, this is quite a small unit and it is often converted into therms, where:

$$1 \text{ therm} = 100{,}000 \text{ Btu}$$

When carrying out comparative costs, the data in Figure 7.16 can be used. However, care must be used in interpreting this data as the efficiency of appliances varies. Also, the calorific value of natural gas, liquefied petroleum gas (LPG), solid fuel and fuel oil varies depending upon the precise composition.

Energy use in catering

The overall use of energy by the British catering industry has been estimated to be 77,770 million megajoules per year (Energy Efficiency Office, 1988). The breakdown of this between sectors of the industry is shown in Figure 7.17. Gas is still the most popular fuel for prime cooking, representing some 80 per cent of the energy used in this activity.

When estimated in terms of the energy consumption per cooked meal, hotel restaurants and high class restaurants are seen to use the most (Figure 7.18). However, it must be borne in mind that the amount of food in snack bars and coffee shops is less than full restaurants and also, the degree of

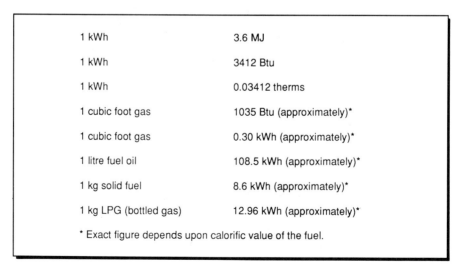

1 kWh	3.6 MJ
1 kWh	3412 Btu
1 kWh	0.03412 therms
1 cubic foot gas	1035 Btu (approximately)*
1 cubic foot gas	0.30 kWh (approximately)*
1 litre fuel oil	108.5 kWh (approximately)*
1 kg solid fuel	8.6 kWh (approximately)*
1 kg LPG (bottled gas)	12.96 kWh (approximately)*

* Exact figure depends upon calorific value of the fuel.

Figure 7.16   *Comparative fuel data*

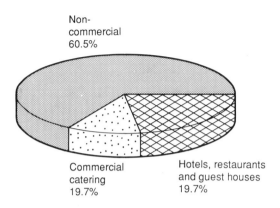

Non-commercial
60.5%

Commercial
catering
19.7%

Hotels, restaurants
and guest houses
19.7%

Figure 7.17 *Comparative energy consumption by sectors of the catering industry*

food preparation and cooking is probably less. These differences would account for some, but not all, of the discrepancies.

The way in which this energy is used varies from one sector of the industry to another, but approximate figures for use are shown in Figure 7.19 (Energy Efficiency Office, 1988).

Electricity

Factors associated with the choice of electricity as an energy source include:

● *Efficiency.* Electricity is a secondary energy source and, as such, it provides a high energy efficiency to the end user. In

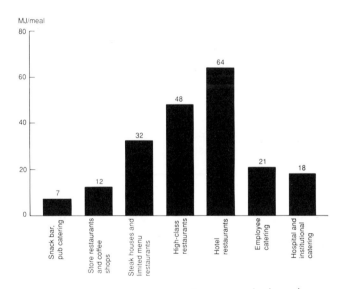

Figure 7.18 *Energy consumption per cooked meal*

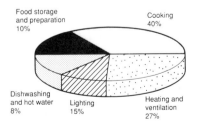

Food storage
and preparation
10%

Cooking
40%

Dishwashing
and hot water
8%

Lighting
15%

Heating and
ventilation
27%

Figure 7.19 *Approximate utilization of energy in catering*

turn this means that less heat is lost to the kitchen and that less ventilation is required.

- *Cleanliness*. As there is no product of combustion, cleaner equipment and kitchens may be achieved.
- *Electronic/computerized control*. With the development of more sophisticated controls, it is often easier to gain full benefit from these with electrically heated appliances.
- Combination appliances. With the increasing development of combination appliances (microwave/forced convection, steam/forced convection, etc.), the use of electricity, at least in part, is required.
- *Versatility*. Electricity can be used for all appliances, including mechanical preparation and refrigeration equipment.
- *Heat output*. Large appliances may need three-phase supplies, which is not always available and which may lead to problems of maximum demand tariffs.
- *Slow response*. Many chefs feel that the response time of electricity is too slow. New developments in heating elements are improving the speed of response of electrical appliances.

Alternating current (AC) electrical supplies to a building may be of two types:

1   Single-phase 240/250 V.
2   Three-phase 440/450 V.

Because three-phase circuits have three live wires and a higher voltage (compared to the single live wire and lower voltage of a single-phase circuit) they can supply energy at higher rates. In general, single-phase supplies are used for lighting circuits, to provide power to socket outlets for small portable equipment and, using radial circuits, to provide power to small to medium-sized electrical appliances. Three-phase supplies are used to provide energy to large electrical cooking appliances and to appliances which have large electric motors.

Electricity supplies enter a building using a service cable, terminating in the main supply fuse. This is connected to the consumer's meter and main distribution panel.

Small kitchen appliances are provided with a flexible lead together with a 13 amp plug which can be used with a single-phase ring main circuit. This is a continuous loop of cable supplying electricity to a number of socket outlets. Larger appliances are individually connected back to a distribution board, using either single-phase or three-phase.

In this system, appliances are provided with individual electrical supplies of the appropriate type (phase and amps) from a supply on a distribution fuseboard. Supply to the distribution board comes from the main distribution board. This is known as a radial supply.

The traditional method of wiring catering appliances is to bring supplies up through the floor screed in a cast iron conduit to a level 23 cm above floor level. A flexible conduit is then used to take the supply to the appliance. This system is difficult and expensive to modify for future changes.

Some new catering installations use a system of flexible cables and sockets for all appliances, both three-phase and single-phase. This allows easy disconnection and reconnection of appliances for cleaning and maintenance, particularly where the appliances are supplied with castors. Where this is associated with busbar electrical supplies, it allows easy modification of a kitchen layout (Kirk and Gladwell, 1988).

Electricity is converted into heat by passing a current through a resistance element. The simplest type of electrical heating element consists of a nichrome wire surrounded by a layer of magnesium oxide and protected by a metal sheath. This is used to produce the heat in ovens, boilers, fryers and grills.

Higher temperatures and faster heat up times can be achieved with a quartz glass tube which comprises a spiral heating element held down the centre of the tube. The latest electrical heating element design is called the halogen lamp. It consists of a spiral tungsten heating element in a quartz glass envelope in which the air has been replaced by an inert halogen gas. These lamps can be operated at very high temperatures and give out large quantities of infra-red radiation. They operate with higher efficiencies than other electrical radiant elements.

Natural gas

Factors associated with gas as a source of energy include:

- *Fast response*. Many chefs prefer to cook on gas because of the fast response time and controllability of the flame.
- *Efficiency*. Because it is a primary source of energy, gas has a lower efficiency to the end user. The waste energy ends up as heat and combustion products, which must be removed from the kitchen. Developments with gas burners, such as surface combustion, catalytic and pulse combustion, are improving their efficiency.
- *Heat output*. Gas appliances provide a large thermal capacity from a single supply source.

Natural gas is composed principally of methane. In most catering appliances, the gas is used in the form of an aerated flame. In this type of flame, gas is mixed with air prior to combustion to give a high output focused flame. Alternatives to the aerated burner are surface combustion burners (used for generating thermal and infrared radiation) and catalytic burners.

Natural gas enters the building through a service pipe, which is terminated with an isolating stop valve. This is connected to the main gas meter from which all supplies radiate.

Natural gas is normally supplied through a piped network. The heat output of a supply depends on both the diameter of the supply pipe and the pressure of the gas. A governor is used to control the latter. The pipe work may be copper or mild steel. The final connection to the equipment may be rigid or it may use a flexible connector. Bayonet connectors have been developed to allow for the rapid disconnection and connection of gas equipment.

Liquefied petroleum gas

Liquefied petroleum gas (LPG) exists in two forms: propane gas and butane gas. Commercial propane, which is composed of 90 per cent propane together with other hydrocarbons is used as an alternative to natural gas. It is distributed as a pressurized liquid, either in bottles or by road tanker. In the latter case, the user needs a storage tank on the premises in a location which is easily accessible to the tanker. Most gas burning appliances are available with the ability to burn propane as an option.

The other form of LPG is commercial butane. This gas burns at a lower temperature than propane and its use is confined mainly to flambé/spirit lamp applications and barbecues.

Steam

Many appliances require a supply of live steam. This may be generated centrally or locally. Central generation of steam is common in many areas of institutional catering.

However, its use is declining. Localized generation may be for a single appliance or for a group of appliances which all require steam such as steaming ovens and steam jacketed kettles.

Controls

Controls on catering appliances control the following physical conditions:

- On/off.
- Time.
- Temperature.
- Pressure.
- Safety.

Controls may be mechanical, electromechanical, electronic, (solid state) or microprocessor. Mechanical controls are used to open and close gas and water pipes (on/off) or to control the volume of flow (variable), such as the gas valve on a gas burner. Mechanical controls may also involve clockwork motors, linked to a gas valve, as a timer on a gas appliance.

As the name implies, electromechanical controls use both electricity and mechanical forces to operate controls. As an example, a timer may use a simple mechanical (clockwork) motor, linked to an electrical switch, as a timer for an electric oven.

Electronic or solid state controls use electric timers and logic circuits to measure and control an appliance. The use of electronic digital control also facilitates the use of digital displays for more precise display of temperature and time.

Microprocessor controls use very large scale integration (VSLI) to build complex computer circuits on small silicon chips. These controllers are programmable and are very sophisticated in terms of complexity and speed. Not only do they allow much

more precise control of time and temperature and a high level of user programmability, they also provide for built in fault diagnostic routines, making servicing much simpler.

Thermostatic control

Probably the most common control on catering equipment is the thermostat. This uses the feedback control loop to control the temperature of ovens, fryers, steamers, refrigerators and many other appliances. A diagram of the feedback control loop was shown in Figure 2.3. The way in which this is applied to the control of temperature in a thermostat is indicated below. The same principle can be used to control pressure, because of the precise physical relationship between temperature and pressure.

The components of the feedback control loop are incorporated into a thermostat as follows:

- *Measure.* Temperature can be measured (or sensed) using a bimetallic strip, a vapour pressure phial, or electrically, using thermistors or thermocouples.
- *Desired value (temperature).* This is set on a dial or digital display on the control panel of the appliance.
- *Comparison of measured and desired value.* In a mechanical control, the relative movement (caused by the bending of a bimetallic strip or the increase in pressure of a liquid as it evaporates) is compared with a position set on a dial.
- *Error signal.* If the measured value is less than the desired value a negative error signal is generated. If the measured value is greater than the desired value, a positive error signal is generated. If the measured value and the desired value are the same, the error signal is zero.
- *Control action.* The control action acts upon the energy supply. A negative error

signal means that the appliance has not achieved its required temperature, so that the control action is to keep the energy supply on. A positive error signal means that the appliance has overshot its required value, causing the control action to switch off the energy supply. A diagram of a typical vapour pressure thermostat is shown in Figure 7.20.

With feedback control, no control action takes place until the process has deviated from its desired value. If there is a long time lag between the control action and the resultant outcome, the process may deviate a long way from its desired value before coming back into control. The result of this is that the output cycles on either side of its desired value, as shown in Figure 7.21. With cheap mechanical and electromechanical controls, the deviation on either side of the desired value can be as high as $+/-25°C$. With a solid state or microprocessor control, the deviation can be less that $1°C$.

Safety controls: flame failure devices

There is a risk of a build-up of explosive mixtures of air and gas, should a gas burning appliance either fail to ignite, or should the flame blow out. To prevent this happening, many gas appliances are fitted with what is known as a *flame failure device* (FFD). An FFD works in a similar way to a thermostat. A sensor, which may be a bimetallic strip, a vapour pressure phial or a thermocouple, is used to detect the heat from the flame. If the heat from the flame is not detected, the FFD responds by closing off the gas supply.

Materials of construction

Iron and steel

Iron and steel, because of their tendency to rust and become corroded, and because of

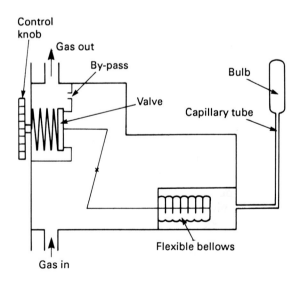

Figure 7.20 *Vapour pressure thermostat to control a gas appliance*

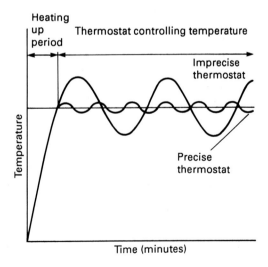

Figure 7.21 *Thermostat cycling*

their relatively poor thermal conductivity (one-quarter that of copper), have a restricted use in the professional kitchen. Cast iron is used to make heavy-based pans for frying, for griddle plates and for similar appliances, such as bratt pans. Mild steel is used to make knives and small utensils.

In order to protect it from corrosion, iron may be coated with a surface layer to improve its corrosion resistance. Some of these coatings are:

- *Porcelain and vitreous enamel*. This has been used both to cover cooking vessels (casserole dishes) and appliances. In recent years a number of imported ena-melled cooking dishes have been found to be contaminated with toxic metals, such as lead and cadmium.
- *Galvanizing*. This is the application of a thin coat of zinc on the surface of iron or steel. This coating is not suitable for situations where the surface can come in contact with food, since the zinc is dis-solved by acids. It is often used as the base or frame of stainless steel prep-aration tables and sinks, because of its cost advantage over stainless steel.
- *Chromium plating*. A thin layer of chro-mium is applied to the surface of steel to give it a bright glossy finish and to protect the steel from corrosion.
- *Polymer coatings*. Materials such as poly-tetrafluoroethylene (PTFE) can be used to coat surfaces which come into contact with food. These polymers can withstand high temperatures, are tough, non-toxic and easy to clean. They are used as non-stick coatings on pans, pots and griddles and similar applications. Unfortunately, the coating does not easily withstand abrasion and even hair-line scratches can ruin the non-stick properties. Because of this, cleaning must be done carefully and every effort made to prevent scratching of the surfaces. Overheating can also damage the polymer.

Stainless steel

Stainless steel is an alloy of steel with other metals to impart corrosion resistance. There are different forms of stainless steel. The best stainless steel for food use is known as 18:8, which refers to an alloy of steel with 18 per cent chromium and 8 per cent nickel. It is available in a variety of finishes — polished, brushed, etc. Also, it can be coloured for front of house applications.

The gauge (thickness) of stainless steel is also important since this controls its strength and durability.

One drawback to the use of stainless steel in a kitchen area is that it can be noisy, particularly when combined with the use of ceramic wall tiles. Stainless steel sinks and worktops may be treated on the underside with a layer of sound deadening material.

Because stainless steel has a relatively poor thermal conductivity, pans are often manufactured with a copper base when used for stove-top cooking.

Copper

This has a high melting point (1083°C) as against the 232°C of tin. Its relative specific gravity or weight per unit volume is similar to wrought iron but three times that of aluminium. It has a high thermal conductivity (three-quarters that for silver), which makes it an ideal material for cooking utensils.

However, copper has a number of undesir-able properties when associated with foods. For example, when exposed to air containing carbon dioxide, it forms a thin, bluey-green skin of verdigris which is toxic. Second, copper is dissolved by acid foods and the copper salts produced are also toxic. Third, copper promotes the oxidative rancidity of oils and fats. For these reasons, the insides of copper cooking vessels are covered with tin, a metal which resists corrosion by air and water and which does no harm to food which comes into contact with it.

There is a danger that old tinned copper cooking utensils may contain lead – if this is the case, the lead can be easily taken up by foods (Reilly, 1976). Lead is a cumulative poison and, if consumed in food over a period of time, can cause serious damage to health.

Pewter is an alloy of tin, copper and antimony. However, there is a danger that old pewter may contain lead.

Aluminium

Aluminium is a relatively soft metal and, because of this, is not as durable as stainless steel when used for pans and food containers, although it can be hardened by the anodizing process. It has a relatively high thermal conductivity (one-third that of copper). Its other advantage for hand-held kitchen utensils is its low density – it is one-half the density of iron, for example.

There are some problems over the use of aluminium in cooking. Aluminium is covered with a thin layer of aluminium oxide, and this is absorbed by many foods where it can, for example, cause a discolouration of white sauces. Aluminium is easily pitted or corroded by foods which contain salts and acids.

Recent research has shown a link between a building of aluminium in the brain and Altzheimer's disease. However, there is no evidence that this aluminium is caused by foods contaminated with aluminium.

Aluminium is also used in the form of aluminium foil in the kitchen, for covering food during cooking and for wrapping food.

Plastics

There are two main groups of plastic materials: *thermosetting plastics* and *thermosoftening plastics*. Thermosetting plastics are moulded from liquid materials, but once they have cooled and set, they cannot be melted again: if they are heated to high temperatures they will burn. Examples are ureaformaldehyde, polyurethane and melamine. Thermosoftening plastics set when cold but revert to a liquid when heated; the cycle of melting and setting can be repeated indefinitely. Examples are polythene, polyethylene, polypropylene, polystyrene, polyvinyl chloride (PVC), polytetrafluoroethylene (PTFE) and nylon. An important property of these plastics is their melting point since this determines if they can be used as food containers and cooking utensils in hot liquids, steamers, pressure cookers and ovens. In general, polythene and polystyrene have low melting points (below 100°C).

Thermoplastics are used for making kitchen utensils, food bowls, cutting boards and table tops in sandwich and salad preparation areas. They are also used for carts and food containers. Foamed plastics (particularly polystyrene) are used for insulated cups.

Thermosetting plastics are used to make unbreakable crockery, and, in the form of plastic laminates, in front of house areas such as table tops and front panels on cafeteria units.

In addition to the above applications, plastics are used for storing and wrapping food. All types of plastic are used from simple polythene bags and cling-film wrapping through to complex laminates used to make sous-vide bags and disposable oven-proof containers. Recent concern has been expressed about wrapping fatty foods in some plastic films, because of the absorption of plasticisers. Moulded plastic containers are used to hold sandwiches and cold snacks. Foamed polystyrene containers are used to hold hot take-away foods.

Wood and paper

There are two types of wood: softwood (from coniferous trees) and hardwood (from deciduous trees). Normally, softwood is used for structural timbers while hardwood is used for furniture and decorative laminates. In general, woods have a porous surface which makes them difficult to clean and may introduce a hygiene hazard. This is why plastic cutting boards are now used in preference to wooden ones.

Various forms of paper are used in the kitchen. Highly refined papers are used in the form of greaseproof paper for lining cake tins, and as food wrapping. Absorbent papers are used in the form of large rolls for wiping spills, hand drying, etc. and in the form of paper towels.

Glass and ceramics

Glass is formed by fusing together mixtures of oxides such as sodium oxide, calcium oxide etc. Glass is used to produce kitchen utensils and tableware. Quartz glass is used in quartz and halogen infrared heating elements. The addition of lead oxide produces lead crystal, glass which has good optical properties which is used for producing high quality tableware.

Ceramics are made by heating clay, in combination with other minerals. The surface may be finished with a white, coloured or decorated glaze to make them non-porous and more attractive. In addition to their use in tableware, ceramics are used to make wall and floor tiles. They are also used as the radiant element in gas catering equipment. The type of clay and the quantity of vitreous material influences the quality and cost of the ceramic. The finest ceramics, with a high degree of vitrification, are the porcelains. This is followed by china clay and ball clay. Low cost ceramic items are made from earthenware.

References and further reading

Energy Efficiency Office (1988). *Energy Savings in Catering*. London: Department of Energy.

Grandjean E. (1973). *Ergonomics of the Home*. London: Taylor and Francis.

Khan M. (1987). *Foodservice Operations*. Westport, Conn.: AVI.

Kirk D. and Gladwell D. C. (1988). Adaptable Kitchens for Colleges of Further Education. *International Journal of Hospitality Management*, vol. 7, part 13, pp. 285–92.

Milson A. and Kirk D. (1980). *Principles of the Design and Operation of Foodservice Equipment*. Chichester: Ellis Horwood.

Pine R. (1989). *Catering Equipment Management*. London: Hutchinson.

Reilly C. (1976). The Contamination of Food by Lead During Catering Operations. *HCIMA Review*, vol. 2, part 5.

8
Types of kitchen equipment

A wide range of equipment is used in all catering kitchens, ranging from small hand tools to large pieces of equipment. It is not the intention to cover the total range of equipment in this chapter, but to give an overview of the major types with an emphasis on giving an understanding of how they work.

Hand tools

Despite all of the developments in catering equipment, a large proportion of all kitchen activities are performed using hand tools. Many of these tools have been used in a largely unmodified form since the days of Soyer and Escoffier. However, the materials from which they are made have changed in line with developments in materials technology.

The choice of suitable hand tools is largely a matter of personal choice on the part of the chef and there are no hard and fast rules determining the best shape and size of individual tools. This section covers the basic items of small hand equipment found in the typical kitchen.

The chef's personal tools are relatively small in number and of them a set of knives is by far the most important. Knives of various sizes are required with which to trim and cut vegetables for garnish, to bone meat, to fillet fish, to slice and to carve.

The choice of a knife depends upon a number of factors:

- The weight and balance in the hand.
- The material of construction of the blade.
- The shape and material of construction of the handle.

For example, many chefs prefer the traditional knife with wooden handle and steel blade to a more modern knife with a hollow ground stainless steel blade and moulded thermoplastic handle. They find in practice that mild steel retains its edge and sharpness better than the stainless steel blade and are prepared to put up with the discolouration of the blade. However, the last few years have seen many developments in the technology of knife manufacture which give stainless steel a greatly improved sharpness.

The same is true in relation to knife handles. From a hygiene point of view, a moulded plastic handle is far superior to a wooden handle in two parts which is fastened by rivets on to the blade. However, the acceptance of these into professional kitchens has been slow because the weight, balance and feel of these knives may not be acceptable to the chef. This is changing because of the increased emphasis on hygiene. Colour coded knife handles are now available, to allow segregation of those used for raw foods from those used for cooked foods.

Basic knives and cutting tools

Normally a chef would have at least three knives of the traditional French pattern, which consists of a rigid blade with a broad heel tapering to a point (Figure 8.1(a)). The blade has a curve to allow a rocking heel to toe movement on the chopping board. The three most common sizes are:

1 7.5 to 8.5 cm blade for trimming and turning vegetables.
2 23 to 25 cm blade for slicing and dicing.
3 28 to 35 cm blade for chopping and mincing, severing poultry bones.

In addition to these knives, there would be:

- A *filleting knife*. A 15 to 18 cm blade, similar in shape to the French knife, but more slender, which is used for removing fish from the bone or trimming meat.
- A *boning knife*. A 15 cm blade, without the broad heel of the French knife and with the blade curving backwards at the tip giving a rounded toe to the blade. As its name implies, it is used for boning meats. The slender blade can be used to cut close to the bone with minimum wastage.
- A *palette knife*. A 23 to 25 cm blade with a rounded toe and with no cutting edges. Its use is for scraping bowls, for turning and removing articles during cookery and for smoothing and finishing surfaces (Figure 8.1(b)).
- A *carving knife*. Long (25 to 35 cm), flexible blades with a straight edge and a rounded toe (Figure 8.1(c)). A knife steel is used to sharpen knives on a regular basis (Figure 8.1 (d)). Knives should be sent away to an expert for resetting or regrinding as necessary. The frequency for this depends upon the use (and abuse) of the knife. Too frequent regrinding will reduce the life of the knife.

Cook's fork

This fork is used for holding joints when carving. They are normally two-pronged, with straight, thin tines and the handle is often fitted with a guard (Figure 8.1(e)).

Peeler

Despite the fact that machines are used in many operations to peel root vegetables, a hand peeler is still required. A number of different designs of peeler are available and choice is a matter of individual preference.

Parsley choppers

Consist of four parallel curved blades, with a handle at both ends which permit a rotary action for rapid chopping (see Figure 8.2(a)).

Choppers and cleavers

These choppers have a 25 to 40 cm rectangular blade and are used to cut through soft bones and connective tissue. The back of the chopper is also used to crack bones (Figure 8.2(b)).

Meat saw

A bow-type saw with a 35 cm blade, used to saw through bones without splintering (Figure 8.2(c)).

Mandolin

The mandolin consists of a rectangular wooden or metal frame fitted with two parallel steel cutting plates. The distance between these two plate can be adjusted to affect the thickness of cut of vegetables which are pushed down the face of the mandolin, across the two blades (Figure 8.4(d)). A variation of the basic mandolin is one which has a built-in stand.

Cutting boards

The use of wooden cutting boards, particularly those with an open porous surface, is considered unsatisfactory by many experts. The porous surface harbours bacteria and is difficult to clean. A number of substitutes to wood are now used, including polypropylene, rubber clay compound and synthetic rubber. While none of these substitutes has exactly the same characteristics as wood, a suitable alternative can usually be found.

Cutting boards should be colour coded to show which one should be used for raw meats, which for vegetables and so on. A common convention is to use:

Red   □ raw meat
Blue   □ raw fish
Green   □ fruit and salad
White   □ dairy products
Yellow   □ cooked meats
Brown   □ vegetables

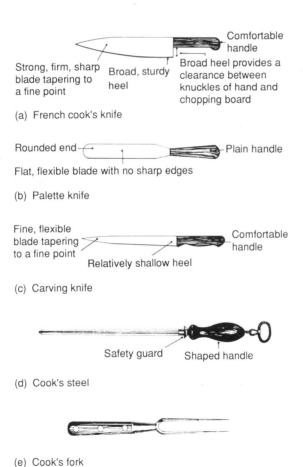

Figure 8.1 *Kitchen knives*
From R. E. Martland and D. A. Welsby (1988). *Basic Cookery*. Oxford: Heinemann.

It is also possible to differentiate between vegetable and salad preparation. The same system may be used for knife handles.

Other hand tools

Whisks

The balloon type whisk is made of strong flexible tinned wires, curving out from a handle, where they are bound together. Whisks vary in size from 15 to 45 cm. They are used for the incorporation of air and for the smoothing of sauces (Figure 8.3(a)).

Wooden/plastic spoons and spatulas

Spoons and spatulas are made from hardwood, such as beech, or from thermoplastics, such as polypropylene. The spoon has a concave bowl whereas the spatula is flat. Spatulas are available in lengths up to 120 cm for use in large boiling pans and bratt pans (Figure 8.3(b) and (c)).

Skimmer

This implement consists of a round, slightly concave perforated disc, set on a long handle at only a slight angle (Figure 8.3(d)). It is used both for taking the scum off the surface of stocks, and for turning foods and removal of pieces for testing. A wire skimmer (Figure 8.3(e)) can be used when deep fat frying for turning and removing small pieces of food.

Ladle

Ladles are made of tinned, chrome plated or stainless steel, or aluminium. They are available in a range of sizes for measuring and portioning liquids and sauces (Figure 8.4(a)).

Serving spoons

Serving spoons are made from the same materials as the ladle. They should be used solely for serving, never for stirring (Figure 8.4(b)).

Steak/grilling tongs

Metal tongs, with the prongs held together by a cross bar, are used for turning and testing meats in grilling (Figure 8.4(c)).

(a) Four-bladed parsley chopper

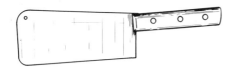

(b) Chopper

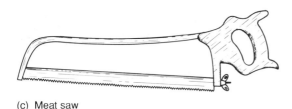

(c) Meat saw

Figure 8.2   *Chopping and cutting tools*
From R. E. Martland and D. A. Welsby (1988). *Basic Cookery*

Other hand tools would include rolling pins, kitchen scissors, apple corers, can openers, trussing needles, cutlet bats, iron spatulas, vegetable scoops, larding needles, piping bags/tubes, sieves, salad baskets, thermometers, scales and poultry secateurs.

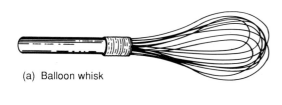

(a) Balloon whisk

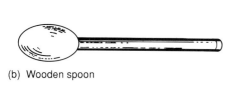

(b) Wooden spoon

(c) Spatula

(d) Skimmer

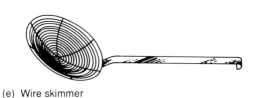

(e) Wire skimmer

Figure 8.3 *Whisking and stirring implements*
From R. E. Martland and D. A. Welsby (1988). *Basic Cookery*

(a) Ladle

(b) Serving spoon

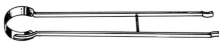

(c) Steak tongs

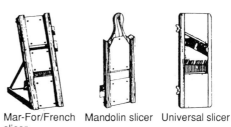

Mar-For/French   Mandolin slicer   Universal slicer
slicer

(d) Hand slicers

Figure 8.4 *Miscellaneous equipment*
From R. E. Martland and D. A. Welsby (1988). *Basic Cookery*

Cooking utensils

A wide range of cooking utensils go to make up what is often referred to as the *batterie de cuisine*. Historically these items would have been made largely from tinned copper, but now a range of materials is used in their construction, such as stainless steel (possibly with a copper base to improve thermal conductivity), vitreous iron and aluminium. Only the major items are included in this description.

Frying kettle (friture)

Kettles are heavy oval or round pans with vertical sides and with handles at the narrow ends. These handles should project well away from the side of the pan so that they remain cool. Fritures are available in a range of sizes, and are fitted with a wire drainer. Additionally, food may be cooked in a frying basket or, alternatively, a nest frying basket may be used to remove small fried items (Figure 8.5(a), (b) and (c)).

Iron frying pan

These pans have a heavy wrought-iron base, 17 to 40 cm in diameter and with sloping sides. Important features are that

- The bottom should be perfectly flat to ensure even cooking.
- That the angle between the sides and base should be coved or rounded for ease of cleaning (Figure 8.5(d)).

The pan is, of course, used for shallow frying such as sautéing of potatoes or onions and the tossing in butter of certain vegetables. The pan is also used for shallow frying of fish.

Omelette pan

An omelette pan is similar to a frying pan, but it has curved sides which help to give an appropriate shape when the pan is tapped at the time the omelette is being finished and rolled. Pans vary in size from 20 to 30 cm (Figure 8.5(e)).

Pancake pan

This is also similar to the ordinary frying pan but with shallower sides and a base diameter of 18 cm (Figure 8.5(f)).

Stew pans

These are cylindrical pans with a single long handle (and possibly with a small lateral handle on the large pans) and lid. They are available in a range of sizes (15 to 40 cm in diameter) and may be deep or shallow. Their use includes all sorts of stove-top work from boiling to stewing – they are the all-purpose kitchen pan (Figure 8.5(g) and (h)).

Shallow stew pan (sauteuse)

This is like a small, shallow stew pan, but with sloping sides. It is used for sautéing vegetables, tossing food in butter or sauce, for the reduction of liquids, and for poaching small delicate foods.

Sauté pan

This is a shallow, flat round cooking vessel with straight vertical sides, which are shallower than the shallow stew pan. It has a long handle and a flat sheet type cover. It is used for the sautéing of meats, particularly where an accompanying sauce is to be made in the same pan (Figure 8.5(i)).

Large pots (casseroles)

These vessels, which are wider than they are high, are fitted with two lateral handles. The capacity varies from 10 to 36 litres. The vessel has a flat round cover with lateral handles (Figure 8.5(j)).

Large stew pan

This type of stew pan is similar to the large pot, except that it is taller in relation to its height. It is commonly used for making sauce, boiling, etc. (Figure 8.5(k)).

Stockpot

This tall cylindrical vessel has a tap fitted into the lower part. It is used for making clear meat, bone or poultry stocks. The capacity of stockpots varies from 20 to 170 litres (Figure 8.5(l)).

Baking sheet

A baking sheet is flat and is usually made of black wrought steel to a size to suit the oven in use. The flat sheet is given a right-angle edge on three sides about 2 cm deep, with the fourth side open so that baked goods can be easily slid from the sheet (Figure 8.6(a)).

Roasting tray

This is a tin-lined, wrought steel, aluminium or vitreous enamel tray, of rectangular shape and short vertical sides. It has handles fitted on the short sides. The size of the tray is related to the size of the oven and to the size of the article to be roasted (Figure 8.6(b)).

Grilling tray

A grilling tray is a heavy metal tray, in the form of a rectangular sheet with all four edges turned up to give a rim of 1 cm. It is used for holding items under the salamander

for cooking or for giving a gratin finish (Figure 8.6(c)).

Colander

This may be made from tinned steel, aluminium, stainless steel or plastic. It is simply a hemispherical shell with a built-in stand. The bowl is pierced with an array of holes, which are less than 6 mm in diameter. It is used for straining liquor from vegetables, farinaceous items, etc. (Figure 8.6(d)).

Vegetable drainer

This item, which is normally made of tinned steel, is similar to a colander but is designed to fit inside a pan, resting on its two handles. It is used for reheating blanched vegetables, etc. (Figure 8.6(e)).

Conical strainer

Conical strainers are available in various sizes (12 to 23 cm) and with fine and coarse strainers, which consist of wire gauze (fine) or perforated metal (coarse). Both types of strainer are used for 'passing' thickened sauces and gravies (Figure 8.6(f)).

Double wire grill or fish grill

A double wire grill comprises two wire grids: one is hinged on one side and the other with handles on the other which are capable of being clipped together. For grilling fish on an open grill the wires, which are set about 15 mm apart, are first wiped and the oiled fish placed on to one grill and trapped in position by folding over and clipping the second grill. The double wire grill can then be placed on the open grill and the fish easily turned by turning over the whole grill (Figure 8.6(g)).

(a) Friture

(h) Shallow stew pan

(i) Sauté pan

(b) Frying basket

(c) Nest frying basket

(j) Casserole, large pot

(d) Frying pan

(e) Omelette pan

(k) Casserole, large stew pan

(f) Pancake pan

(g) Deep stew pan

(l) Stockpot

Figure 8.5   *Pots and pans*
From R. W. Martland and D. A. Welsby (1988). *Basic Cookery*

Wire pastry rack

These wire stands consist of a simple rectangular wire grid on short feet. They vary in size from 30 by 23 cm to 60 by 45 cm. They are used particularly in pastry areas, for cooling foods removed from the oven and for fondant work and sugar dipping. They are also used in larder areas for chaud-froid and aspic work (Figure 8.6(h)).

Other cooking utensils include fish kettles, bains-maries and double boilers.

Moulds

Dariole mould

These are small, round flat-based moulds used for single portions of savoury dishes or for charlottes, bavarois, crème caramels, etc. They are approximately 6 cm in diameter and 7 cm deep. Originally they were made from tinned copper, but now they are more likely to be tinned steel (Figure 8.7(a)).

Charlotte mould

Made from the same types of material as the dariole mould, these moulds are used for both hot and cold charlottes. They are flat bottomed, straight-sided moulds. The sides have a slight slope. They vary in diameter from 10 to 20 cm (Figure 8.7(b)).

Savarin moulds

These moulds are used for producing ring-shaped baked goods, aspics and mousses, and consist of a circular ring-shaped mould with a raised centre (Figure 8.7(c)).

Flan rings

These rings consist of a simple round hoop which is 2.5 cm deep, with each rim turned over for strength. The ring is used in combination with a baking sheet which acts as the base to the ring (Figure 8.7(d)).

Cake hoops

Hoops are similar to flan rings, but are deeper.

There are many other moulds used in the kitchen, such as the timbale mould, the jelly mould, ice pudding moulds, raised pie moulds, tartlet moulds and patty tins.

Cooking appliances

Boiling tables

Boiling tables may be countertop, freestanding or combined with an oven in the form of a range (Figure 8.8). They are used for heating utensils such as stewing and frying pans for boiling, stewing, shallow and deep frying. The most convenient height for a boiling table is generally accepted as about 860 to 870 mm.

Boiling tables may have gas or electric solid plates, gas open burners or electric rings. The traditional solid top boiling table is a direct descendant of the traditional coal range. It has a central hot spot or 'bull's eye', with a gradual reduction in temperature towards the edge of the plate. This gives a range of cooking conditions from fast cooking to simmering without needing to adjust controls. Great flexibility is also possible over the size of pots and pans which can be used. Its disadvantages are that it:

- Gives off large quantities of heat into the kitchen.

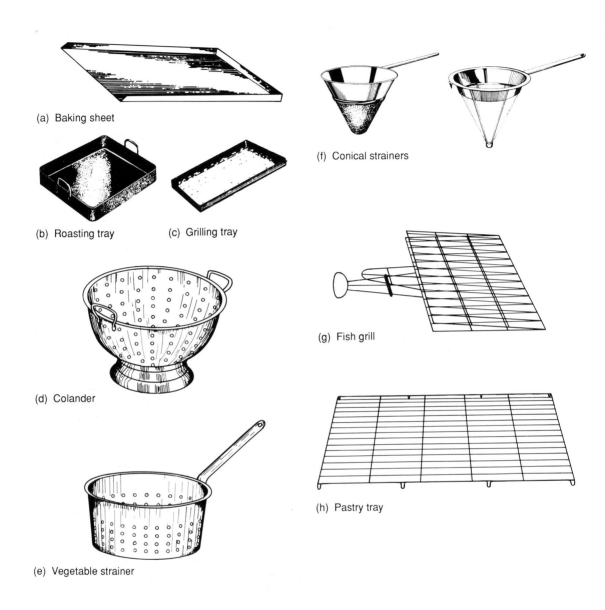

(a) Baking sheet

(b) Roasting tray

(c) Grilling tray

(d) Colander

(e) Vegetable strainer

(f) Conical strainers

(g) Fish grill

(h) Pastry tray

Figure 8.6   *Sheets and trays*
From R. E. Martland and D. A. Welsby (1988). *Basic Cookery*

● Takes up a lot of space relative to the volume of food which can be produced.

Open burners and rings are less flexible in terms of sizes of pots and pans but are more energy efficient than the solid top, since only those burners in use need be on. They are quick to respond to a change of control setting.

(a) Dariole mould

(b) Charlotte mould

(c) Savarin mould

(d) Flan ring

Figure 8.7 *Moulds*
From R. E. Martland and D. A. Welsby (1988). Basic Cookery

It is possible to obtain boiling tables with a mixture of solid plates and open burners/rings.

The halogen hob

One new development in the boiling table is the use of the halogen hob. The hob uses a halogen lamp mounted below a vitreoceramic (a ceramic material with a high glass content) plate, which is marked to indicate the correct location of pans on the hob (see Figure 8.9). These hobs use infra-red radiation to heat the base of the pan, which gives rapid heating up times and high efficiencies.

The induction hob

Another new development of the boiling table is the induction hob. This is similar in appearance to the halogen hob, but operates on a very different principle (Figure 8.10). Induction hobs are available as back-bar units, with two-, three- or four-ring boiling tables or combined with an oven.

Electronic circuits produce low-frequency alternating currents which are passed through a coil of wire mounted just below a ceramic cooking surface. However, without the presence of any ferromagnetic material, the current flow is low, as is the power consumption. When the base of a pan (containing a high proportion of ferromagnetic material) is placed on the ceramic cooking surface, the current flow increases and a magnetic field is developed, which passes into the base of the pan. Here it is converted directly into heat. As soon as the pan is removed, the electric current and magnetic field decline giving instantaneous energy control.

General-purpose and roasting ovens

Ovens may be provided as part of a range, as free-standing units, on a stand to raise the

Tutorial topic

Collect together leaflets and catalogues on hand tools used in the catering industry.

Analyse the hand tools in terms of cooking/preparation applications, materials of construction, methods of cleaning, ease of cleaning, skills required to use and cost.

For each, suggest the types of food, preparation methods and dishes for which the equipment is most suited.

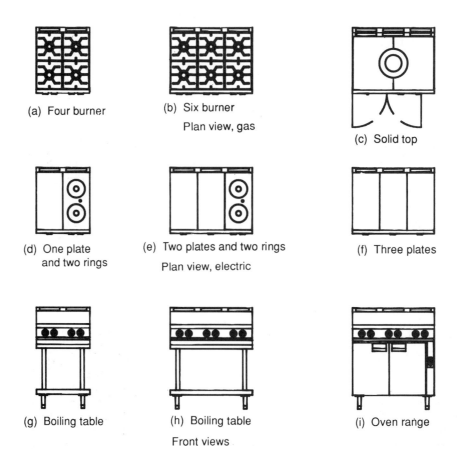

(a) Four burner

(b) Six burner

Plan view, gas

(c) Solid top

(d) One plate and two rings

(e) Two plates and two rings

Plan view, electric

(f) Three plates

(g) Boiling table

(h) Boiling table

Front views

(i) Oven range

Figure 8.8 *Boiling tables and ranges*

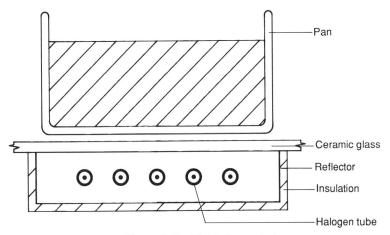

Figure 8.9 *The halogen hob*

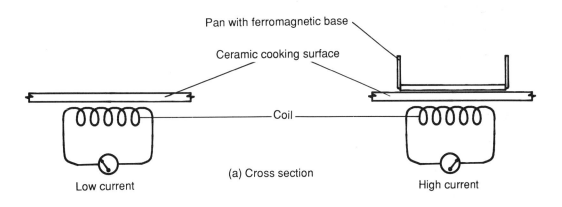

(a) Cross section

(b) Plan view

Figure 8.10 *Induction hobs*

working height, or stacked to increase the utilization of floor space. They may utilize natural convection, radiation or forced convection.

Natural convection ovens utilize gas burners or electric heaters to induce convection currents inside the oven space. Even in a so-called natural convection oven some radiation will be present and, the higher the cooking temperature, the higher will be the proportion of radiant heat. These ovens are general-purpose in nature since they can be used for a large number of cooking methods: roasting, baking, braising, stewing etc. (Figure 8.11). Ovens may have side-hinged doors (single or double) or drop-down doors.

For large-scale production, variants of the general-purpose oven are used, including the rotary oven, the reel oven and the travelling oven. The rotary oven has a horizontal hearth which rotates about a vertical axis. Reel ovens also rotate, but use hinged platforms which rotate around a horizontal axis, causing the platforms to rotate like a ferris wheel. The travelling oven uses a conveyer belt to take food items through the oven.

Ranges

A range is a combination of a boiling table with a general-purpose oven (or sometimes a convection oven). It represents a very traditional and popular design which has developed from the first range designed by enclosing the solid fuel fire.

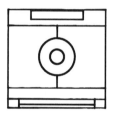

(a) Plan view

Medium-duty six burner
range with side-hung doors (b) Front view

Heavy-duty solid top range
with drop-down door

Figure 8.11 *General-purpose oven ranges*

For many years this was the key appliance in catering. It is often combined with other appliances such as the grill. For the small kitchen, *restaurant ranges* are available, which have ovens, boiling tables, grills, griddles and deep-fat fryers in a single range unit.

The oven range is now giving way in importance to other types of equipment. The oven at floor level is very inconvenient and dangerous and alternative arrangements using an oven on a stand, to bring it up to working height, together with a separate boiling table is often preferred.

Forced convection ovens

Forced convection ovens utilize a fan or blower to circulate heated air over the food (see Figure 7.8). Models which simply stir the air are less effective than those which cause uniform flow of air over all shelves. Some convection ovens use multiple fans or fans which change directions periodically to make the temperature throughout the oven more uniform.

The more efficient heat usage in forced convection ovens permits cooking at a lower temperature and in a shorter period of time than using natural convection, allowing economies of energy, space and time.

Forced convection ovens can cause food to dry out more than is the case with natural convection. Many forced convection ovens are fitted with a humidity spray to counteract this effect. In some cases, where crust development is required, the humidity is turned off, but in other cases, such as the roasting of meats, the humidity spray is turned on.

Forced convection ovens may have cooking computers to control time and temperature in the oven and to measure the temperature of a roasting probe. The computer can be programmed with preset times and temperatures for particular products, including programming times for an individual shelf.

Baking, pastry and pizza ovens

Although the ovens described above can be used for baking, where large quantities of bread products are produced specialist baking and pastry ovens may be used. Bread baking requires a high temperature and a high level of radiant heat. This is best provided using an oven which has a shallow hearth. This means that the bread will receive intense radiation, both from above and below. In order to prevent shielding of this radiant heat, only a single shelf is provided.

Where greater production volume is required, the ovens can be stacked, to give the equivalent of several shelves. Where a combination of general-purpose, baking and pizza ovens are stacked, they are sometimes referred to as *deck ovens* (see Figure 8.12).

Closely related to the baking oven is the pizza oven. Like bread, pizza also requires intense radiant heat and a high temperature. Because the pizza is a thin product, the hearth can be even more shallow than in the baking oven.

Impingement ovens

Impingement ovens use a chain conveyer belt to pass foods through vertical forced convection jets of hot air (see Figure 7.10). These jets of hot air, which are directed on to the surface of the food, produce intense rates of heat transfer. In this way, they allow the rapid cooking of items such as pastry goods and pizzas. Because of the intense surface heating, they cannot be used to cook thick foods.

Infra-red continuous ovens

These ovens use a chain conveyer belt to carry food between gas or electric infra-red heaters. They are used mainly for products such as pizzas. They have similar cooking properties and limitations as the impingement oven.

Roast and hold ovens

There are two main types of roast and hold ovens. One type is a modified convection oven with a core food temperature probe. It is programmed to heat the food (usually roast meats) to a defined centre temperature, at which point it switches to hold mode, where it holds the food at a lower temperature in order to reduce shrinkage.

The second type of roast and hold oven uses dark infra-red radiation from the walls of the oven to roast at low temperatures (66 to 100 °C). Although the cooking time is longer than conventional roasting, the shrinkage and weight loss of meat is considerably less. It also uses less energy. As with the first type of roast and hold oven, it has a probe for measuring core temperature and automatically reduces to a hold temperature when the desired temperature is achieved.

Microwave ovens

Of the many changes in catering technology over the last quarter of a century, the advent of the microwave oven is notable. When first introduced, caterers were interested but did not always realize their best application. Today they are in widespread use, but their main use is for reheating foods rather than for prime cooking (Figure 8.13).

Because of the poor uniformity of microwave heating, many ovens are fitted with turntables, which move the food through regions of high energy and low energy.

The rate at which heat is generated in the food depends partly upon the nature of the food itself. Therefore, it is not always satisfactory to reheat dishes involving a variety of types and sizes of food. Another problem can be the reheating of frozen foods because of the difference in the rate of heating of ice and water. Ice is a poor absorber of microwave energy, whereas water is a good absorber. Because of this, water heats up much more rapidly. Thus, in defrosting frozen food a technique (sometimes called *pulse power*) of alternately switching on and off the energy is used. This allows heat which builds up in areas of the food to be redistributed by conduction.

The rapid heating potential of microwave ovens is recognized in fast-food operations, pub catering and night staff meals. Remembering that microwaves do not brown food, some of their other applications include:

- 'Flashing' à la carte dishes just prior to their service to the customer.

(a) Single oven

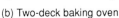

(b) Two-deck baking oven

(c) Three-deck baking oven

Figure 8.12   *Baking ovens*

- Defrosting and/or reheating of frozen dishes.
- Reheating chilled dishes.
- Cooking vegetables.

Microwave ovens may be fitted with cooking computers to allow programming of times and power levels. Buttons on the control panel may be preset to required cooking/reheating programmes for individual products.

Many caterers use domestic microwave ovens in a commercial situation. This can lead to problems because of:

- The relatively low power level of domestic ovens.

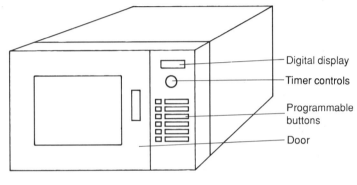

(b) Microwave oven

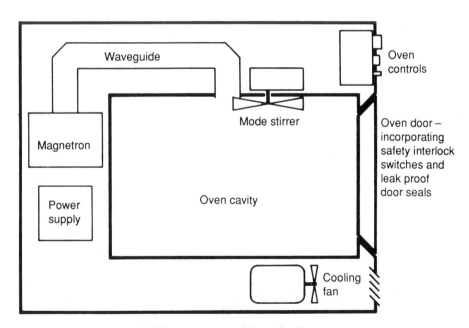

(a) Microwave oven with mode stirrer

Figure 8.13   *Microwave oven*
(a) From A. Milson and D. Kirk (1980). *Principles of Design and Operation of Catering Equipment.* Chichester: Ellis Horwood

- A deterioration in performance when these units are run for long periods of time.

Both of these factors can lead to food not achieving the desired temperature and the introduction of food poisoning risk. For these reasons, catering microwave ovens should always be used.

Microwave/convection oven combination

Since microwaves heat rapidly within the body of the food and forced convection browns the outside, the combination of the two into a single appliance can prove very effective – particularly with an à la carte menu. Items such as chickens can be roasted from chilled in approximately 10 minutes. With this appliance, most items on an à la carte menu can be cooked to order, reducing the level of wastage. The limitation to this type of oven is that it cannot handle large volumes of food.

The convection heat may be provided by gas or electricity.

Cook-chill regeneration ovens

There are three main types of cook-chill regeneration oven. One utilizes quartz tube heaters placed between all shelves in the oven. The quartz tubes produce infra-red radiation, which gives a better penetration of the food than does visible radiation (Figure 8.14).

The second type of regeneration oven is a development of the convection oven. The third possibility, particularly suited to sous vide, is the use of the combination oven (see below). For small quantities of food, the microwave may also be used.

Proving ovens

Proving ovens are not really ovens, but consist of thermostatically controlled high humidity cabinets for proving yeast raised products.

Smoking ovens

These are ovens with a base compartment for holding hardwood chips. The compartment is heated to generate smoke. The amount of smoke in the oven is controlled using an

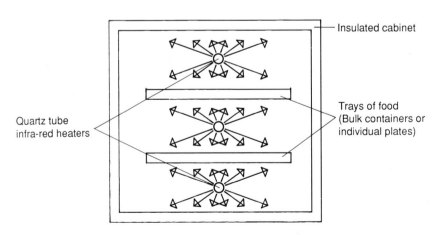

Figure 8.14 *Infra-red cook-chill regeneration*

adjustable vent. Some smoking ovens operate with a high humidity.

Pans, kettles and steamers

Boiling pans and kettles

These are large stainless steel pans which may either be fitted with a tilting mechanism or may be fixed. The latter type has a draining tap at the base of the pan. Small pans may be countertop, while large pans are floor mounted (Figure 8.15).

The pans may be directly heated by gas or electricity, or they may have a water or steam jacket. This jacket gives a more uniform and controlled temperature and is used for cooking items such as delicate sauces, which might otherwise burn. The steam may be generated in the base of the appliance. Alternatively, either a separate steam generator or a central steam supply within the kitchen may be used.

Large boiling pans may be fitted with a mechanical stirrer. This prevents food building up on the wall of the pan where it might otherwise burn. It also saves labour and reduces the risk of burns to the operator.

The trend to batch cook in smaller quantities, the increased use of frozen vegetables, and developments in steamers has caused a reduction in the demand for the larger boiling pans. However, there is a role for the smaller boiling pan for soups, sauces, and custards. Several small boiling pans give much more flexibility than one large one. These small boiling pans can be mounted on a table containing the steam generator.

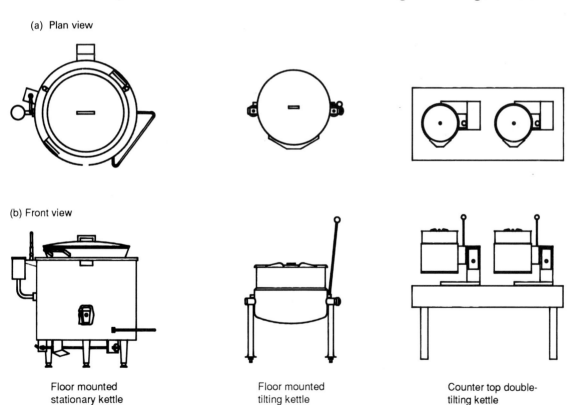

(a) Plan view

(b) Front view

Floor mounted stationary kettle

Floor mounted tilting kettle

Counter top double-tilting kettle

Figure 8.15 *Boiling pans and kettles*

Bratt pans or tilting skillets

Bratt pans consist of a shallow rectangular (or sometimes circular) cast iron or stainless steel pan with a tilting mechanism. The pan can be used for a very wide range of cooking methods, from shallow frying to boiling, braising and sautéing (Figure 8.16).

Steaming ovens

The traditional atmospheric steamer, using natural convection steam at 100°C can produce high-quality steamed foods, but it is relatively slow and, particularly when using small batches, energy inefficient. However, a number of radical developments have maintained the importance of the steamer in the modern kitchen (Figure 8.17).

Pressure steamers

By increasing the pressure of steam both the temperature of the steam and the boiling point of water rise. For example, at a pressure of 15 p.s.i., the temperature of steam is 121 °C. At this temperature the cooking time of food is reduced significantly. This allows large volumes of food to be batch cooked in small quantities, which improves quality and energy consumption. The steam may be generated internally in the cooking vessel or from an external steam generator. The latter gives the minimum cooking time.

One problem when using pressure cookers is that it is impossible to check when the food is ready because of safety interlocks. On account of this, and the short cooking times, precise timing is required.

Convection steamers

One of the problems with the atmospheric steamer is that the natural convection currents in steam are slow moving, which leads to the lengthy cooking times associated with steaming. If the velocity of the steam is increased using forced convection, cooking time and energy consumption can be reduced significantly.

Two methods are used to introduce forced convection. One way, which is a similar method to that used in a convection oven, is to introduce a fan into the back of the oven. The alternative method is to use an external steam generator and to inject the steam,

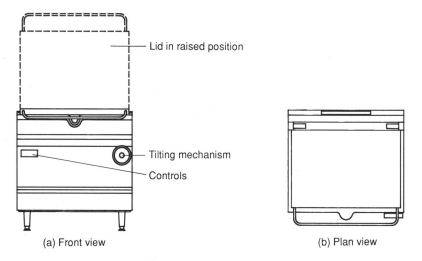

(a) Front view

Lid in raised position

Tilting mechanism
Controls

(b) Plan view

Figure 8.16   *Bratt pan*

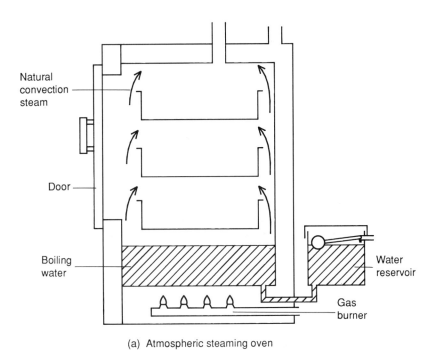

(a) Atmospheric steaming oven

(b) Pressure steamer with external steam generation and steam jets

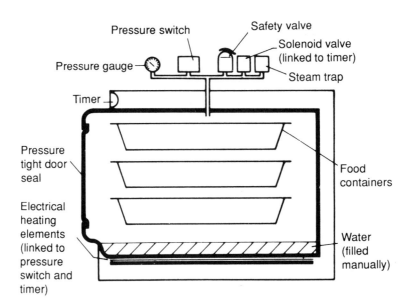

(c) **Pressure steamer with internal steam generation**

Figure 8.17   *Steaming ovens (cross-section)*
(b) and (c) from A. Milson and D. Kirk (1980). Principles of Design and Operation of Catering Equipment.

through jets, into the cooking chamber. Because the steam condenses, there is no carry-over of flavours between foods (Figure 8.18).

It is now possible to purchase pressure/ pressureless convection steamers with sophisticated computerized controls. This type of steamer saves space and is suitable for use in a kitchen which needs both, but does not have room for, a pressure steamer and a convection steamer.

Combination ovens

The description of the convection steamer above draws parallels with the design of the convection oven. Also, when discussing the convection oven, the frequent need for high humidities was discussed. There are many advantages to be gained from combining together the convection steamer and the convection oven in a single appliance – the *combination oven* (Figure 8.19).

The combination oven can be used in one of three ways:

1   As a convection oven.
2   As a convection steamer.
3   As a *combination* of steam and forced convection air.

Fryers

Fryers are used for deep-fat frying. The vat or tank of frying oil is heated either externally or internally. Internal heating may use either electric immersion elements (Figure 8.20(a)) or gas immersion tubes. The benefit of the immersed heating element is its high rate of thermal efficiency, because all of the heat from the element goes into the oil.

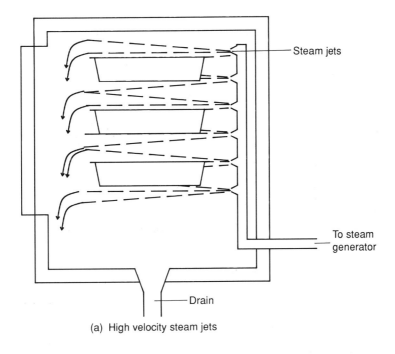

(a) High velocity steam jets

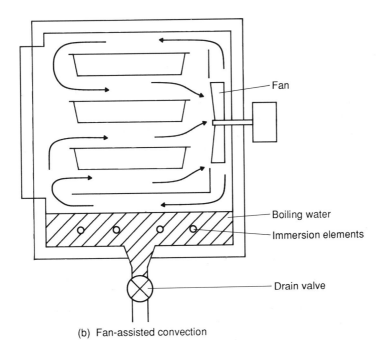

(b) Fan-assisted convection

Figure 8.18 *Convection steamers*

Another advantage is the development of a cool zone below the element. Because the oil heats mainly by convection, the heat rises up through the vat of oil, leaving cooler oil below the element.

Many modern fryers have this cool zone – an area in the base of the frying vat where the oil is cooler and where particles of food accumulate. Removing these particles from the high temperature oil helps to extend the life of the frying oil. As an alternative to the use of immersion elements to produce the cool zone, many fryers use a V pan fryer with external gas burners (Figure 8.20(b)).

Modern fryers require very high levels of heat input. This is necessary to recover the temperature of the oil as rapidly as possible. When, for example, a basket of frozen chips, is lowered into the hot oil, the temperature of the oil immediately drops. Both the frying time and the quality of the product depend upon a rapid recovery of temperature. If the temperature remains low, the food will both absorb a lot of oil and take a long time to cook.

Fryers also have a drain valve to allow easy removal of the oil for filtering and replacement. The use of oil filtration systems

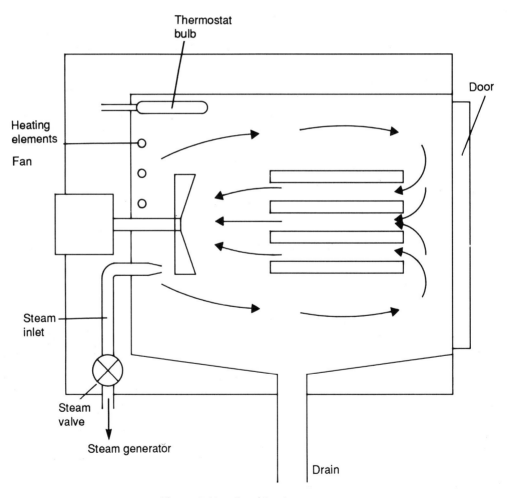

Figure 8.19 *Combination oven*

is now increasingly common in catering operations which produce large volumes of fried food, since it increases the life of the frying oil. Filtration systems may be either mobile units or they may be built into a suit of fryers.

Computerized fryers

Fast-food fryers are often fitted with frying computers and automatic basket lifts. By monitoring the temperature of the oil, the computer can ascertain when the food is ready, whatever the initial temperature and quantity of the raw food. The computer then activates the basket lifts. Once the computer has been programmed it can automatically compensate for variations in the initial temperature and quantity of product placed in the basket. It does this by measuring the rate at which oil temperature is recovered.

Pressure fryers

The pressure fryer found early application in fast-food and take-away business because of its ability to produce high-quality items in a short period of time. When frying under a pressure of 15 p.s.i., the boiling temperature of water in the food is raised to 120 °C, so

that the food cooks at a much faster rate. Also, because of the high humidity, the food does not dry out, a common problem with deep fat frying. The most successful application is for producing fried chicken.

Food is placed in a deep pan of heated oil, and a pressure-tight lid is clamped down so that water from the food builds up as steam inside the vessel (initially air must be vented from the vessel). The pressure is regulated until the end of the heating time, when the pressure is automatically released (Figure 8.21).

Continuous fryers

Continuous fryers consist of a long vat of oil, with a metal chain conveyer passing through the oil. Normally they are used in very large catering operations to produce large quantities of fried food. There are smaller versions available for frying doughnuts; these have a flipper bar to turn the product over half way through the cooking process.

Oil filtration machines

These machines may be either mounted into a suite of fryers or free-standing mobile units. The oil is pumped from the cooking vat

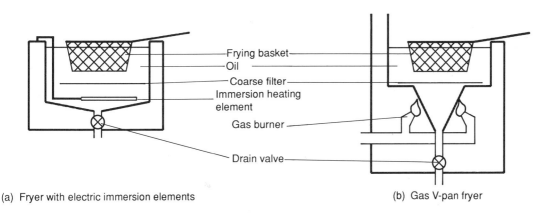

(a) Fryer with electric immersion elements

Frying basket
Oil
Coarse filter
Immersion heating element
Gas burner
Drain valve

(b) Gas V-pan fryer

Figure 8.20   *Frying equipment*

through a series of filters and back into a clean vat. Filtration extends the life of the frying oil by removing particles of food.

Griddles and fry plates

The griddle consists of a flat cast iron plate which is heated from below. It can be used to cook a wide range of food items which otherwise might be grilled or shallow fried. In addition to items such as hamburgers and steaks, it can also be used to cook breakfast items, such as bacon, sausages and eggs. Some griddle plates have very wide temperature fluctuations across the plate, which makes it difficult to use the whole area. Modern griddle plates are divided into sections, each of which has its own thermostatic control (Figure 8.22).

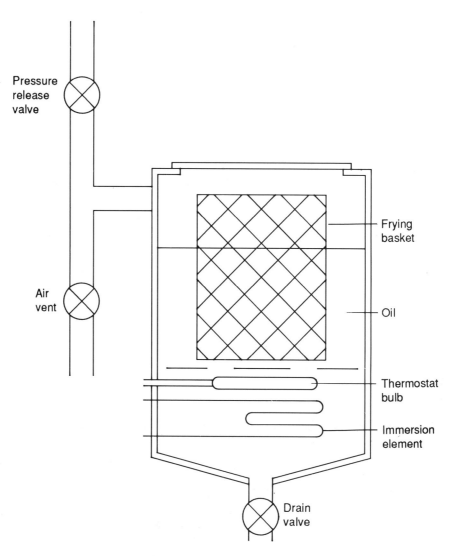

Figure 8.21   *Pressure fryer*

Griddle plates are sometimes provided as part of a boiling table or range. In some cases it is possible to remove this griddle plate, and use the heating elements as additional open burners.

Grills

Intense radiant heat is required from a grill. This may be achieved using electric radiant elements, quartz or halogen tubes. Alternatively, radiant heat can be generated with gas, using metal frets, ceramic plates, or ceramic surface combustion burners.

Grills may be employed using heat from above, heat from below or a combination of the two. Those heated from above are sometimes referred to as salamanders. Food is placed either on a wire toasting rack or on a cast iron brander plate, so called because it produces brander marks on steaks. It acts as a source of heat which is transferred to the food by conduction. In this way the food is cooked from above by radiation and from below by conduction (Figure 8.23).

The rate of cooking in grilling is controlled both by the intensity of the radiant heat but also by the distance between the food and the radiant element.

Grills heated from below produce radiant heat by heating mineral lava (pumice) formed

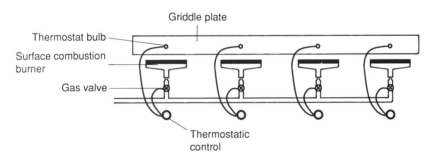

Figure 8.22 *Thermostatic griddle plate*

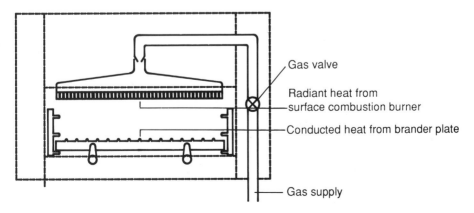

Figure 8.23 *Grill or salamander*

in the shape of charcoal bricks. These bricks simulate charcoal cooking and, for this reason, the appliance is often referred to as a chargrill. Some grills used for barbecuing may employ charcoal as the source of fuel and radiant heat.

Barbecue grills are similar to char grills, but they are usually designed to work from bottled liquid petroleum gas so that they can be portable. They may use lava rocks or charcoal.

Contact grills are also used where food is sandwiched between two heated metal plates, the bottom plate being fixed and the top plate hinged along one edge. In terms of their method of operation these are actually closer to griddles than they are to grills.

Chain grills/broilers

These continuous grills (or broilers) consist of a metal chain conveyer belt which passes between gas or electric infra-red heaters. Food is placed on one end of the belt and the speed of the belt is adjusted to ensure that the food is cooked by the time it leaves the grill compartment. They are used in fast-food operations for cooking hamburgers and buns.

Toasters

Toasters also use radiant heat. In fact, grills are often used to produce toast in hotels and restaurants. Specialist toasters for bread and buns may be of the pop-up type, or rotary toasters. In the latter, slices of bread are fed on to an endless power-driven chain and passes between vertical radiant surfaces.

Specialist appliances have been developed for toasting sandwiches. These may be similar to a grill, but with heating elements on both sides, or they may be in the form of a contact grill, where the food is toasted by clamping it between two horizontal heated metal plates.

Stockpot stands

Electric and gas heated stockpot stands are of strong construction and are designed to withstand heavy usage. Gas stockpot stands are available with open burners and in multiples of the single unit. The height of the stand is normally 610 mm, but some may be available down to 455 mm (Figure 8.24).

Preparation equipment

Mixing machines

The most widely used mixer in catering consists of a stationary bowl, with a mixing element which follows a planetary path as it moves around the bowl. The element must come as close as possible to the walls of the bowl in order to sweep away food sticking to the walls (Figure 8.25). Mixers have capacities from 5 litres to 150 litres.

A variety of mixing elements is used for general mixing, for the incorporation of air (whisking) and for dough kneading. A different speed is required for each element. Mixers may have a number of fixed speeds, or they may be continuously variable.

Mixers often have attachment points for a wide range of food preparation equipment

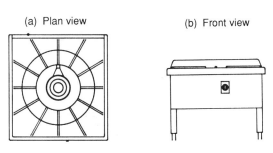

(a) Plan view   (b) Front view

Figure 8.24 *Stockpot stand*

such as mincing machines and vegetable preparation machines.

Vegetable preparation machines

Vegetable preparation machines are used to slice, dice and grate a range of vegetables. Interchangeable discs are used to change the thickness of slice or coarseness of shred. Vegetables are fed by gravity from above and pass the horizontally rotating cutting/ shredding discs. A combination of two discs is required to produce diced and chipped products (Figure 8.26).

Vegetable peelers

These are used to peel potatoes and other root vegetables. Their importance has declined with the increased availability of pre-prepared vegetables.

Peelers consist of a vertical cylinder coated on the inside with an abrasive material. The base, which rotates, also has an abrasive coating. It also has ridges to lift up and rotate the potatoes to ensure even peeling. A steady stream of water is run through the machine to wash the potatoes and to remove soil and peel from the machine (Figure 8.27). The sink into which this waste is discharged should be fitted with a basket strainer or a

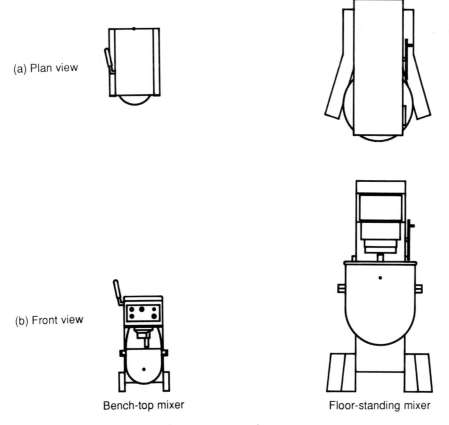

(a) Plan view

(b) Front view

Bench-top mixer

Floor-standing mixer

Figure 8.25 *Food mixer*

waste disposal unit in order to prevent blocked drains.

Small portable potato peelers may be used on a worktop adjacent to a sink. Larger machines are mounted on floor stands.

Care is required in the use of potato peelers to prevent excessive waste.

Food processors/vertical cutter mixers

These types of mixers consist of a plastic or metal bowl with a rotating blade in the base. The speed of the blade can be varied and a number of types of blade can be used – metal with a sharp cutting edge for chopping, plastic for beating and aerating. Food processors vary from small countertop models to the large *vertical cutting and mixing machines* (VCM) used for tasks such as puréeing large volumes of soup. Large machines may have a tilting mechanism to allow easier discharge of the product (Figure 8.28).

Food processors may be combined with vegetable preparation machines, in which case the bowl is interchangeable with the slicing/dicing attachment.

Where the processor is required to purée food which has been cooked in a boiling pan, rather than remove it from the pan into a VCM, it may be more convenient to use a *turbo-mixer*. This mixer consists of a rotating knife blade which is mounted on the end of a U-shaped stainless steel tube, designed so that one end can be dipped into the cooking vessel. The unit is mounted on a trolley so that it can be used throughout the kitchen.

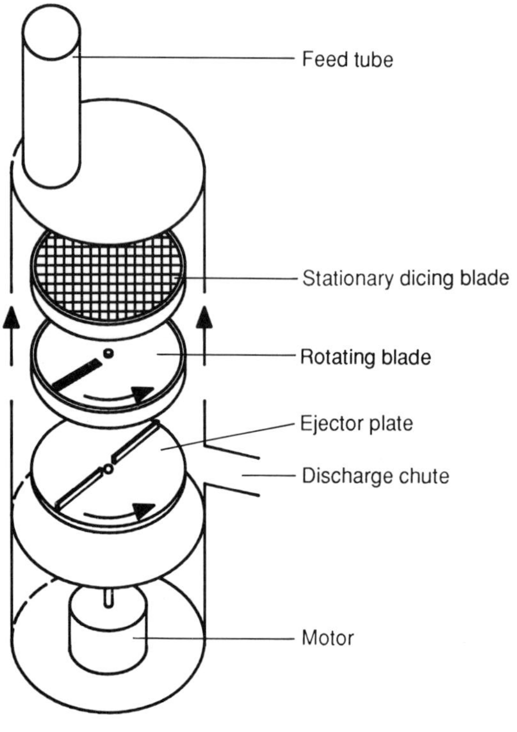

Bowl choppers

A rotating bowl moves food beneath a rotating knife, which cuts across the path of the rotating bowl. The appliance has a lid with safety interlocks to prevent access to the rotating blades. It is used for cutting meats, for producing purée, for chopping vegetables and for making breadcrumbs.

Slicing machines

There are two main types of slicing machine: gravity feed; and automatic feed. In the gravity feed machine a sloping platform carries the food into the path of the circular rotating cutting blade. An adjustable plate is used to vary the thickness of the slice.

With the automatic slicing machine the plate is horizontal rather than inclined, and

Figure 8.26   *Vegetable preparation machine*

Feed tube

Stationary dicing blade

Rotating blade

Ejector plate

Discharge chute

Motor

the food is carried by mechanical force into the slicing blade.

Preparation tables

Easy-to-clean preparation tables constructed of stainless steel are now universally used in catering. They may be mounted on an open stand, on a stand with a shelf, with drawers or with a cupboard underneath.

Tables for use against walls usually have an upstand at the back which is some 100 mm high. Tables which go into corners also have this upstand along the edge which goes against the wall. Centre tables do not have the upstand, but are turned down on all edges.

Preparation tables may be bought as modular units, with depths of 600, 650 or 700 mm. Alternatively, they may be custom made to fit a particular work space.

Sinks

Sinks are a requirement of all kitchens: they can be divided into hand-wash sinks, preparation sinks and pot-wash sinks. In addition, there may be a sink for dishwashing and a mop sink.

Sinks are usually made from stainless steel and may have one, two or three sink bowls. They may also have a draining board.

Racking

Racking is required in kitchens to hold pots, pans, baking sheets, measuring jugs and other utensils. Modular racking systems are now common; they may have solid or wire shelves and the height of these shelves can be adjusted.

Other preparation equipment includes can openers, chipping machines, mincing

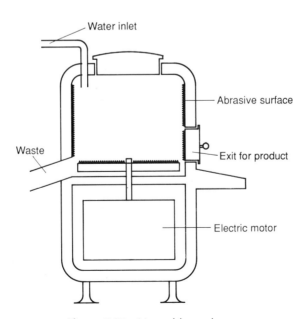

Figure 8.27   *Vegetable peeler*

machines, bread slicing machines, bread buttering machines, coating machines (for breadcrumbing), patty forming machines (for hamburgers), pastry rolling machines, pastry case stamping and filling machines, dough dividers and juice extractors.

Dishwashing equipment

There are now dishwashers for all sizes of establishment. Machines are of two main types: batch machines where all the processes of pre-rinsing, washing, rinsing and sterilizing take place in a single tank, and multi-tank machines, which have separate regions for each activity, with baskets passing in sequence from one stage to the next (Figure 8.29). In principle, there are eight basic functions of dishwashing (Walstrom, 1989):

1   Scrapping sorting and stacking on racks.

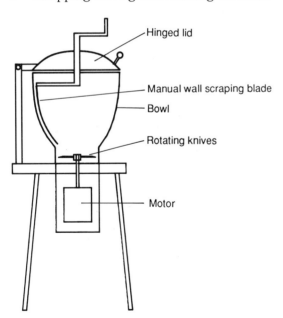

Figure 8.28   *Vertical cutter mixer*

2   Pre-rinse (external to dishwasher).
3   Pre-rinse (internal).
4   Pre-wash.
5   Chemical wash 60 °C.
6   Power rinse.
7   Final rinse 80–85 °C.
8   Drying.

The washing action depends upon a combination of three factors:

1   Mechanical action (jets of water).
2   Water temperature.
3   Chemical action from detergents.

Low temperature detergents are now available to give a similar washing action, but at a lower temperature than conventional dishwasher detergents. If the final rinse water is less than 80 °C, chemical agents are required to ensure the destruction of vegetative cells of bacteria.

For establishments where washing is carried out by hand, a double sink is required, with one bowl for washing and the other for sterilizing (in which the water must be at a minimum of 77 °C for at least two minutes. However, because of the labour saving, most establishments now have a dishwashing machine.

For full-size dishwashing machines, a standard 500 mm by 500 mm rack is used. Racks are available for plates, cups, glassware and cutlery. A rack can hold:

- Nine soup or desert bowls.
- Sixteen main course plates.
- Twenty-four side plates.
- Twenty-five cups.
- Thirty-two saucers.

Undercounter or countertop batch machines are available for the smallest establishment and for bars. The next size up is the free-standing front-loading batch machine.

These machines can wash ten to twenty-five racks per hour.

Pass-through batch machines reduce the amount of handling required. Dirty and clean tables on either side of the machine allow baskets to be loaded, pushed through the machine and unloaded. The dirties table often has a scraping ring and a sink, fitted with a pre-rinse spray and waste disposal unit. Pass-through machines are available in straight line and corner models. They can wash twenty to sixty racks per hour.

With increased capacity, a multi-tank dishwasher is required which uses separate sections for each of the washing processes. The machines may also have a drying section,

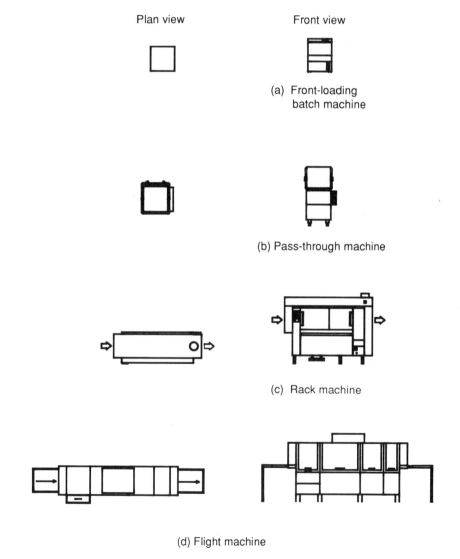

Plan view   Front view

(a) Front-loading
batch machine

(b) Pass-through machine

(c) Rack machine

(d) Flight machine

Figure 8.29 *Dishwashing machines*

utilizing a hot air blower, at the end of the wash cycle.

These are of two main types of multi-tank machines: rack machines; and flight machines. In the case of rack machines, crockery and cutlery are loaded on to racks which are pulled through the machine. Conveyorized or roller sections are used to load and unload the machine. These may operate using gravity or they may be motor driven. Depending on the number of tanks in the machine, they can handle between sixty and 200 racks per hour.

Flight machines utilize a conveyer belt through the dishwasher. This conveyer has plastic plate holders, which hold items of crockery at a suitable washing angle. As an alternative, the crockery and cutlery may be loaded into baskets, which are carried on the conveyer.

Most dishwashers are electrically heated and powered. Where a supply of hot water is available, a dishwasher can be supplied with a hot fill. Machines are also available which can utilize steam supplies.

A temperature of between 60 and 71 °C is required for initial washing, although developments with low temperature detergents are changing this. For rinsing and sterilizing a temperature of 80 °C is required. In situations where the water pressure is low (less than 2 bar or 30 p.s.i.), a booster pump is required.

Specialized machines are available for washing glassware and for washing pans and trays.

In large installations it may be economic to use conveyer handling systems. These can be used to convey trays from the restaurant (including elevator sections to travel over door openings) to the tray sorting area. This may be particularly useful in conjunction with self-clearing systems.

The dirties end of the dishwasher may have a pre-rinse sink, complete with spray and a waste disposal machine.

Pre-rinse sprays consist of a reinforced flexible hose mounted over a sink. The supply end is connected to a tap, which may provide hot and/or cold water. The other end has a spray gun with a manual trigger. The powerful spray of water can be used to wash food debris off plates prior to washing. This improves dishwasher performance and reduces water and detergent consumption.

Waste disposal machines

Disposal machines are used in the kitchen and dishwash areas. Food is washed through high-speed rotating blades before being discharged into the waste pipe. Small machines may be mounted in the base of a standard sink and large machines are mounted in a trough. They can also be incorporated into the dirties section of dishwasher tables.

Compactors

Compactors are becoming increasingly important to the caterer because of the increased use of packaged foods and of disposable plates, cups and food containers. Compactors used a hydraulic ram to reduce the volume of the waste and to pack it into plastic covered bales.

Mechanized pan scourer

Scourers are often used to remove burned-on food from pots, pans and containers. They consist of a wire brush which is rotated at high speed. It is mounted on the end of a sheathed flexible drive shaft, the other end of which connects to an electric motor. The machines can either be mounted over the potwash sink or they can be used on mobile trolleys.

Refrigeration equipment

Refrigeration is an essential part of all catering operations. It includes frozen and chilled refrigeration in stores, and is used for preparation work in the kitchen and in the service area (Figure 8.30).

Broadly speaking, there are two temperature zones: -18 to $-20°C$ for frozen foods and 0 to $5°C$ for chilled foods. However, in medium to large operations, the chilled storage will be subdivided to give separate store areas and temperatures for dairy products, raw meats and fish, cooked meats, salad items, wines etc. (see Figure 5.9).

For bulk food storage, walk-in or reach-in stores may be used. Walk-in cold stores may be installed in a building, but it is now more common to use modular cold rooms. These are built on site from manufactured insulated panels, allowing a wide variety of store sizes (Figure 8.30(b)).

Reach-in cabinets consist of factory manufactured units with one, two or three doors. Many of the new cabinets are designed to take gastronorm trays and/or wheel-in trolleys. Because of the importance of temperature control many cabinets are fitted with digital temperature displays. Compressors and condenser coils may be mounted at the base of the unit, on top of the unit or at some distance away from the unit where the air is cooler (Figure 8.30(a)).

In the kitchen, chilled storage is often required for holding food which is awaiting preparation, which is in preparation or which is finished and being held for service. This refrigeration may be provided in the form of reach-in cabinets or under-worktop refrigeration. Under-worktop refrigeration provides

the chef with convenient and safe food supplies and minimizes walking. Specialist worktops have been developed with refrigerated cupboards and bain-marie type cut-outs, for the preparation of salads and sandwiches. They may be fitted with drawers or cupboard doors to suit the needs of the operation (Figure 8.30(c)).

For food which is awaiting service, reach-in cabinets or refrigerated cupboards with cold wells (a refrigerated version of the open bain-marie) may be used. Reach-in cabinets are available in the form of pass-through units, allowing easy transfer from kitchen to servery.

For cook-chill and cook-freeze systems, refrigeration is required to rapidly chill or freeze the food. The most common method of doing this is to use the *blast chiller* or *blast freezer* which uses forced convection air (at $-10°C$ for blast chilling and at $-40°C$ for blast freezing). This air is blown over the surface of food which is held in standard trays on shelves or trolleys (Figure 8.31).

As an alternative to blast chilling with cold air, it is possible to use liquid nitrogen at $-196°C$ or liquid carbon dioxide at $-78°C$). The lower temperature of these fluids can significantly reduce the chilling/freezing time.

For sous vide, an alternative to blast chilling is the use of *immersion chilling*. Sealed bags of food are immersed in a tank containing a mixture of water and ice. The water is circulated through the tank to give conditions of forced convection. This gives very rapid chilling for the individual pouches of food used in sous vide.

Mobile racks and carts

One of the most common activities in the kitchen is the movement of food from one place to another. In most cases this move-

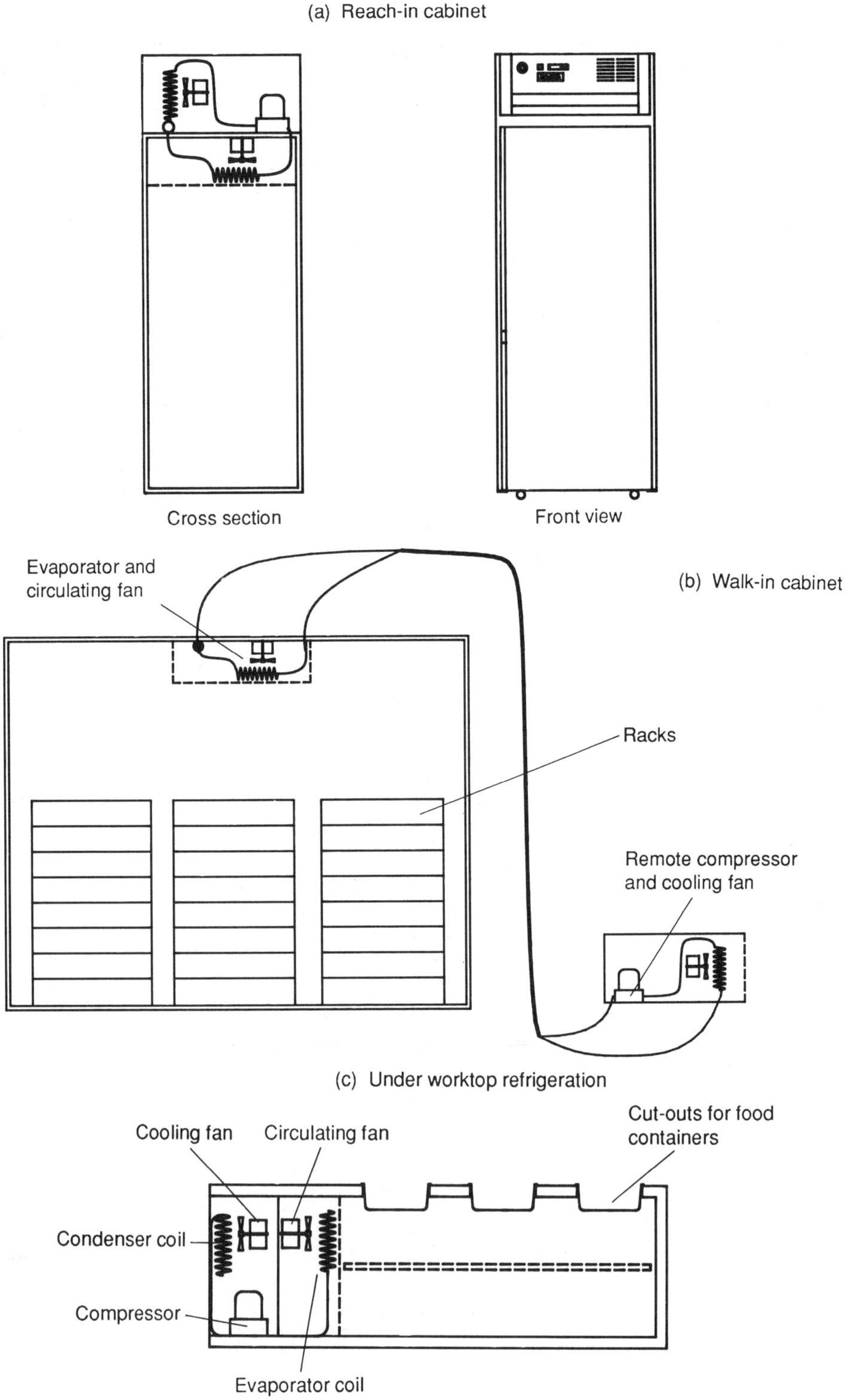

(a) Reach-in cabinet

Cross section

Front view

Evaporator and
circulating fan

(b) Walk-in cabinet

Racks

Remote compressor
and cooling fan

(c) Under worktop refrigeration

Cut-outs for food
containers

Cooling fan   Circulating fan

Condenser coil

Compressor

Evaporator coil

Figure 8.30 *Refrigeration equipment*

ment involves a person carrying that food. Use should be made of trolleys and racks and standardized containers, which can be used to move more efficiently.

Large convection ovens, steamers, blast freezers, blast chillers and combination ovens use trolleys for loading and unloading.

In many kitchens, mobile bins are used to hold bulk ingredients such as flour and sugar. These lidded, rectangular bins can be stored under a preparation table.

Service and holding equipment

Service and holding equipment may be utilized either in the kitchen where they function as the pick-up station for waiting staff, or in the restaurant where they are used in self-service, self-help and buffet arrangements.

In the kitchen, a service line consists of a combination of hot cupboards, bains-marie, plate warmers, ambient cupboards, refrigerated cupboards and cold-wells. The units

often have an overshelf and warming lamps over the heated section. They may also have a tray slide on the front of the unit.

In the restaurant, similar units are used to those in the kitchen but the units are often customized, with a high level of decorative finish to make them attractive and to act as a food merchandiser. They are also fitted with a glass 'sneeze guard' and shelves supporting heating lamps.

The units may be connected together in the form of a suite, including ambient sections with display cabinets, beverage sections, tray holders, cashier units and cutlery stands. In some situations, mobile display units are used, so that the arrangement of buffets can be varied to suit each type of function.

Hot cupboards and bains-marie

Hot cupboards are used for holding crockery, service dishes and prepared food. Because of

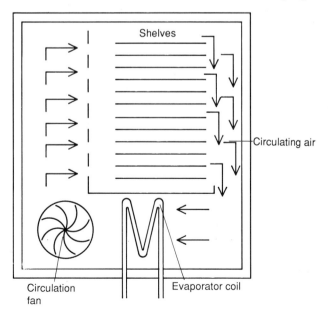

Figure 8.31 *Blast chillers and freezers*

the trend towards small batch cooking, the volume of storage for hot food has diminished. These cupboards are heated by gas or electricity and utilize natural convection. Temperatures must be sufficient to maintain food safely but without too much drying out (63–75 °C). It is important that temperatures are uniform throughout the hot cupboard, without the presence of cool spots: this can pose a hygiene hazard. Hot cupboards may have solid heated tops (hotplates), or they may be combined with bains-marie. They may also be in the form of mobile heated trolleys, which can be use to transport food.

In food display cabinets, the hotplate may be made of stainless steel or, alternatively, it may be covered with decorative ceramic tiles or ceramic sheeting. Tiles retain heat well but the grouting can harbour bacteria.

The traditional bain-marie consists of an open bath of hot water, designed to hold pans of sauces, etc. at a safe temperature. However, nowadays the bain-marie is often designed to hold standard drop-in food containers. The development of modular container systems leads to great flexibility in the sizes of containers which can be placed in a standard cut-out in the top of the bain-marie (Figure 8.32). Bains-marie may be wet or dry. Wet bains-marie give a more uniform heating to the food containers, but where there are no convenient water supplies or where mobility is required, dry bains-marie are often preferred.

Refrigerated display units

These consist of countertop display units for salad bars, cold buffets and cold desserts, together with a refrigerated storage cupboard. The countertop may have a stainless steel cold well, or it may be covered with ceramic tiles. Alternatively, an ice bed might

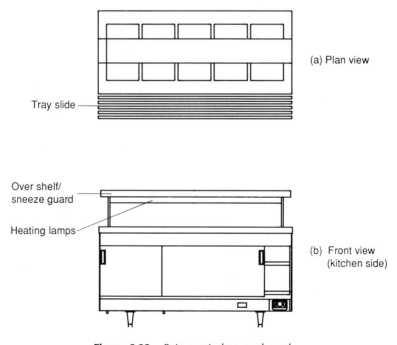

Figure 8.32   *Bain-marie hot cupboard*

be used, in which case the unit is fitted with a tank to collect melted ice.

Lighting of cold display units needs to be carefully planned, to make sure that radiation from lamps does not cause heating of the food. Cold fluorescent tube lamps are best for this purpose.

Refrigerated display cabinets mounted on plain cabinets or on bars are often used to both hold and display cold desserts and gâteaux.

Plate warmer

Warmers are used to hold and dispense heated plates. The plates are held in a heated cabinet and stacked on a spring loaded platform. The platform is designed so that the top plate on the stack is raised to the level of the top surface of the servery. The plate warmer units may be free-standing, mobile, or built into servery units. They are designed to work with a specific size and weight of plate or bowl.

Tray assembly systems

For operations such as hospitals, where a large number of plated meals must be assembled under hygienic conditions, use may be made of a conveyorized system. Work stations are located by the side of the conveyer for all items of food on the menu, together with crockery and cutlery (see Figure 8.33). They may be used for assembling meals which are ready for immediate consumption or for assembling cook-chill meals.

When assembling meals for immediate consumption, a method is needed to keep hot food hot, and to keep cold food cold. Hot food may be kept hot through the use of heated pellets held under the plate or by using insulated trays. Ambient and chilled foods may either be placed in separate trolley sections from the hot food or in separate compartments in the insulated trays.

When the foods have been assembled, they must be transported to the wards using trolleys. In the case of some types of cook-chill system, the trolley may also act as reheating equipment. This has the advantage that meals can be transported while still cold and reheated close to the ward at the latest possible time.

Beverage equipment

Water boilers and tea and coffee making

There are three main types of gas and electric water boilers (Figure 8.34):

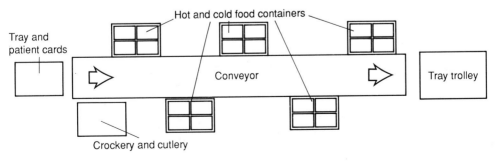

Figure 8.33 *Meal assembly system*

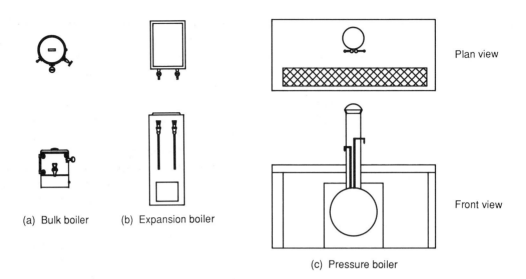

Plan view

Front view

(a) Bulk boiler   (b) Expansion boiler

(c) Pressure boiler

Figure 8.34   *Water boilers*

1   Bulk.
2   Expansion.
3   Pressure.

Operational demand determines the type selected. Prolonged service throughout the day and evening calls for boiling water at short notice at any time. Expansion and pressure boilers can provide this continuous flow, with pressure boilers providing the greatest volume. Pressure boilers can also provide steam for heating milk.

Counter sets (or café sets as they are often called) consisting of a water boiler with milk and coffee urns are available. However, many people now prefer independent filter coffee systems. These may be of the pour and serve type for situations where the demand is low or intermittent. Alternatively, coffee and tea may be made from concentrates.

For making coffee, independent filter coffee making machines are often preferred. These vary in capacity from the single jug, portable pour and serve machines up to large countertop filter coffee machines which are plumbed in. Specialist espresso coffee machines are now used in many catering operations. They can make individual cups of

fresh coffee and provide a supply of steam for heating milk.

Machines are also available for heating and dispensing frozen, canned or powdered concentrated tea and coffee. These machines are often used in self-help cafeteria systems. They are designed to dispense a measured volume directly into a china or disposable cup.

Cold beverage systems

Several types of cold beverage machines are available, which usually have both a holding and merchandising function. They may also be used in self-help cafeteria systems.

Still fruit juice machines

These machines consist of a plastic display tank holding the fruit juice (canned or frozen concentrates) which is continuously agitated and refrigerated. The juice is dispensed from a tap.

Carbonated beverage machines

These beverage machines are used to produce a range of carbonated drinks by mixing a concentrated flavoured syrup with refrigerated water and carbonating it with carbon dioxide. Ice machines are often built into or located adjacent to these machines.

Milk machines

A refrigerated cabinet is used to hold bulk packs of milk. A plastic spout fastened to the bulk pack passes through the dispensing tap on the machine. In this way, the milk does not come into contact with either the cabinet or the tap ensuring a high standard of hygiene.

Ice making machines

Ice making machines may either be countertop or floor standing. Prepared ice, which may be in the form of various sized cubes, flakes or crushed ice, is held in a bin.

Ice cream machines

Soft ice cream and frozen yogurt machines are available in a range of sizes, with capacities from 5 to 30 litres. Mixes are available which are poured into the machine where they are frozen and aerated simultaneously inside a cylindrical drum. *Milk shake machines* are similar to the above.

Vending equipment

Self-help equipment for use in cafeterias has been discussed above. This section covers coin operated vending machines, which are now commonly used to provide food and drinks at remote sites and at all hours of the day and night. These may be hot drink machines, cold drink machines, ambient snack machines, or chilled food machines. There have been great improvements in coin mechanisms leading to greater reliability and the ability to give change.

Hot drink machines may use powdered ingredients or fresh brew systems. Powder machines have separate containers for each type of drink. They are portioned into a mixing bowl which is provided with the required volume of hot water. The mixed drink then goes to the cup station. Machines using ground coffee and leaf tea are also available.

Cold drink machines may dispense cans of cold drinks. Alternatively, they may produce the drink from a concentrated syrup, refrigerated water and carbon dioxide.

Ambient snack machines dispense packaged snack foods such as crisps, nuts and confectionery. The cabinet provides two functions: a display of the products on sale; and a mechanism for dispensing the chosen product, using a peg or spiral coil mechanism.

The same functions are required for chilled-food vending machines. The meals must be held at a safe refrigerated temperature (related to the shelf life of the product). The machine must have an interlock to take the machine out of service, should the temperature rise to an unacceptably high temperature. Chilled meal vending is often accompanied by a vending machine for reheating the food.

One new development is the use of cashless vending system in the form of plastic cards and card readers. The plastic cards can be charged with the equivalent of an amount of cash and recharged with cash at machines located close to the vending machine. Every time a product is dispensed from the vending machine, the cash value on the card is debited by the appropriate amount. The same cards can be used in cash registers as part of an industrial, college or school catering operation.

Tutorial topic

Collect literature from a number of equipment manufacturers on one type of appliance.

Analyse this literature in terms of the factors covered in Chapter 7.

Identify any references to *specifications*.

Estimate the capacity of each appliance, using the methods described in Chapter 7.

References and further reading

Milson A. and Kirk D. (1980). *Principles of Design and Operation of Catering Equipment*. Chichester: Ellis Horwood.

Modlin R. A. (1989). *Commercial Kitchens*. Arlington, Virginia: American Gas Association.

Pine R. (1989). *Catering Equipment Management*. London: Hutchinson.

Walstrom J. (1989). Dishwashing Equipment. In *Catering Equipment Management* (Pine R., ed.).

9
Kitchen planning

A kitchen plan or layout should be determined by catering policy, starting with:

- The menu as the factor which dictates what items should be produced.
- The quantity of production and the method of production (see Chapters 3 and 4).

Chapter 3, which covers menus, indicates that the menu is 'marketing in action' and a guide to meal merchandising. The menu is also the blueprint of a catering operation and may be accepted as the starting point when designing kitchens and selecting appliances. However, there are many constraints which make the kitchen planning process complex. These constraints include:

- Availability of capital finance.
- Availability of space.
- Availability of staff.
- Skill levels of staff.
- Restrictions on building services.

In determining kitchen layout (as well as organizing subsequent work within it) certain fundamental intentions remain constant, whatever the operation. It is possible that traditional kitchen organization along sectional or partie lines may be compatible with achievement of the fundamental aims, but it is unwise to start with such an assumption. Kitchen planning must not be obscured by 'traditional' thinking and when undertaking it, preconceived notions should give way to a logical approach. Principles applicable in designing any production or assembly plant should be applied to kitchens.

Equally, care should be taken when attempting to copy some new venture or system which appears to work elsewhere. We have seen in Chapter 2 that a successful system is much more than just a collection of parts, but is a totality. Often the mistake is made of copying the kitchen layout and equipment specifications from an existing operation, in the hope that this will recreate the success: this usually does not work.

Catering intentions

Basic catering intentions might be summarized as:

- Receiving a variety of commodities.
- Partial or complete preparation followed by cooking, reheating, portioning and other dispensing methods.
- Minimizing the distances moved by materials, equipment and people and the elimination of risks of cross-contamination.
- Regulating the food supply in meal form within limitations of economy, time, locality and quantity but so that food and service is acceptable, attractive and hygienic.

- Providing the flexibility to match the demand of consumers.
- Minimizing space requirements.
- Providing a satisfactory working environment.
- Complying with legal requirements of both the building and the catering process.

The conceptual plan

All aspects of food service planning hinge on the above considerations. The planner must be careful not to introduce too much detail at an early stage in the planning process, which might obscure these basic issues. The process should start with a *conceptual plan*, which provides an overview of the way in which the catering system will operate, as discussed in Chapter 2.

The conceptual plan begins with the marketing and merchandising policy decisions concerning:

- The customer and the customer's specific needs in terms of time of day, acceptable price and food requirements.
- The menu – style, content and communication to the customer.
- The service style – how the food is to be delivered to the customer.
- The relationship between production and service, as discussed in Chapter 4.

Continuing cost inflation affects every industry. Catering involving labour, food and fuel is vulnerable to price escalation. Coupled with this, shortage of skilled staff and higher rates and rentals, particularly in city centre locations, spur the caterer to seek new answers to production problems. Trends stemming from today's economic problems include:

- Greater mechanization.

- Simplified operations.
- Increased use of convenience foods.
- Use of new commodities.
- Development of new cooking appliances and methods.
- Reduced size of food production (kitchen) areas.
- Use of mechanical handling equipment, such as conveyors.
- Use of central kitchens supplying food to a number of service points.
- Use of computerized controls on equipment.

Luxury hotels and restaurants may appear to be least affected by these considerations; but even at this level there are adaptations in approach to kitchen planning designed to optimize the utilization of higher paid and scarcer staff and in the increased exploitation of pre-prepared commodities. Coffee shops, speciality restaurants, self-carving and self-help buffets are some manifestations of change. This is reflected in kitchen plans which involve fewer staff and more pre-prepared commodities, even at the highest level; in other areas of the industries these principles are long established.

As was discussed in Chapter 2, old style relationships between production and service have, in some cases, been replaced by alternative systems involving central kitchens and the use of cook-freeze or cook-chill. Industrial and institutional caterers seek to reduce meal production costs by judicious use of modern systems, equipment commodities and methods. These areas have also been greatly affected by the trend towards lighter meals, together with more snacks and salads. The constant endeavour is to smooth out the peaks of production during meal times each day, and to minimize staffing requirements for unsociable hours – evenings, nights and weekends.

Food purchasing policy also affects kitchen planning, because of its impact on storage and preparation areas. The increased use of pre-prepared foods in the kitchen has considerably reduced the need for preparation areas within the kitchen. On the other hand, the increased use of frozen and refrigerated foods has increased the need for refrigerated storage.

The influence of marketing and merchandising

Greater emphasis on marketing and merchandising in all sectors of the catering industry is reflected in:

- Selling prices based less on meal production costs and more on value to customers of the total food service offered.
- Greater use of point-of-sale promotional material.
- Development of specialities either of dishes or forms of service giving character to an establishment.

Present trends in kitchen layout seem destined to lead to closer contact between actual points of food service and customers. This is seen in a number of ways, such as the greater involvement of customers in the service (and even cooking activities) and an increase in the exploitation of the 'theatrical' nature of cooking. These factors have an effect both on the type of equipment used and on the layout of facilities. Once holding and cooking equipment move into 'front-of-house' areas, much more thought needs to be given to the aesthetics of their design and of their effect on the environment.

The other major influence on marketing of the catering operation is the effect of location. It is beyond the scope of this book to discuss factors influencing the location of the restaurant, which is the chief determinant of the location of the kitchen. The exception to this may be where a central kitchen, or commissary, is used to produce and supply foods to a number of catering outlets. Here, the decision about location of the central kitchen is determined by the pattern of distribution — the distance moved by delivery vehicles and the physical (geographical) relationship of the various end kitchens (Dilworth, 1989).

Information required

Before beginning kitchen planning, answers to various questions are needed, such as:

- What type of meal will be offered?
- How many persons will be served?
- When will these meals be required?
- How many sittings are there to be for each meal, or in an all-day service, how long will each person be seated?
- What will be the extent of tea, coffee and food service for other areas in addition to the restaurant?
- Is allowance to be made for special functions?
- What area of floor space is available?
- What is the position of windows, ventilation, drainage, water supply?
- Are there any constraints on electricity, gas and other services?
- What type of service is proposed — self-service, cafeteria, waiter or waitress service?

This information can be used to determine the methods of production and service, the quantities of food production required (average and peak), the processing stages, the timing of these stages and the equipment needs.

The planning team

In the detailed planning of catering areas, initial planning should not be the concern of one person. It normally involves a *planning team*, made up as indicated in Figure 9.1. This represents a full team for a large project. In general terms the architect would 'manage' the project, although now quite frequently the catering consultant takes this role. The catering consultant together with representatives of the catering organization would develop the conceptual and operational plans, including important factors such as hygiene. The interior designer, together with representatives of the catering organization would develop the theme and detailed plan for the restaurant.

The architect would cover detailed building work, compliance with building codes, fire codes etc. and coordination with the construction company. The mechanical and electrical consultants would handle planning of the building services – ventilation, water, drainage, gas, steam (if applicable) and electricity.

The importance of teamwork in the planning process becomes evident, when viewed in terms of the discussion in Chapter 2 about the nature of a system and its parts. All members of the planning team need to be fully briefed about the plan, as it develops, to give a unity of design and to ensure that all of the parts work together.

Despite managerial representation on planning teams, planners may still neglect adequately to consult the catering supervisor or chef in regard to this and other aspects of kitchen design. This creates two problems. In the first place the detailed day-to-day operation of the kitchen may be neglected by the planning team; this is unfortunate because a plan, no matter how pleasing aesthetically, must function as a dynamic entity. Second, catering supervisors and chefs who are not adequately consultant may have no commitment to the success of the newly planned kitchen.

Area required and location of the kitchen

While there are no hard and fast rules for determining the floor area required to produce and serve food for a specified number of customers, figures are available giving typical areas. These figures can be used as a rough guideline and to determine if special measures are required because of too much or too little space.

Kitchens are sometimes reduced in size in order to provide more space and increase seating in the restaurant. While this is sensible from a revenue generation point of view, this reduction does not necessarily increase the trading capacity of restaurants. This is because the kitchen, as much as the dining room, can determine what numbers can be served during a service period. Reduction in kitchen size must, therefore, be planned to maintain (and even increase) productivity and still result in a satisfactory

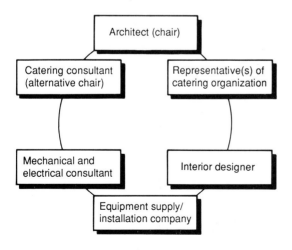

Figure 9.1 *The planning team*

workplace for employees. Cramped kitchens lead to delays and faults in service and these flaws may ultimately deter customers.

In spite of these important reservations, the trend over the last thirty years has been to reduce the size of the kitchen. This has been possible because of the factors shown in Figure 9.2.

These factors among others make the calculation of kitchen area difficult. Briefly stated, kitchen areas vary according to the type and number of meals provided and on the method of production. There is an economy of scale in that, as the number of patrons increase, so the kitchen area per patron decreases as does the ratio between kitchen area and restaurant area. Figure 9.3 gives traditional estimates of kitchen area requirements, but these can be reduced, using the techniques identified in Figure 9.2. These figures include storage, preparation, cooking and service areas, but do not include cafeteria serveries, staff facilities or offices. Within the kitchen space, the approximate breakdown into functions is shown in Figure 9.4, but with the same reservations as with the kitchen area.

Restaurant areas can be estimated in a rather more precise way, providing we know the maximum number of covers, the average seating time and the style of service (Lawson, 1979). The basic figures for seating areas are shown in Figure 9.5. To this must be added an allowance for service aisles, trolley or tray stacking areas, waiter/waitress stations, servery areas and queuing areas.

Location of the kitchen

The location of the kitchen within the building is critical from an operational point of view, but even in new buildings it is not given sufficient attention. In order to provide the logical flow from deliveries to food service discussed below, the relationship between deliveries, kitchen and restaurant is important. The kitchen requires good access for the delivery of food and for the removal of waste. These access points should be separated and well away from guest entrances and exits.

Ideally, there should be five different entrances to the kitchen:

1 Staff entrance to cloakroom.
2 Goods entrance to stores.
3 Garbage/refuse removal.
4 Waiting/service staff to restaurant.
5 Waiting/service staff from restaurant.

In practice, this complexity is often not possible and some compromise has to be made. An important aspect of entrances to a

---

- Increased use of pre-prepared foods.

- Increased availability of mechanical preparation equipment.

- Increased productivity of new types of catering equipment.

- Reduction in the size of menus.

- Changes in working practices within the kitchen.

Figure 9.2 *Factors leading to a reduced kitchen area requirement*

kitchen is that of security. The chef's or supervisor's office should have good visibility of as many of these entrances as possible.

Storerooms and kitchens should be located in a cool part of the building (facing north or north east) and with good natural daylight. Windows should be located so that they do not cause sun glare or solar gain.

The distance and ease of access between kitchen and dining areas(s) should be considered. Quality of food and speed of service depends, among other things, upon good communications and transport between these two areas. While the use of lifts and dumb waiters can overcome some of the problems of having kitchen and restaurant on different floors, these create operational problems and should be avoided if possible.

The work flow is necessarily complicated when one kitchen must service a number of food outlets in a building.

Hygienic design

In Chapter 6 the, importance of food hygiene and of the influence of kitchen design on this was discussed. From an ideal point of view, there would be a straight line flow from raw material to finished product, with no back-tracking. The dirty (precooking) activities would be separated from the clean (post-cooking) activities. This would include different staff or a change of uniforms. All materials and surfaces likely to come into contact with food would be easily cleaned, including the sides, behind and underneath equipment. Any spaces which cannot be cleaned would be sealed to prevent build-up of food and to eliminate insects and rodents. There would be no cracks, joints or screw heads on equipment and smooth curves would be used rather than internal right angle bends. The

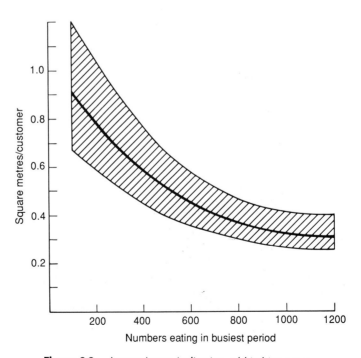

Figure 9.3   *Approximate indication of kitchen areas*

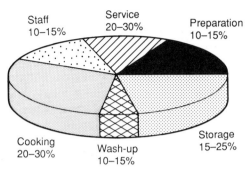

(a) Main areas as a percentage of total area

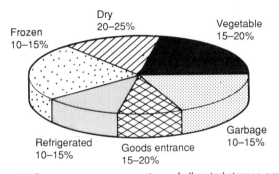

(b) Stores areas as a percentage of allocated storage area

Figure 9.4   *Allocation of areas within the kitchen*

Type of catering	Area required (square metres per cover)
School meals	0.8
Cafeterias	1.0
Fast-food	1.0
Family restaurants	1.2–1.5
Silver service	1.2–2.0

Note: These figures exclude aisles and service access, self-service areas and self-help (buffets, breakfast bars, salad bars etc.).

Figure 9.5   *Approximate indication of seating areas*

possibility of water back-siphoning would be prevented (ICMSF, 1988a).

The garbage removal area should be screened and be provided with a hard floor surface sloping to a drain. A water supply should be provided to allow washing out of containers.

Work and method study

A layout is based on good work flow from the receipt of raw materials at goods entry to the dishes finally brought to the servery for the guests. Also, the productivity of a kitchen is greatly increased if individual work areas are designed to minimize the movement of staff. Work and method study provides the catering planner with techniques which are invaluable to achieving good work flow and to the design of efficient work areas.

Work and method study techniques can be used to improve existing working methods or to plan new ones. They answer the basic questions of any production or service system:

- What is done?
- Why is it done?
- Where is it done?
- When is it done?
- How is it done?

Using these questions, it is possible to ascertain if each task is necessary or whether it can be eliminated or combined or whether the sequence can be changed or simplified.

One major aspect of work and method study is the use of recording techniques. Most of these techniques can be used to record the stages in an operation for materials, people and equipment. For example, flow process charts the flow of a product through the stages of transportation, operations, storage and delay. It is possible to take each item on a menu and produce a flow process chart (Figure 9.6).

Another important recording technique is the flow diagram. Here, lines are drawn on a plan of an area to show the direction and volume of movement of people and/or materials within the area. This provides a good visual indication of the volume of movement between points, but it also shows cross-flows (Figure 9.7). Where a large volume of movement is found between two areas or work centres, these areas should be located as close together as is possible. At the same time cross flows should be eliminated as far as is practicable.

Multiple activity charts are another useful work study technique. These charts record the relationship in time between events. Charts may be drawn for staff, materials (menu items) or equipment. A hypothetical chart for catering equipment is shown in Figure 9.8. These types of diagram are useful in rationalizing the equipment needs, in allocating staffing duties and similar resource issues.

Another aspect of work and method study is the design of work centres and the layout of individual work spaces. Techniques are available for recording the activities involved in carrying out any activity or process. A principle of design is that all required materials and equipment should be located within easy reach of employees. A knowledge of basic anthropometric data makes it easier to do this (Goldsmith, 1979).

Flow of work

The basic flow of work is shown in Figure 9.9. Intelligent disposition of preparation machinery, sinks and work benches may reduce the total daily 'kitchen mileage' covered by the food and cut down unnecessary 'travelling' by staff. Thus, a perfect kitchen from this point of view is one in which raw and cooked materials undergo minimum movement and only cover the same route once. There should be no back-tracking of food or staff to prevent the risk of bacteriological contamination of cooked food by raw food.

One of the first tasks in developing a layout is to identify the *work centres* which will exist in a kitchen. The nature of the work centres will vary according to the nature of the menu and production system. From a theoretical point of view, there are two types of production layouts:

1 Product layout: with this layout, each work centre is responsible for making a specific product; each work centre has its own equipment which may lead to some duplication. An example would be the layout of a fast food store.

2 Process layout: here each work centre performs a particular process; all materials which are required to undergo this process are transported to this centre. Examples would be the use of frying, baking or chilling areas in a layout.

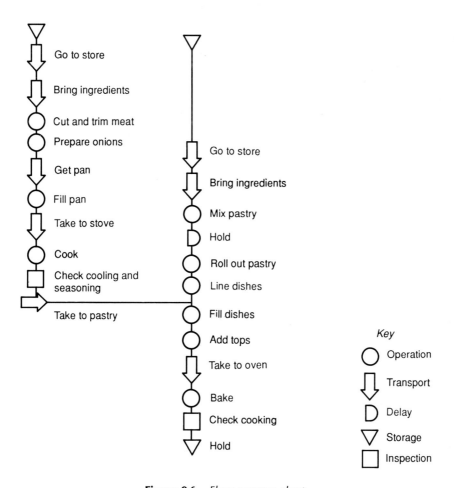

Figure 9.6 *Flow process chart*

Techniques are available for determining the correct relationship between work centres (Kirk, 1989a). These techniques are designed to:

- Identify all work centres.
- Identify the approximate size of a work centre, based on staff and equipment needs.
- Determine the relationship between these work centres.

A common way of doing this is to classify relationships between any two work centres as:

Very important relationship.
Important relationship.
Slightly related.
Non-related.
Undesirable for close relationship.

These relationships can be shown in the form of a chart, as shown in Figure 9.10. This information can then be used when organizing the relationships between work centres on the plan, as shown in Figure 9.11. When transposing this information to the plan, attention must be given to both the area of each work centre and the need for traffic lanes and work aisles. The information can be derived from flow process charts or from work study measurements of activity.

In practice, this type of exercise is often not required, because of the simplicity of relationships and because of the common practices in most kitchens. The difficulty of

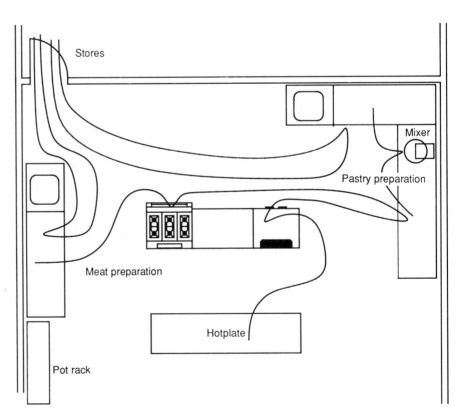

Stores

Mixer

Pastry preparation

Meat preparation

Hotplate

Pot rack

Figure 9.7 *Flow diagram*

kitchen planning is often to produce this logical flow within a particular building envelope. Layout becomes even more of a problem when the location of equipment is governed by existing constraints such as drainage and supporting pillars. The use of activity relationship charts is justified when planning large production kitchens, where there are multiple food outlets and when designing kitchens for a chain of restaurants.

In a traditional kitchen, the work centres were often located in separate rooms. Today this division is much less common, other than for activities such as dish-washing. Use is made of half height walls to physically divide an area but to retain visual and verbal communication. This in turn has led to the development of multi-function open plan preparation areas with the elimination of physical barriers.

Traffic lanes and work aisles

In order to ensure efficient flow through the kitchen, adequate and properly devised traffic lanes and work aisles are indispensable. A *traffic lane* represents the major route used by product as it passes through the process. It provides straight flow lines for the receipt, preparation, cooking and serving of product, together with the ancillary but important

Time	Range	Oven	Fryer	Mixer
9.00				
9.15				
9.30	▨			▨
9.45	▨			▨
10.00	▨			▨
10.15	▨			
10.30				
10.45		▨		
11.00		▨		
11.15		▨		
11.30		▨		
11.45				
12.00				
12.15				
12.30				

☐ Not in use   ▨ In use

Figure 9.8 *Multiple activity chart*

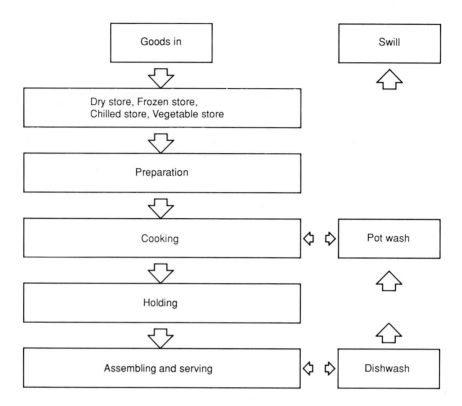

Figure 9.9   *Flow chart of kitchen activities*

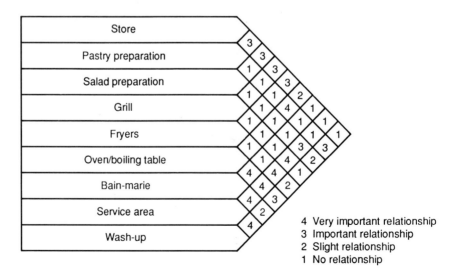

Figure 9.10   *Activity relationship chart*

tasks of waste removal, dish-washing and pot washing. Distances between key points such as goods entry, stores, preparation, cooking and servery should be as short as is practicable and compatible with the nature of traffic. For example, where the use of trolleys is envisaged, this information should be used when determining aisle widths.

Work aisles represent areas in the kitchen where staff carry out work. Ideally, the main traffic flow should avoid work aisles, which desirably should be at right angles to the main traffic routes.

The widths of traffic lanes and work aisles are governed by ergonomic factors. Typical values for the width of these spaces is given in Figure 9.12.

The basic layout of kitchens and work centres

Using the information provided so far in this chapter, it is now possible to carry out the development of the basic layout. This is normally drawn at a scale of 1:50, which means that 1 mm on the plan is equivalent to 50 mm in real life. For people who are unsure about the use of scales, graph paper with 1 mm divisions can be useful.

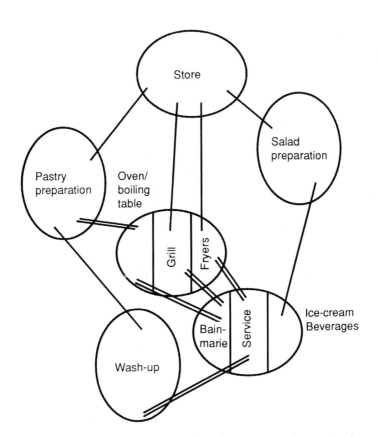

Figure 9.11   *Location of work centres based on activity relationship chart*

A number of additional techniques are useful at this stage. Plastic templates (drawn to a scale of 1:50) can be used to draw furniture, bathroom fittings, WCs and hand-basins. Cut-out templates representing the size of pieces of catering equipment are of value. Even this does not help some people, who find it difficult to relate a two-dimensional plan to what the three-dimensional outcome will be. Here, the use of scale models can help. Another helpful aid is for architects or catering consultants to produce three-dimensional drawings (isometric or perspective), which give a clearer indication of what the kitchen will look like.

Another useful technique is to use transparent overlays, which can show information such as food movement, staff movement, the layout of utilities (gas, water, electricity and drains) and so on. These are similar to the flow diagrams of Figure 9.7. The movement of staff and food can be ascertained through the use of flow process charts.

From the information given above on work spaces, traffic lanes and work aisles, it is possible to deduce some general layouts for work centres. Some examples are shown in Figure 9.13. Other possible arrangements can be worked out in a similar way.

When using the central location of equipment, either as a single line or as a parallel back-to-back arrangement, two layouts are possible. They are:

1   The *linear* or *(perpendicular) layout*.
2   The *transverse layout*, as shown in Figure 9.14.

The linear arrangement can give good flow of materials from the kitchen to the servery area. The transverse arrangement can segregate raw from cooked food effectively and reduce back-tracking, but it can act as a barrier to efficient flow through the kitchen.

600–800 mm	Space for person working at preparation table, sink or for countertop cooking.
1200–1400 mm	Space in front of equipment with drop down door and for tilting equipment.
750 mm	Minimum for work aisle.
1500 mm	Minimum for main traffic lane.
1000–1500 mm	Allows two persons to pass.
1500–1800 mm	Allows trolley to pass one person.
1500–1800 mm	Allows trolley to pass between two persons working back to back.
900 mm	Minimum clearance between equipment and work tables (preparation area located opposite equipment)
1000–1200 mm	Minimum in front of cooking equipment to which food is conveyed by trolley.
800–900 mm	Person with tray.

Figure 9.12   *Work aisles and traffic lanes*

When designing lines or suites of cooking equipment, another issue is where to locate the associated preparation area: the two possibilities are shown in Figure 9.15. The associated work area may be located by the side of the appliances or, alternatively, it may be located opposite. This can be effective from an ergonomic point of view, except that staff must rotate through 180 degrees in moving from preparation area to cooking equipment.

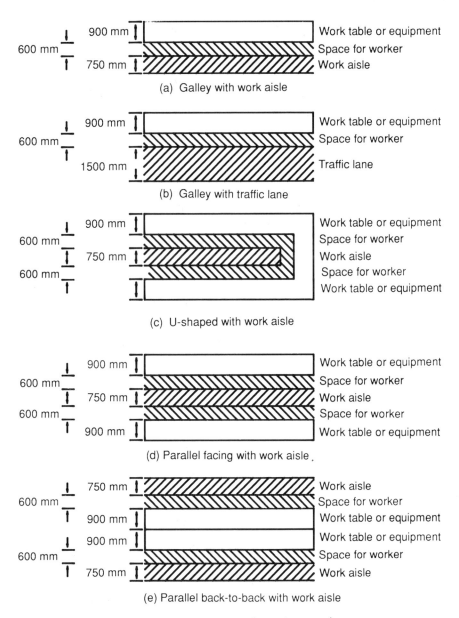

Figure 9.13 *Space requirements for various work centres*

It also means that they cannot keep an eye on food being cooked when doing preparation work. The arrangement becomes unsatisfactory when the gap between the two also acts as an aisle. The most convenient location for preparation space is usually by the side of the appliances, since this minimizes movement and reduces the distances over which hot foods must be carried. It also reduces the area of the work centre. One disadvantage of this arrangement is that it often increases the area of ventilation

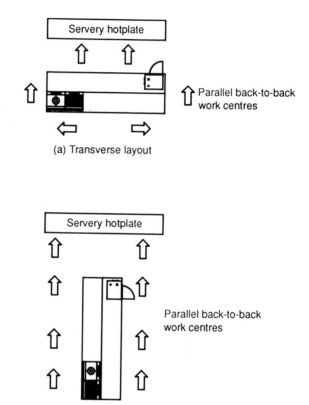

Figure 9.14   *Transverse and perpendicular central islands*

Tutorial topic

Estimate the space requirements for the following layouts:

1   A parallel back-to-back kitchen which has preparation tables facing both banks of equipment, and with a work aisle.

2   As 1 above, but with traffic lanes in place of the work aisles.

canopy which has to be provided. It also increases the length of the cooking line. A modification of this is to have preparation tables at right angles to the cooking equipment.

Passages and ancillary offices and facilities

Before considering factors applying within the kitchen itself it should be noted that passages to and from the kitchen must be unobstructed, both for the entry of goods, the exit of containers, the removal of waste and the movement of staff. Changing rooms, staff toilets, hand-washing facilities, supervisor's/chef's office, kitchen porter facilities and possibly a staff dining room all have to be remembered for inclusion at the planning stage.

Good receiving facilities

External space is needed for the parking of delivery vans. At the goods entry point for the larger kitchen, sufficient space is required for receiving and checking goods, to accommodate a weighing machine, checking table, stand-up desk and space for delivered goods prior to storage. Space may also be required for parking hand trucks and/or trolleys. Smaller kitchens will not require all of these facilities.

In some circumstances, a raised delivery platform is of value to allow foods to be moved on trolleys directly from a delivery vehicle into the goods reception area.

Space must also be provided for the storage of refuse and waste. Ideally, a separate exit should be used for this from the one which is used for goods delivery. Often paladins, or similar swill containers, are used outside the kitchen to hold food waste. If

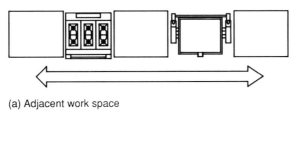

(a) Adjacent work space

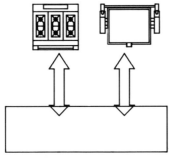

(b) Opposite work space

Figure 9.15 *Cooking lines and associated preparation areas*

paladins are kept in an outside yard, a provision is required for washing both the containers and the floor. Often paper and plastic waste is compacted to reduce its volume.

Storage

Coupled with the aim of smooth flow from goods entry to dishing at the servery is the provision of storage space appropriate to a kitchen's size. The nature of supplies (types, quantities, delivery frequency, delivery containers, storage containers) will have been determined as a part of the food policy. Suitable storage capacity and conditions must be provided for all the various types of raw materials including dry goods, fruit, vegetables, raw meat, poultry and fish, cooked meats, dairy produce and frozen foods. Obviously, finishing kitchens (as a part of cook-freeze and cook-chill operations) have very specific requirements.

As is the case with kitchen area, recommendations of the correct storage area for each type of raw material is fraught with difficulty. The relative amounts of dry storage, fruit and vegetable storage and refrigerated storage depends so much on the individual food policy and on the local delivery situation. Many of the recommendations are based on the practice of twenty or thirty years ago, but the patterns of food delivery and availability of processed and refrigerated foods has changed considerably. Also, there is now a move to reduce stock levels, in order to minimize inventory costs.

Some important trends are:

- The increased use of frozen foods both raw materials (fish, meat, poultry and vegetables) and partially or fully prepared foods (confectionery and baked goods, ready cooked individual items and completely cooked meals).

- The increased use of chilled foods — particularly deserts, gâteaux and ready meals.

- Increased dry store provision for dehydrated, canned and ready-mixed products, such as soups, sauces, pastry mixes and pie fillings.

- A corresponding decrease in the amount of vegetable and fruit storage, with the exception of salad items, which are a growing part of most menus.

- A decrease in the storage capacity of raw meats and fish and a change from large joints to pre-portioned cuts.

- The use of mobile modular racking systems in stores to allow adaptability and ease of cleaning.

Typical recommendations for food storage varies between 15 and 25 per cent of the kitchen area. However, where possible, the calculation of store volume based on turnover, delivery intervals and package sizes gives a more accurate estimate of storage capacity.

In some situations there is one main store from which all goods are issued to the kitchen(s). In other situations goods may be delivered directly to the kitchen or department and departments may have their own day stores. A number of points may be made: one is that the use of a central store, which issues goods to departments greatly improves control over stores; however, the use of day stores at a departmental level can greatly reduce staff movement and increase food hygiene. These two are not mutually incompatible, but problems arise when departments build up their own stores of goods because it makes stock control and production planning more difficult. In general, the holding of stock beyond that required for immediate (daily) use should be discouraged.

Vegetable storage

The ideal storage temperature for most vegetables is 9 to 12 °C and the room should be ventilated. However, many salad items keep better under refrigerated storage. Where dirty vegetables are used, the vegetable store should be isolated from other areas of food storage. It should be located close to both the delivery bay and to the vegetable preparation area of the kitchen, so that the vegetables do not have to pass through other areas.

A danger in vegetable storage is deterioration through close packing in warm unventilated corners. Raised platform accommodation, preferably slated metal, should suffice for storing sacks of potatoes and other root vegetables. Open mesh racks should also be provided for other vegetables so that they are kept cool and exposed to the circulating air.

Dry storage

A dry store is used to accommodate grocery items such as canned and packaged goods. Its temperature should be 9 to 10 °C achieved either by natural ventilation or by air conditioning in summer and it should be located close to the delivery bay.

In many kitchens the dry store takes up approximately one-quarter of the total stores volume. Dry stores are normally walk-in and utilize metal racking systems for storage; adjustable shelves allow maximum space utilization. Mobile stainless steel shelving units are flexible and hygienic. Where trolleys are to be used, this must be allowed for when calculating store volume.

Metal or plastic storage bins for flour, sugar, dried cereals or other items stored in bulk should be mounted on wheels or castors for easy movement to preparation areas and for ease of cleaning.

The store should be equipped with weighing machines of an appropriate capacity to suit the weight of goods issued. A desk and 'office' area may also be required for store-keeping records.

Dry stores should be proofed against vermin of all kinds and birds. Materials which are resistant to the gnawing of rodents should be selected where possible. The storeroom should be lockable and well ventilated.

Refrigerated storage

Because changes in catering operations style are rapid and capable of many permutations, it is impracticable to give precise guidance about how much refrigerated storage a kitchen requires. At one extreme, a system may be entirely dependent upon frozen or chilled foods, at the other end of the scale a kitchen may use no frozen foods and a restricted amount of chilled foods. Most kitchens lie somewhere between these two extremes.

Small kitchens may have just one cold room (at 5 °C) for all chilled food storage together with a frozen food cabinet. Larger establishments require separate chilled stores for raw meat, raw fish, and high risk products (dairy and cooked meats). The advantage of this is that, in addition to reducing the risk of cross-contamination, ideal storage temperatures and humidities can be provided to suit each commodity. For example, although raw meat and raw fish require similar temperatures (−1 to +1°C), fish requires a higher humidity than meat. Additionally, separating items can reduce flavour transfer.

The choice between reach-in and walk-in refrigeration should be based on storage capacity. For a small operation single or double door reach-in cabinets provide the best solution. They also provide the easiest separation of commodity types as outlined above. Small walk-in cabinets are inefficient as the ratio of access volume to storage volume is high. At best, only about half of the storage capacity of a walk-in refrigerator is useful.

However, for a large operation, the duplication of a large number of reach-in cabinets is costly and inefficient of both space and energy and walk-in cabinets become the best solution. As a rule-of-thumb, walk-in stores become feasible above 300 to 400 meals.

Other storage areas

Storage must also be provided for a number of other materials. For example, most kitchens carry a wide range of detergents and cleaning materials, which must be stored away from food materials.

Storage is required for all items of crockery, tableware and cutlery and for serving dishes, serving flats and so on. These are normally stored close to both the dish-wash area and the service and restaurant areas. Another increasing important store requirement is for disposable paper and plastic plates, plastic cutlery, aluminium foil and disposable plastic containers.

Preparation areas

Vegetable preparation area

The requirements of a vegetable preparation area depends upon the volume of vegetables and salads served and on the nature of the purchased commodity. For small operations and/or where large volumes of pre-prepared vegetables are used, a sink and preparation table will suffice, together with some way of

handling waste and trimmings; this may be a bin, or the work centre may incorporate a waste disposal machine. An electrically-operated potato-peeling machine is usually justified. In addition, many kitchens now have vegetable preparation machines.

The vegetable preparation area should be located close to cooking equipment used for vegetables – boiling tables, tilting kettles and steamers.

Preparation of fish, meat and poultry

Few kitchens now have full butchery departments which can handle sides of beef, etc. Much of the meat, fish and poultry requirement is purchased in portion-controlled cuts. Breaded, ready-to-fry portions can further reduce preparation time and space. As a minimum, a sink and preparation table is required. Access to preparation equipment such as a mincer attachment on a mixer and a bowl chopper is useful. In larger kitchens, the meat preparation area may have its own equipment (from a hygiene point of view, this is better) and it may have other specialized equipment such as sausage fillers and patty moulders, depending on the menu. A marble slab is often used for fish preparation.

Pastry and bakery preparation areas

In the smallest kitchen, and where much use is made of ready-to-bake and ready-to-serve pastry products, pastry and bakery areas may consist of preparation tables, a small mixing machine and access to oven space. Larger kitchens may have their own bakery or convection ovens located in this area. Where large amounts of pastry are being prepared, electrically-operated pastry rollers can be of value, as can die stamping machines to produce pie bases. A marble slab is often required where there is a lot of hand pastry work.

If bread or other dough-based products are to be made, a proving oven will be required and possibly other specialized equipment for portioning and moulding loaves and rolls.

Cooking areas

An analysis of the menu should reveal the type and capacity of cooking equipment required (see Chapter 4). This analysis should be summarized according to the different cooking processes as follows:

- Roasting and baking.
- Boiling.
- Grilling and toasting.
- Steaming.

- Deep frying.
- Shallow and griddle frying
- Making of soups, stews and stocks.
- Plate and food holding in hot cupboards, bains-marie and refrigerated storage.
- Beverage making.
- Hot water for culinary purposes.

An analysis of the menu should provide information about the requirements for each of the above cooking methods, both the average and peak production requirement (kg/hour or litres/hour). A chart might be used, such as that shown in Figure 9.16. The exact appearance of this chart will depend upon the type of menu. A fixed menu will relate to specific dishes, while a cyclic menu will have main menu categories.

Having established these basic cooking methods and food quantities, this can be translated into types and sizes of equipment, using the principles established in Chapters 7 and 8. Cooking and serving high-quality

Menu: Lunch										
Menu item	Portion size (kg/litres)	Cooking time (hours)	Number of portions	Quantity (kg/litres)	Production method* 1, 2 or 3	Cooking method	Method 3 average production capacity*†		Method 1 peak service capacity	Appliance
							Batches	Capacity		
Beef curry	0.1 kg	2	150	15 kg	3	Braising/ boiling	1	15 kg		Bratt pan
Apple pies	0.15 kg	1	80	12 kg	3	Baking	2	6 kg		Convection oven
Chipped potatoes	0.1 kg	0.15	150	15 kg	2	Frying			8 kg/hr	Deep fat fryer
									15 l/hr	Water boiler
Tea	0.31		120	36 l	2	Boiling				
etc.										

Notes:

* Production methods:
1 to demand   Capacity based on peak service rate.
2 to order   Capacity based on peak service rate.
3 to schedule Capacity based on average production rate.

† Average production rate = quantity/number of batches

Figure 9.16 *Cooking capacity assessment*

food in large quantities, and to a strict time schedule, is an exacting task, even under the most favourable conditions. By the correct choice of cooking equipment, purely physical strain can be eased. Moreover, the favourable environment of an adequately equipped kitchen leaves greater scope for exercising skill, maintaining quality and controlling costs. In making decisions about the numbers of appliances to be used, multiple activity charts (Figure 9.8) can be used to determine if there is any possibility of sharing equipment between menu items.

Economical cooking depends upon using appliances designed for a specific purpose, and deployed to meet average conditions. In a new kitchen it is important to guard against putting in too much equipment. The ideal is to prepare, cook and serve food with the minimum of appliances in active use. The effect of this 'menu justification' policy is to keep down capital outlay as well as to minimize running costs.

Modern, high-capacity catering equipment is expensive but, provided that it is properly planned into the kitchen, its cost can be justified. There is a danger that a kitchen will be designed on conventional lines, with large amounts of conventional equipment, to which is then added some of the newer high throughput equipment. This is an expensive solution, both in terms of capital and space.

Decisions need to be made about whether to locate all cooking equipment in a central line or island, or whether to locate equipment in work centres. In many situations a hybrid of the two provides the best arrangement. Thought must also be given to equipment disposition (see Chapter 7), and to the degree of mobility in the kitchen. At its most basic level, some mobile equipment, such as mixers and food processors, may be mounted on castors to enable them to be shared between work centres. This is useful when a work centre cannot fully justify its own machine. On a more sophisticated level, some kitchens

are now planned so that all equipment is mobile; this allows disconnection and movement of equipment to simplify cleaning procedures. It also allows rearrangement of equipment to suit a particular menu or production plan.

Location of equipment is often strongly influenced by the building and its services. While in theory it is possible to use any piece of equipment anywhere in a building, in practice some locations are practically impossible (or very expensive) because of the need to lay new drains, to provide long ventilation ducts or bring in new energy services. For this reason, early discussion with the mechanical and electrical consultant is essential. However, it is important that the kitchen planning process is not over-influenced by these capital cost considerations. The effect of location on the efficiency of the kitchen during its life is equally important and the catering consultant and representatives of the catering company need to be fully aware of this cost compromise.

Food service areas

There are three basic methods of serving food, but with a large number of variations possible. These three methods are:

1 Waiter/waitress service.
2 Self-service/self-help.
3 Counter service.

Waiter/waitress service

With waiter/waitress service, it is common practice to provide a service line or hotplate, which acts as the link between the kitchen and waiting staff. The service line would have hot, chilled and ambient food storage, together with storage of hot and cold tableware, service flats and service dishes. It also may have an overshelf (possibly with heating lamps mounted under this) and a tray slide on the front, on which waiting staff can assemble their order (Figure 9.17). In addition to the hotplate area, there would also be a pantry or stillroom area where waiting staff can prepare beverages, toast and similar items.

Self-service

A number of arrangements of self-service areas are possible, starting with the simple straight-line counter (Figure 9.18(a)). Once the number of customers exceeds the customer rate of a straight line servery, which is six to nine customers per minute (Lawson, 1979), a number of possibilities exist. One is

to create a bypass area, to allow customers to pass around slow activities, such as plating the main entrée items.

Another alternative is to duplicate a part or all of the servery. For example, a sandwich, snack or beverage area can be taken out of the main servery and located in a second cafeteria line (Figure 9.18(b)). This eases the situation where there is a large demand for a simple meal of a sandwich/snack and beverage. Where there are large demands for full meals, the whole line may be duplicated using parallel lines, convergent lines (Figure 9.18(c)) and divergent lines (Figure 9.18(d)). With all of these, one line can be closed during slack periods.

In order to break up the queue and to direct people straight to their choice of food a number of alternatives have been used. The *echelon* servery is similar to a straight-line counter, but the queue is disrupted by setting the servery units at an angle (Figure 9.18(e)). Even greater disruption of the queue is

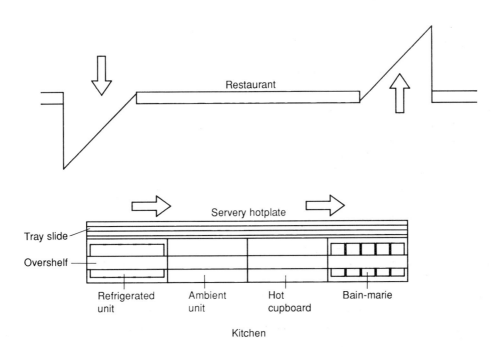

Figure 9.17 *Waiter/waitress servery hotplate*

achieved using the *free-flow* or *scramble* system (Figure 9.18(f)). With both the echelon and free-flow systems, some of the servery counters may utilize self-help. For example, salad bars are now very popular.

Counter service

One type of counter service, which may be incorporated into self-service lines or as an independent unit is the call order or back-bar servery. Typically, this consists of two paral-

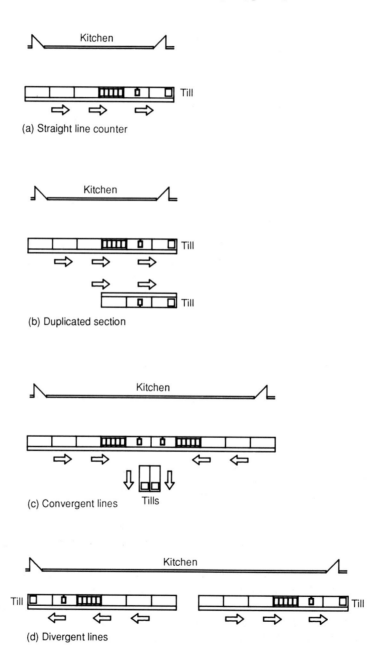

(a) Straight line counter

(b) Duplicated section

(c) Convergent lines   Tills

(d) Divergent lines

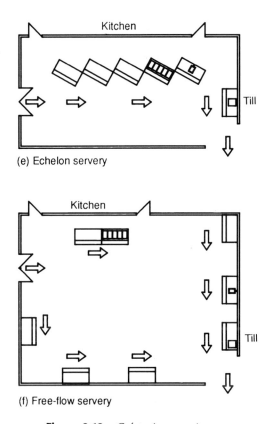

Figure 9.18 *Cafeteria serveries*

lel counters, one against a wall and holding preparation and cooking equipment and the other, against which the customer queues, holding beverages and the cash register.

The service counter in many fast-food operations is rather different in concept to traditional servery lines. While there are a number of possible arrangements, the two most common types are shown in Figure 9.20. One uses multiple queues and duplicated till points, each of which is independent. The other uses a single queue leading to one ordering cash point. The staff member at this point communicates details of the order to preparation staff (using voice or computer systems). The customer picks up the order as he/she moves down the counter.

Another interesting service development, which utilizes a combination of fast-food and free-flow concepts is the *food court* (Figure 9.21). This may be operated as a collection of fast-food units all sharing a common seating area. This allows a family to make a wide range of selections.

Dishwashing areas

The design of a dishwasher area depends upon the number of crockery and cutlery items to be washed within a period of time. For very small operations, an undercounter dishwasher together with associated tables may suffice, such as the barwashing system shown in Figure 9.22. Beyond this scale, a pass-through dishwasing machine, with a dirty and clean area can be used. This may be

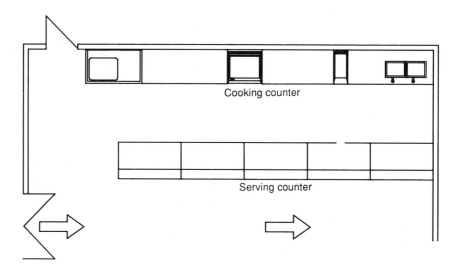

Figure 9.19 *Back-bar counter*

configured as a straight line (Figure 9.23) or a corner (Figure 9.24) arrangement.

Rack machines and flight machines can handle very large volumes of dirty dishes, but much greater thought needs to be given to the dirties area in particular. One possibility is to use a tray stripping area at right angles to the dishwasher feed, as shown in Figure 9.25. The stripping table often has a shelf over it to take empty racks which are filled with plates, cups and cutlery as they are removed from the trays.

Another possibility is to use a continuous conveyor system in conjunction with flight dishwashers, as shown in Figure 9.26.

Ventilation

Staff and kitchen efficiency are affected by heating and ventilation and thus productivity may be hampered or enhanced. Kitchen ventilation must meet three requirements:

1   Maintenance of comfortable working conditions.
2   Prevention of condensation.
3   Confining cooking smells to the kitchen.

Additionally, where high risk foods are being handled (such as in cook-chill systems) temperature control may be required to control microbiological growth. In these situations, an environmental temperature of 10 °C or less is recommended.

We can differentiate between two types of ventilation: *background*; and *localized*. Background ventilation relates to the movement of air in the total kitchen. It is normally provided using extractor fans together with vents allowing air to enter the kitchen. Typically, in a kitchen, twenty to thirty air changes per hour are required. However, some of this will be provided by the localized ventilation.

Localized ventilation may be provided in several ways but, in a kitchen, the most common method is to use a canopy. The canopy may be mounted on a wall or suspended from the ceiling. Localized canopies may be provided over individual appliances, such as dishwashers, or large canopies may be used over banks or lines of equipment. Typically, localized canopies extract air at the rate of 0.3 to 0.45 cubic metre per second.

Whatever the location of a canopy, its edge should project beyond the cooking

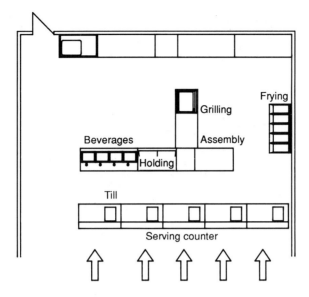

(a) Duplicate till points

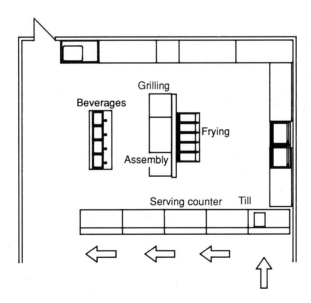

(b) Single till point

Figure 9.20 *Fast-food counters*

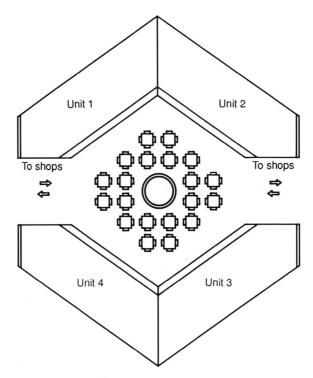

Figure 9.21   *Food court*

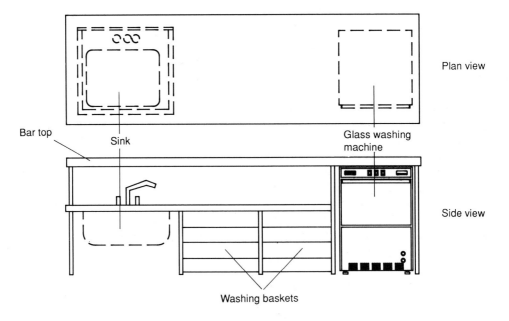

Figure 9.22   *Bar glass wash area*

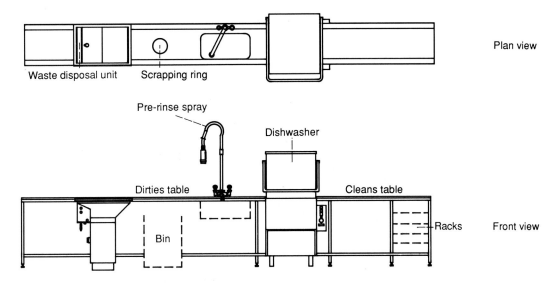

Waste disposal unit   Scrapping ring   Plan view

Pre-rinse spray

Dishwasher

Dirties table   Cleans table

Bin   Racks   Front view

Figure 9.23 *Batch machine – straight line arrangement*

equipment by at least 45 mm on the side where oven doors open and 35 mm on the other sides. They should be at a height of 2 m above floor level. The rate of extraction and supply of make-up air requires the specialized knowledge of the mechanical and electrical consultant or of a canopy supply company.

Canopies are usually made of three materials: metal; glass; or plastic. Whatever the material of construction, they should be functional, pleasing in appearance, easy to clean and not introduce a fire hazard. They should be fitted with a small gutter around the bottom edge to deal with any condensation caused before the canopy heats up. Normally, this condense gutter need not be connected to a drain, as evaporation is rapid. Canopies often incorporate bulkhead lighting. Grease filters in canopies should be easy to clean, either by removal and washing in sink or dishwasher, or by automatic 'in-place' wash-down systems. Many canopies are now fitted with fire detection and fire extinguishing systems.

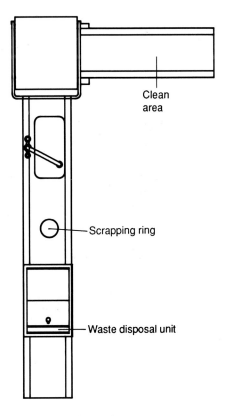

Clean area

Scrapping ring

Waste disposal unit

Figure 9.24 *Batch machine – corner arrangement*

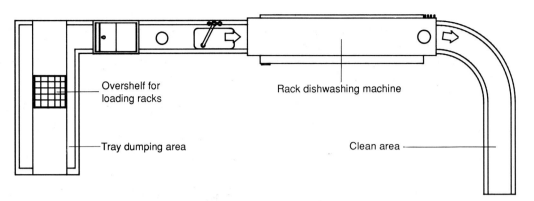

Figure 9.25 *Rack machine with tray clearing area*

Water supplies

Three types of water supply are required in a kitchen:

1 Cold, non-drinking water for staff rooms, toilets, showers, wash-up areas, pot-wash, wet bains-marie, hand washbasins and as a feed to the hot water system.

2 Cold drinking water (mains water) for water fountains, food preparation and cooking areas.

3 Hot water, at various temperatures produced by a central boiler (possibly with a number of local calorifiers at different temperatures) for hand washbasins and preparation sinks.

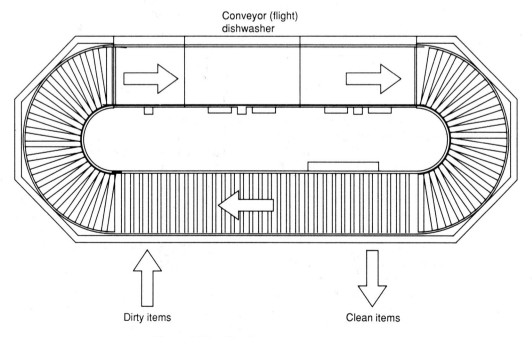

Figure 9.26 *Continuous conveyor system*

In addition to the above, some specialized supplies may be required such as softened water (for appliances such as combination ovens) and high pressure supplies (for pressure steamers and dish washing machines). These supplies may be localized to a single appliance if there is only a single requirement within the kitchen.

Where mobile equipment requires a water supply, bayonet fittings can be used in conjunction with reinforced hoses.

Drainage

In addition to the need for plumbed waste connections to sinks, there may also be floor drains in the form of open gulleys (covered with a metal grille) or circular drains. These floor drains are useful in wet cooking areas and for floor washing. It is important that the floor is sloped to take water to these drains. Some appliances, such as steaming ovens, require a vented drain connection to prevent any danger of back-siphoning.

Drainage can be provided to mobile equipment, using a tun dish or screw-in sockets mounted in the floor.

Kitchen drains are often fitted with a grease trap, which will retain fats and other solid material. These are normally located outside the kitchen and should be easily accessible for maintenance.

Flooring

Interesting developments in floor surfaces continue, but it is still hard to find the 'ideal' floor material. A floor material should have the following characteristics:

- Ease of cleaning.

- Non-slip, particularly when wet or greasy.
- Non-tiring to the feet of employees.
- Attractive appearance.

The traditional floor consists of kiln-fired quarry or terrazzo tiling. This provides a good surface, but it is slippery when wet, and the grouting between the tiles can harbour dirt and bacteria. Carborundum particles may be added to improve its non-slip performance. Many of the new floor materials are laid as a continuous screed to eliminate joints. They can be made less slippery by the incorporation of carborundum chips, which stand proud of the surface. Where slipping is a problem with existing floors, it is possible to coat most types of surfaces with a rubber-based compound which will make it much less slippery.

Skirtings and corners should be coved to facilitate cleaning and to eliminate joints which can harbour pests.

Walls

Kitchen walls should meet the following needs. They should be:

- Easy to clean.
- Of attractive appearance.
- Be able to reflect light.

There are many wall surfaces including plastics and washable paints which give good results in kitchens. Nevertheless, glazed ceramic wall tiles retain high popularity. There are problems with these tiles. For example, they glaze and crack and reflect noise.

Alternatives to ceramic tiles, such as plastic sheet materials, overcome many of the problems of tiles and their use is increasing. The joints between the sheets of material are sealed with a silicone compound, avoiding the use of nails, screws or cover strips.

Lighting

Adequate lighting is necessary for many kitchen activities. Some kitchens are in basements or semi-basements and, in any case, may not be sited to obtain the best natural light. Artificial lighting is almost invariably required. Kitchen and servery lighting is important not only to support efficient operation, but also in promoting cleanliness. Not only is the intensity of lighting important, but also the direction of the light (to prevent glare) and the colour of the light (to prevent distortion of food colours).

Recommended lighting levels (ICMSF, 1988a) are 540 lux for inspection, 220 lux for work rooms and 110 lux in other areas.

A planned fluorescent tube installation is likely to give uniform intensity, minimum shadows and low energy costs. The only problem with fluorescent tubes can be that of colour distortion. Where this is a problem, colour corrected tubes can be used.

Colours of lights, especially in the service area, must be considered since incorrect colour can change the presentation of food and adversely affect diners. Because of its complexity, advice on lighting, within the context of servery and dining areas, should be discussed with an interior designer.

Colour

The effect of white tiles, polished stainless steel and high levels of illumination can produce a very stark environment in kitchen and servery areas. While introducing colour in the form of decorated tiles and coloured stainless steel, increase the cost of a kitchen,

it may have a beneficial effect on employees. However, colours which have a high reflective value (pale or pastel colours) should be used rather than strong or dark colours.

Ceilings

Treating kitchen ceilings to obviate moisture condensation is somewhat easier with paints available today. Ceiling heights need no longer be excessive, for air change by artificial ventilation is a common means of promoting airy work places. However, very low ceilings should be avoided for the kitchen, both from the air circulation and psychological point of view. A floor to ceiling height of not less than 3 m may be considered reasonable.

Suspended ceilings incorporating washable ventilation panels are now available. These panels can be removed and passed through the dishwasher.

Staff facilities

Staff facilities must be provided, unless adequate facilities are available at a convenient location in the building. At a minimum these facilities must provide a room to change, storage for outdoor and working clothes, toilet(s) and a hand washbasin.

The number of toilets is determined by the Sanitary Convenience Regulations 1964, which gives the minimum number of facilities related to the number of employees. For operations with less than five members of staff, one closet only is required. Above this number, separate facilities are required for male and female staff.

Staff should not be allowed to eat in kitchen or servery areas. If it is not possible for them to eat in the main dining areas, a separate staff dining room must be provided.

Computer-assisted design

Computer-assisted design (CAD) is now commonly used for kitchen planning (Kirk, 1989b). A number of advantages are available to the professional planner through the use of CAD.

- The possibility of using a single drawing to produce plans at different scales.
- The availability of symbol libraries from catering equipment manufacturers to provide fast accurate drawings of specific items of equipment (Figure 9.27).
- The rapid redrafting of plans as they are adapted.
- The use of layers on the drawing (equivalent to transparent overlays allows one basic drawing to be used for a number of purposes, such as outline drawings, full scheme drawings and service (utility drawings).
- A high level of drawing presentation.

The use of three-dimensional CAD, although less common, provides a number of other advantages, including the development of walk-through models of kitchens and restaurants. These help the non-planner visualize the plan in a very realistic form.

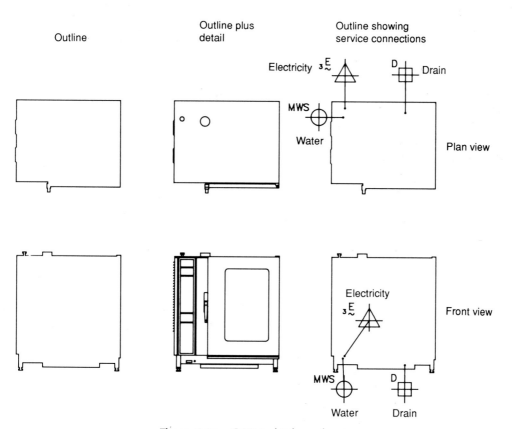

Figure 9.27 *CAD in kitchen planning*

Tutorial topic

Design a menu, suitable for a cafeteria school meals service.

Assuming that 500 pupils per day are to use the facility, approximately how much space will be required?

Based on your menu, decide on the appropriate work centres, together with types of equipment and capacities.

Assuming that the kitchen is to be rectangular in shape (the sides having a ratio of 2:1), design a layout of the kitchen and servery at a scale of 1:50.

References and further reading

Axler B. H. (1979). The Work System. In *Foodservice: A Managerial Approach*. Boston: W. C. Brown, pp. 171–209.

Birchfield J. C. (1988). *Design and Layout of Foodservice Facilities*. New York: Van Nostrand Reinhold.

Dilworth J. B. (1989). *Production and Operations Management – Manufacturing and Non-manufacturing*. New York: Random House, pp. 549–75.

Goldsmith S. (1979). Anthropometric Data. In *New Metric Handbook – Planning and Design Data* (Tutt A. and Adler B., eds.). London: Architectural Press, pp. 23–31.

HCIMA (1989). *Kitchen Floor Safety*. Technical Brief No. 3. London: HCIMA.

ICMSF (1988a). Hygienic Design of Food Operating Areas. In *The Hazard Analysis and Critical Control Point System to Ensure Microbiological Safety and Quality*. Oxford: Blackwell, pp. 62–80.

ICMSF (1988b). Hygienic Considerations in the Design and Use of Equipment. In *The Hazard Analysis and Critical Control Point System to Ensure Microbiological Safety and Quality*. Oxford: Blackwell, pp. 81–92.

Kirk D. (1989a). Layout Planning. In *Catering Equipment Management* (Pine R., ed.). London: Hutchinson, pp. 63–72.

Kirk D. (1989b). Kitchen Planning I: Overall Considerations. In *Catering Equipment Management* (Pine R., ed.). London: Hutchinson.

Kirk D. and Gladwell D. C. (1988). Adaptable Kitchens for Colleges of Further Education. *International Journal of Hospitality Management*, vol. 7, part 3, pp. 285–92.

Lawson F. (1979). Catering Design. In *New Metric Handbook – Planning and Design Data* (Tutt A. and Adler B., eds.). London: Architectural Press, pp. 165–73.

Nichols J. L. (1987). Floor Safety in Commercial Kitchens. *Journal of Royal Society of Health*, vol. 4, pp. 148–50.

Spears M. G. and Vaden A. G. (1985). *Foodservice Organizations*. New York: Wiley.

10

Kitchen maintenance and energy management

Maintenance costs are as real as those for food, wages or other regular expenses and, if this is not recognized, serious trouble may result. Preventative maintenance measures are cheapest in the long run, yet too often minor repairs are neglected until they become major ones, with major costs. No one buys a car without taking maintenance schedules and service intervals seriously: the same is rarely true of catering equipment.

Appliances and plant not well-maintained may become inefficient, increasing energy costs and decreasing employee productivity. When a refrigerator, mixing machine or a slicer is inoperative it is difficult to measure resultant damage to efficiency or business in pounds and pence, but damage and cost there undoubtedly is.

Cleaning is inextricably linked with maintenance and is, indeed, a part of it. Replacement, too, is an integral factor in maintenance and cleaning. We unhesitatingly replace an old car or van when repair bills are too high, but many kitchens retain old refrigerators or other machinery and pay highly in maintenance costs. It is not unknown for restaurants to have to restrict their menu or even close if key items of equipment fail.

Many top companies now consider all of these factors at the time they make a purchase decision on a new piece of equipment. Rather than just looking at capital costs, they look at all costs over the life of the equipment – its maintenance costs, the cost of energy, the cost of cleaning and so on.

One of the problems of kitchen maintenance is that of determining the responsibilities of the kitchen management and staff towards kitchen maintenance, as against the duties of maintenance staff or the plant engineer.

Maintaining and keeping the kitchen in a clean condition is primarily the chef's or catering manager's responsibility, whatever the manner in which this duty may be delegated. Today, this assumes greater significance than ever because:

- Kitchen cleanliness is governed by statutory requirements more stringent than ever before; similarly, kitchen safety.

- It has never been so difficult to recruit the staff needed to keep the kitchen clean.

Preventative and remedial maintenance

In large organizations, policy decisions as to whether kitchen plant and machinery is to be maintained under contract by manufacturers, distributors or service companies is made by senior management, rather than at unit management level. The catering manager and/or head chef should be aware of company policy.

Many companies now operate a system of *preventative maintenance*. This system uses a routine schedule of service work carried out by in-house or contracted engineers, which takes place before a breakdown has occurred. The essential components of a programme of preventative maintenance include (Dilworth, 1989):

- Regular inspection, at predetermined time intervals, together with a system of record keeping to assess the condition of the building fabric and equipment.
- A programme of lubrication, adjustment, painting and cleaning.
- A schedule of servicing to all major items of equipment, including the replacement of parts, before breakdown occurs.

However good the programme of preventative maintenance, breakdowns will still occur, and for this reason a system for *remedial maintenance* is required, which covers procedures for all plant and equipment when breakdown occurs. An analysis of the operation can determine the effect of breakdown of any appliance on the operation. The effect of a breakdown of some appliances is more critical than for others. For example, in the case of breakdown of some specialized appliances, the operation may have to be closed down or restricted. As another example, the breakdown of refrigeration equipment may involve loss of perishable foods. The programme of remedial maintenance must take these factors into account when establishing the required speed of response to a breakdown.

Mechanical equipment

In larger establishments, or where the catering is part of a larger organization, the chef or catering manager can call on the services of a maintenance or engineering department (Borsenik, 1979). This would be true of large hotels, industrial catering and hospitals. The small restaurateur is not in this position and must rely on service and maintenance companies.

As far as maintenance of mechanical equipment is concerned, all that is really required on the part of unit management is an efficient system of regular checking and reporting:

- By the catering manager, chef, or other nominated employee, so that faults and repairs needed can be promptly reported.
- Less frequent, but nevertheless regular, inspection and service from either the internal engineering/maintenance section or by a contracted service company, including those inspections by manufacturers under maintenance contracts, or as part of the sale guarantee or renting agreement.

In medium- or small-sized establishments, engineering services may be on a small and even negligible scale and, further, there may be a reluctance to have maintenance agreements made under contract with a manufacturer, distributor or service organization.

Under these circumstances, even greater vigilance is necessary by the kitchen staff, under the direction of the head chef or catering manager. This is required to ensure that all working equipment is kept in proper repair and, of extreme importance, that safety devices are complete, in working order and in use.

There are, in many kitchens, members of the staff who have considerable flair for effecting 'on the spot' or temporary repairs. There are often great dangers in self-help of this kind and a prudent rule is that catering managers, chefs and staff should confine themselves to noting, checking and reporting faults where they occur rather than attempting repairs which they have not been trained to do. There are also legal ramifications of condoning this practice under the Health and Safety at Work Act.

Maintenance log books

One way of ensuring that electrical, manually operated and other equipment is kept continually under check and review by responsible staff is for a maintenance log book to be kept, under the general direction of the catering manager or head chef.

There are a number of ways in which this form might be drawn up, but it should make provision for the following:

- A complete list of all equipment and all cooking equipment having moving parts.
- The items listed should be grouped according to the frequency with which routine and major inspections are either recommended by the manufacturer or considered advisable by management or maintenance staff.
- An indication of the person responsible for carrying out the routine or major

inspection or, alternatively, the date when the next service is due.

Such a log book might be set out as shown in Figure 10.1. Often it is most convenient to have one book for each department and to allocate a separate page for each piece of equipment. The book can then be submitted to the catering manager or head chef on a regular basis.

General repairs record

Apart from the mechanical equipment, the kitchen department contains much that requires supervision and attention. Floors, wall tiles, paintwork, plumbing, cupboards and fixtures, locks and keys are among the items which can aid or impede efficiency and improve or mar working conditions.

It is important that the need for repair and maintenance is noted immediately and recorded. In large organizations, where there is a maintenance department, a report or requisition of work needed is sent to this department for action. For this purpose, a multi-part form might be used or, alternatively, a maintenance record book might be kept. The latter approach is also useful for the smaller organization, where building maintenance and repair must be carried out by a contractor. In this case, a simple maintenance record might take the form shown in Figure 10.2.

A system of recording maintenance and repair work which is required is a convenient and effective means of ensuring that necessary action is taken. It not only ensures that minor items are not overlooked and develop into major ones, but it is also useful as a historical record, proof against changes of staff and as an indication of recurring sources of trouble where they exist.

Equipment:			
Make and reference number:			
Where located:			
Person responsible:			
Frequency of inspection:			
Date	Initial of person responsible	Comment	Initial of Head Chef

Figure 10.1   *The layout of a maintenance log book*

Date	Work to be done	Action taken	Date	Cost estimate	Contractor	Date completed	Actual cost

Figure 10.2   *A simple maintenance record form*

Training in the use of equipment and machinery

The way in which equipment and machinery is used affects both its life and its need for maintenance and repair. Misuse may cause immediate breakdown of an appliance, such as when a spoon or metal implement is accidentally dropped into a bowl chopper. In addition to this, sudden and drastic types of event, misuse may decrease service intervals or reduce the life of an appliance. For example, a water softener which is not maintained may result in the serious damage of a combination steamer. It will also increase detergent requirement in a dishwasher.

Because of this, and for reasons of safety (see Chapter 6), the correct use of equipment should be included in training programmes. On-the-job training programmes should include the correct use of all appliances and this should be reviewed at frequent intervals. The provision of simple instructions adjacent to appliances can be helpful, particularly where staff do not use these appliances on a regular basis.

Routine points for checking in smaller establishments

In large organizations, responsibility for regular checking of the building fabric and equipment will normally be delegated to a head of department, but in a smaller establishment this responsibility may be held by the catering manager or head chef. Whoever holds this responsibility may find the use of a checklist to be of value for routine inspections. Some of the points which might be covered in a routine checklist are shown in Figure 10.3. In carrying out a maintenance check, some of the factors associated with specific equipment is shown in Figure 10.4.

Cleaning routines

The importance of cleanliness from the point of view of hygiene was discussed in Chapter 5. In addition to the hygiene factor, cleanliness is also important because of its effect on morale, staff working conditions and equipment life.

Work routine is vital and it is important to ensure that a rhythmic pattern of cleaning from hour-to-hour, day-to-day, week-to-week and from section-to-section is clearly established. In order to ensure that cleaning takes place at the desired time, and using the correct cleaning materials for the type of soil and the nature of the soiled surface, cleaning routines are required.

Before this can be done, a thorough analysis of cleaning needs is required. Cleaning materials are costly, as is the labour spent on cleaning, and it is important that these resources are effectively used. All surfaces should be analysed in terms of:

- The composition of the material.
- The nature of the soil.
- The hazard analysis.

This analysis should determine the nature of the detergent used, its concentration and method of application (type of machine or by hand etc.), responsibility for the task and the frequency of cleaning. This information should be incorporated into a written cleaning routine for all jobs involved in food preparation and service. The value of written records of work routines can be gauged from a number of factors:

1   Continuity and the ease of handing over duties both at operative and supervisory levels.
2   The discipline of noting down the cleaning requirements is a positive help in analysing, assessing and reviewing what

needs to be done and the best time to do it.

3 Written routines can be developed into checklists, to be used by employees as an aide-mémoir which will ensure that they stick to the prescribed detergents, cleaning machines and frequencies of cleaning.

Visual reminders of cleaning duties, such as wallcharts or racks (as discussed in Chapter 5), are of great value in the busy kitchen.

Energy management

In Chapter 7 we saw the importance of energy consumption to the catering industry and its increasing cost to the operation. Many hotel and catering companies have

---

Daily

Rubbish and swill removal.
Clearance of obstruction: exits (emergency doors operational); passage ways; aisles; stairs etc.
Accessibility of the fire-fighting equipment.
Toilet and washroom inspection.
Storage procedures being followed.
Note for repair or replacement broken tools, equipment etc.

Weekly

Electrical power leads to equipment (replace at first sign of wear or damage).
Guards on mechanical equipment (immediate repair of defects, note possible future weaknesses/breakages).
Flooring check, including underneath equipment (repair cracks, breaks and replace tiles).
Grease traps and gulleys cleaned and disinfected (more frequently than weekly, as necessary).
Check all safety installations.
Check all stairs for structural faults, lighting levels, etc.
Check that water softening equipment is functioning.

Monthly

Thorough equipment and machinery check (linked with the maintenance log book or cards).
Check floor bolts of machines and equipment (looseness causes vibration damage and possible accidents).
Check for damage to painted surfaces, where this is giving protection.

Quarterly

Check labels of fire extinguishers and ensure freshness of contents.
Check kitchen wall and surrounds for repairs.

Half-yearly

Arrange for inspection of electrical circuits and for the replacement of worn wiring or parts.

Figure 10.3 *Some points for a maintenance checklist*

recognized the danger in escalating energy costs and have sought to control consumption, using an energy management programme. It has been estimated by the Energy Efficiency Office that 'with moderate improvements in efficiency and some rationalization in the use of equipment, savings in excess of 20 per cent are achievable'.

One technique, which is particularly suitable for the catering industry is *monitoring and targeting*. This means establishing methods of recording consumption, and establishing targets for future consumption against a set of energy saving measures.

The first step in establishing an energy management programme is to appoint an *energy manager*, who may be the property director, the maintenance manager, the financial director, or some similar senior person within the company. In addition to this an

---

Electrical equipment

Keep clean and grease free (grease may infiltrate wiring elements and short the unit).

Refrigerators

Check door gaskets, and replace any worn gaskets immediately (leaking door seals will reduce efficiency and overwork the compressor).
Do not allow ice to build up, because of faulty manual or automatic defrosting.

Microwave equipment

Check door seals for build up of spilled food, arrange for door seals to be checked for leaks every six months.

High-pressure steam equipment

Check door gaskets for signs of wear or damage; note visual signs of escaping steam from around door seals, etc.

Motors on equipment

Keep free from dust and dirt; ensure that lubrication is completed according to maintenance schedules.

Gas equipment

Remove food spills from burners and aeration inlets; check that flames are blue, never yellow tipped, check operation of spark ignition and flame failure devices.

Kitchen exhausts

Ensure that ducts are cleaned and chemically treated at least twice a year; clean grease filters in hoods on a regular basis.

Knives and tools

Ensure the regular arrangement of grinding and resetting.

Figure 10.4 *Specific maintenance points*

energy committee should be established, which should have representatives of operational, maintenance and financial departments. For a chain operation, energy management should be directed down to unit level by the use of energy budgets, incentive schemes and delegated responsibility down to unit management. In practice, persuading the busy unit manager of the importance of energy costs can be a very difficult problem.

The energy audit

The energy audit is an essential part of an energy management programme, since it 'serves the purpose of identifying where a building or plant facility uses energy and identifies energy conservation opportunities' (Thumann, 1983). In order to be of value, the energy audit should be a regular ongoing activity, not a one-off exercise to identify conservation opportunities.

activities involved in an energy audit:

- Collect fuel consumption per billing period. This allows energy cost for the various fuel types to be established. Converting all energy consumptions to the same basic unit allows measurement of the total consumption. If this is continued over a period of time, it demonstrates changes in energy consumption. A form which might be used for recording energy consumption is shown in Figure 10.5.
- In a large operation or chain it is possible to establish energy cost centres (that is, for a hotel, energy centres might be heating, air-conditioning, domestic hot water, mechanical equipment, foodservice, lighting, swimming pool, refrigeration). Where possible these energy centres should have their own energy meters to allow auditing down to the level of the energy centre.

Month	Electricity		Gas				Heating oil			Total		Degree days	Covers
	kWh	£	Cu. ft	Therms	kWh	£	Litres	kWh	£	kWh	£		
Jan. Feb. Mar. Apr. May June July Aug. Sep. Oct. Nov. Dec.													
Yearly summary													

Unit: _____   Year: _____

Figure 10.5 *Energy audit form*

- Relate monthly consumption to average monthly climate (using heating degree days for heating demand, cooling degree days for air-conditioning demand) and the level of business activity (number of covers or sales volume per month).
- Carry out equipment surveys – identify every piece of equipment which utilizes energy, record its pattern of daily use, its power rating (kW or Btu/hour) and its diversity (the percentage of time the appliance is consuming energy when it is switched on). A suitable form for an equipment survey is shown in Figure 10.6.

Once it has been established, an energy audit allows:

Appliance	Fuel	Power kW	Diversity % (1)	Date	Hours off	Hours on In use	Out of use	Daily energy consump kWh (2)
Steamer	Gas	20	50		3	2	3	50
Fryer	Elec.	15	50		5	2	3	22.5
							Total kWh	72.5

Notes:

(1) Diversity = $\dfrac{\text{average rate of energy use} \times 100}{\text{power rating}}$

A typical figure is 50% for cooking equipment and 20% for refrigeration. More accurate figures can be obtained from manufacturers.

(2) Energy consumption (kWh) = $\dfrac{\text{power rating (kW)} \times \text{diversity} \times \text{hours on}}{100}$

Figure 10.6 *An equipment survey form*

- Establishment of budgets for future performance.
- Monitoring of performance against targets.
- Evaluation of energy saving strategies, investments etc.
- Development of computer models of the energy system, to evaluate alternative strategies.

Energy policy

An energy policy provides a long-term strategy to control energy costs. Based on an energy audit, the current position and trends in energy consumption can be reviewed. Figures can be compared with industrial averages or, in the case of chain, inter-unit comparison can be used.

In general terms, these strategies might include:

- *Review of energy sources and rates.*
- *Good management practices.*
- *Capital investment to reduce energy consumption*

The long-term strategy can identify improvements, implement some or all of these improvements and monitor the effect of these changes, using the ongoing energy audit. This process requires a prioritization of potential changes, based on:

- The magnitude of savings resulting from these changes.
- On the pay-back time of any investment.

A possible prioritization, based on a hierarchical scheme, is shown in Figure 10.7.

One of the clear factors which arises from an energy audit of hotel and catering operations, is the presence of a high energy base load which is independent of the level of business activity. In other words, energy costs have a high fixed cost element and a low variable cost, as shown in Figure 10.8. To some extent, this is inevitable because, for example, a restaurant must be heated and illuminated, even if it has only one customer. However, other areas of energy use, such as that of catering equipment, should be more directly related to the level of business activity than is often the case. As we saw in Chapter 6, cooking represents some 40 per cent of energy consumption in catering.

Review of energy sources and rates

The energy policy should include a review of relative cost per unit of energy based on full

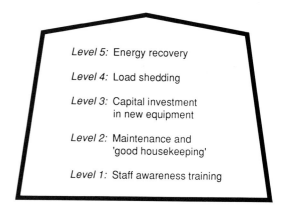

Figure 10.7   *Energy conservation hierarchy*

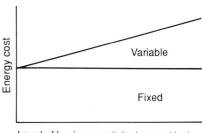

Figure 10.8   *Energy costs in hotels and restaurants: fixed versus variable*

life costs. While it is often expensive to switch from one type of fuel to another and thus achieve benefits from short-term changes in fuel cost, these costs should be reviewed as part of a long-term policy.

Utility rates, where these are the subject of contract negotiation, should be evaluated to determine that the best rate is available, based on the usage pattern of an operation. Full use should be made of lower cost energy such as off-peak rates (electricity) and interruptible rates (gas).

For companies which pay a *maximum demand charge* as a part of their electrical tariff, the effect of this on the cost of electricity should be reviewed. With this type of tariff, the cost of electricity is based not just on energy consumption (kWh) but also on the peak or maximum rate of consumption (kW or kVA) during the billing period. Where the maximum demand tariff is introducing a high penalty, manual or automatic load shedding might be considered – that is, the switching off of high consumption/low priority appliances when power levels rises above a preset value.

Energy conservation measures

Good management practices

There are many examples of the use of good management practices, or 'good housekeeping', to reduce energy consumption. In particular the practice of switching off equipment, heating and lights which are not needed can help to reduce the high base load for energy.

In restaurant kitchens, energy consumption is considerably higher for cooking appliances than it is for other activities. Therefore we should start by concentrating on the large energy consumers in the kitchen,

based on the equipment survey, carried out as a part of the energy audit.

Sensible use of equipment can make a difference, that is, switching on an appliance just before it is required and switching it off when finished. This relates both to cooking equipment, dishwashing equipment and ventilation canopies. In the case of the latter, fans on ventilation canopies should be run at their maximum speed only when essential, otherwise the extraction system is removing large volumes of air from the kitchen which must be replaced by make-up air which needs heating in winter.

It is important to use full loads in most types of catering equipment such as ovens, steamers, dishwashers, etc.; using part batches increase the energy cost per unit of product, as shown in Figure 10.9. It can also be seen from this diagram that overloading an appliance can also reduce efficiency.

Doors on ovens and refrigerators should be opened for as short a time as possible.

It is often possible to cook a particular dish using a number of alternative appliances. The choice of appliance can have an effect on energy consumption, as indicated in Figure 7.1. For example, roasting in a convection oven rather than conventional deck oven, or cooking vegetables in convection steamer or

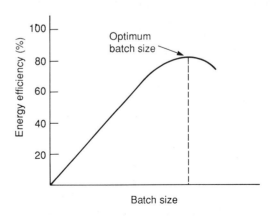

Figure 10.9 *Effect of batch size on equipment efficiency*

combination steamer, rather than on an open top range can reduce energy costs.

Management of staff should form a part of energy policy. Many companies have introduced training and incentive schemes linked to energy management. It is also sensible to hold regular energy awareness meetings.

Checks on the maintenance of equipment should cover such things as thermostat settings, building and equipment maintenance, boiler efficiency, heating ventilation and air conditioning controls, the repair of leaking taps and the replacement of worn door seals on ovens and refrigeration equipment. Other examples include checks on the defrosting control on refrigeration equipment, burner settings on gas appliances, water treatment-(softening) equipment, the replacement of insulation and the cleaning of filters in ventilation systems. Boilers should be descaled at regular intervals.

Capital investment to reduce energy consumption

Investment in energy management must produce a competitive return on capital investment, when compared to other capital investment programmes (Thumann, 1983). Since businesses require pay-back times of less than three years, investment in energy management tends to concentrate on the short term.

In general, it is much cheaper to build energy conservation into a new building, than it is to retrofit into an old building.

New energy efficient equipment, with a lower energy consumption (kW/kg of food) and short preheat times can be cost effective, particularly when replacing older appliances. Much of the conventional equipment in kitchens has a very high energy consumption. Newer designs (convection ovens, induction hobs, convection steamers, tilting bratt pans/skillets) can reduce energy consumption.

Location of refrigeration equipment condensers can have a significant effect on energy consumption. The efficiency of refrigeration depends largely on the difference between the temperature of the condenser and the ambient (surrounding air) temperature. Many refrigeration appliances have their condensers on top of appliances, which is where the warmest air in the kitchen accumulates. Efficiency is improved if the condenser is moved out of the kitchen area, that is, on to the roof.

The introduction of variable speed fans on ventilating systems can reduce energy consumption, not just because of energy to the fan, but, more importantly, because it reduces the volume of make-up air required.

Alternative energy sources, such as solar energy, heat pumps and cogeneration systems should be considered. Solar still has very long pay-back times and in many parts of the world is not reliable enough. Also, there is a mismatch between availability of solar energy and the building heating season. However, summer heating is needed for facilities such as swimming pools and domestic hot water.

Heat pumps

Heat pumps are very effective where electricity is the main energy source. A heat pump can provide the equivalent of three units of energy for every unit of electricity. Also, heat pumps can be a very effective as a means of recovering energy (see below). A heat pump uses the mechanical refrigeration cycle (as used in refrigeration equipment) in order to extract waste heat at a low temperature and to increase its temperature to make it useful for preheating hot water for domestic purposes.

Combined heat and power (cogeneration)

A combined heat and power system, which is the simultaneous generation of heat and electricity, can reduce overall energy costs. There are now compact cogeneration systems, which are suitable for the small hotel and restaurant. It does need a careful feasibility study to prove real full life benefits. A cogeneration system consists of a gas or fuel oil powered engine which drives an electrical generator. It is cooled by a water supply and this water is preheated for domestic purposes (see Figure 10.10). One benefit can be to reduce peak demand for electricity and hence the maximum demand penalty. In some situations it is possible to sell surplus electricity back to the grid (Homer, 1989).

Investment in the building, through the use of new insulation materials, double- and triple-glazing, solar films, motorized window shading systems, and alternative lighting systems can all show satisfactory pay-back times, under the correct circumstances.

Computer-based energy management systems can be very effective in most types of building, but in hotels in particular (Kirk, 1987). They provide:

● Space heating optimization: the computer calculates when the heating should be switched on and off based on external temperatures, internal temperatures and knowledge of previous performance of the system.

● More precise, and more localized thermostat controls: the building can be zoned and the heating period/temperature for each zone controlled.

● Electrical tariff management: automatic peak demand (load shedding) and power factor control can be built into the system.

● Better management through faster and more accurate energy use data and reporting.

In addition, the computer-based energy management system may perform other building management functions, such as security and fire monitoring.

Investment in heat recovery systems

The principles of heat recovery are that:

● Waste heat must be of high quality (that is, at a high temperature and not dispersed over a large area).

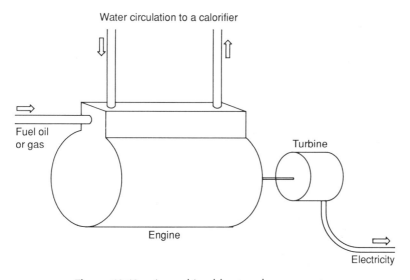

Figure 10.10 *A combined heat and power system*

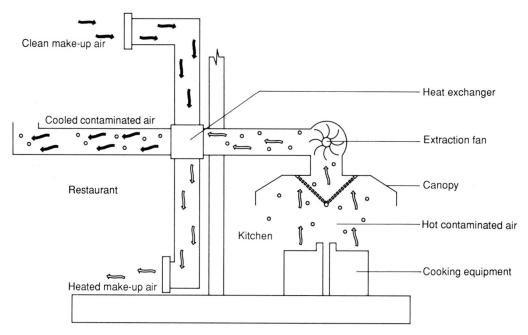

Figure 10.11   *A combined heat and power system*

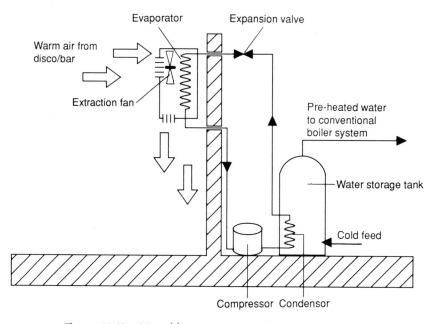

Figure 10.12   *Use of heat pump in energy recovery system*

- There must be a closely related use (related that is both in time and distance) for the recovered heat.
- The cost of recovery (capital and running) must be less than the cost of conventional energy.

Heat exchangers

Heat exchangers are normally required to separate waste heat from its associated contaminants. There are a number of types of heat exchanger, such as the thermal wheel, the air-to-air heat exchanger, heat pipes, and the run-around-coil. Heat pumps can also be used as a form of heat exchanger. They have the advantage over most other heat exchangers in that they can increase the temperature of the waste heat.

Sources of waste heat include:

- Kitchen and dishwashing ventilation systems.
- Waste hot water (dishwashing).
- Public area ventilation/air-conditioning systems in restaurants, leisure centres, discos, etc.
- Lighting.
- Refrigeration equipment.

Possible uses for the recovered heat include:

- Domestic hot water.
- Swimming pools.
- Space heating.

Heat exchangers can have efficiencies of 70 to 80 per cent. Normally, heat recovery cannot supply all of the heat requirements for any of the above applications and it must be utilized in conjunction with a conventional heating system. In general, heat recovery is much more cost effective when it is used in a new building, since it is more expensive to incorporate into an existing building. A schematic diagram of an air-to-air heat exchanger

used to recover heat from a kitchen canopy and return it to the restaurant is shown in Figure 10.11.

Of the above methods of heat recovery, heat pumps are the only way in which the quality (temperature) of the waste heat can be increased. Small heat pumps have now been developed which are ideal as part of air-conditioning systems in situations where there is a need for domestic hot water. For example, a bar or disco in a night club may use a heat pump as the air-conditioning system and return the recovered heat to the domestic hot water system for the kitchen or toilets, as shown in Figure 10.12. Used in this way, heat pumps can often produce very short pay-back times.

References and further reading

Aulbach R. E. (1984). *Energy Management*. The Education Institute of American Hotel and Motel Association.

Birchfield J. C. (1988). *Design and Layout of Foodservice Facilities*. New York: Van Nostrand Reinhold.

Borsenik F. D. (1979). *The Management of Maintenance and Engineering Systems in Hospitality Industries*. New York: Wiley.

Dilworth J. B. (1989). *Production and Operations Management*, 4th edn. New York: Random House, pp. 491–501.

Energy Efficiency Office (undated). *Energy Savings in Catering*. Department of Energy.

Fessler R. (1983). Energy Audit of Food Service Facilities. In *Handbook of Energy Audits*, 2nd edn (Thumann R., ed.). Atlanta, Georgia: The Fairmont Press, pp. 342–62.

Homer S. (1989). Boiler Works. *Caterer and Hotelkeeper*, 7 September.

Kirk D. (1987). The use of computer-based energy management systems in hotels, *International Journal of Hospitality Management*, vol. 6, part 4, pp. 237–42.

Liepens I. (1989). Equipment Cleaning. In *Catering Equipment Management* (Pine R., ed.). London: Hutchinson, pp. 106–16.

Newborough M. and Probert S. D. (1988). Energy Conscious Design Improvements for Electric Hobs. *Journal of Foodservice Systems*, vol. 4, pp. 233–57.

Pine R. (1989). *Catering Equipment Management*. London: Hutchinson, pp. 117–22.

Singer D. D. and Hunt R. O. (1980). Energy Use in the Catering and Food Industry. In *Advances in Catering Technology* (Glew, G., ed.). London: Elsevier Applied Science, pp. 85–94.

Taylor D. (1980). The Implication of Energy Usage in Catering Design. In *Advances in Catering Technology* (Glew G., ed.). London: Elsevier Applied Science, pp. 95–100.

Taylor D. (1989). Energy Efficiency and Utilisation. In *Catering Equipment Management* (Pine R., ed.). London: pp. 124–30.

Thumann A. (1983). *Handbook of Energy Audits*. Atlanta, Georgia: The Fairmont Press, pp. 97–119.

Unklesbay N. and Unklesbay K. (1982). *Energy Management in Foodservice*. Westport, Connecticut: AVI.

Index

Work centres, 183–4
Work and method study, 182–7

Yersinia enterocolitia, 68